Have a very Merry Christmas & Pleasant years Ahead!

The Trails To Attrition

Adam M. Mullin

Wasteland Press
www.wastelandpress.net

Wasteland Press
Shelbyville, KY USA
www.wastelandpress.net

The Trails To Attrition
by Adam M. Mullin

ISBN: 978-1-60047-152-0
First Printing – November 2007
Cover design by Adam Mullin

Printed in the U.S.A.

Why was I here staring, and distancing myself,
Flipping back to see what I had already seen
        Again and again?

Rousing in my judgment in a sensation trying
To grasp at what was suppose to be caught
        As if the author knew what he meant.

As if I knew the author,
    As if I was the author,
        As if each page were of my own.

Concerning what I thought was true,
    Was not invalid but valid, the feeling is real,
        The page holds a function in my mind.

What I see, he cannot tell me, for his words
    Become mine, and I hesitate to turn as if
        This clue is a turning point.

For if I were to suspect that I knew him well,
As he were to know me not, then respectably
    I would expect the same.

So I become by the beginning
And start by the end. And leave
Where I left off again and again.

In Remembrance of:

All those who have passed during and after the Katrina Conflict,
Rita & Wilma In Louisiana, Mississippi, Alabama, and Florida.

Professor Katherine Adams' husband, John L. Adams.

Ethel Freeman.   Kurt Vonnegut.

Lucky Mullin.   Michi.

All those who have left us, and always remember the strongest
Tie between poetry and our World, to see things beyond what
They are through the Dark and Doomed, and when all is
At a standstill and you've just considered taking a Loss,
Take on the next journey, the new journey,
The Revolution, the Symbolic Transformation,
The beginning of an epic,
Life and the World around it.

THE POEM'S WHOLE

You're the one, you're my life
The reason time takes flight.
Oh my blue horizon light, how ethereal
Your diamond, your seven seas, you're seven seas
Organized in every angle
Of the heart, of the soul, of the reason
My life takes whole.
Jupiter (if every wit is wit
As truth could not be buried,
As my love for you is),
Takes justice; balanced when married.
Oh, the balance of the waves,
Delivery on the borne of air,
And lights at every angle;
My life is born to you.
Twelve arms made up of
Two limbs and a starting point
Hold us back.
My life takes fact.
It does not listen, though I love more.
If Mercury could give an ear, I'd deliver
Merriment at ease,
But before you know it, my life takes peace.
And every hint and angle edged,
No sanded rock, as winter sinks,
And narrowly rising grass ups endlessly into the sky;
My life takes why;
I take how. I see the see, I've seen the sea.
But out of seven, only one seems fit to be.
I take my anchor; wind on high, but steady,
My life takes ready—
Without warning,
I run to life blooming like lavender brushing in haste,
But my life takes taste,
And I am gone.

Chapter One
THE TRAIL OF QUESTIONS

LOVE IS WHAT WE LIVE FOR   from *Pulchritude for the Mind*

Every new beginning, has a different path
Paths that take us further
Beyond the greatest math.
Every chance is different, from choices that we take,
We live for peace and harmony,
Yearning for camaraderie,
Love is what we create.

Love is what we live for,
Love is what we live by,
Sharing our togetherness,
Sharing our true path,
Standing side by side,
We live, we love, we fly.

Every drop has a ripple,
That echoes from the past,
Starts a new beginning, as the first wind upon a mast,
Every struggle for the solution,
Each step that pushes us along,
We live with our relentlessness,
Love makes us strong.

Love is what we live for,
Love is what we live by,
Sharing our togetherness,
Sharing our true path,
Standing side by side,
We live, we love, we fly, we fly.

We fly above the zeniths,
High into the stars,
Comets race right with us,
Venus unites with Mars,
Broken pieces of the puzzle,

Fit perfectly in place,
Balanced in the unity in everlasting grace.

Love is what we live for,
Love is what we live by,
Sharing our togetherness,
Sharing our true path,
Standing side by side,
We live, we love, we fly.

- - - - - - - -

FAULT ON LOVE

Translucence bitters
Timeless fades,
Passions corrupt,
Where emptiness's maze;

I sit upon two
Great narrows,
One stretched closed–
Its openness holds carols,

A grave embarked with
Love's name, Heart,
An eye sore,
Torn from me, once apart.

Their name detests mist.
Permanence,
I once held, lost.
So many the expense

Held at my fault for
Everything
I did commit;
Trials, Judged by gathering

My lies! Fore soothe

They were done.
But love, gave out.
On me, I, it, then none.

Love is what I
Lived for? To
Joust politics,
Ideas, not importune.

I loved, which is
Not a lie.
And this is yet, the
Same Path, to fall, rise, die.

Forget Love, its
Hindrance, not
Impatience, who
Scorned me, killed me, made rot

Of all the dreams,
Towards the
Other. Kept her free,
Heart, I lost, did not see

Before, I gave
Them false traits
Thine own despair to
Impartial them my hates.

Suicide saves
Problems; most.
If only a wish called:
To see Heart's cherished ghost.

THE MESSAGED

MONDAY NIGHT

ViceroyElmo: (8:34 pm ET)
    Hey Wendy! How's it going?

Ventanababe: (8:36 pm ET)
    I don't want to talk to you.

ViceroyElmo: (8:36 pm ET)
    Well then why not? Hey did—

Ventanababe: (8:37 pm ET)
    I don't think you heard me.

ViceroyElmo: (8:38 pm ET)
    Heard you? I have open
    Eyes onto this typed page.
    This is not a cup-to
    Cup, walkie-talkie of
    Mumbled talk and other—

Ventanababe: (8:40 pm ET)
    No rhyme. Eric, I told you to stop, yield and end.

ViceroyElmo: (8:40 pm ET)
    Come on, you hang up on me
    When I call. You say it's
    An ended line, or the
    Battery died. I don't.

Ventanababe: (8:44 pm ET)
    Eric, I have school to
    Do. I'm busy—

ViceroyElmo: (8:45 pm ET)
    You know, it's the eighth
    Time.

Ventanababe: (8:46 pm ET)
    Hmmm? The time for what to
    Harass me? To say how
    Much you think I'm a gold—
      En goddess?

ViceroyElmo: (8:49 pm ET)
      Look, I've tried it all, all
    My pulls a man could push,
    All my tricks are used up.
    Poetry has died for
    You. Petals have eroded
    For you. Valentine's Day
    Was an empty scorned flute

        Sipped and shattered. I am
        Alone.

VentanaBabe: (8:55 pm ET)
        Aren't all men? Adam's sin.

ViceroyElmo: (8:55 pm ET)
        It is my fault. C'mon
        I adore you. I'll sin
        For you.

VentanaBabe: (8:59 pm ET)
        Don't you work? Do you care
        About what your parents
        Go through to get you where
        You are?

Viceroy Elmo: (8:59 pm ET)
        Know how my parents met?

VentanaBabe: (9:00 pm ET)
        In a phone booth, your dad
        Masturbating on one
        End and your mother
        Counting each minute in
        Dollars?

ViceroyElmo: (9:02 pm ET)
        No, it was Vietnam.
        Hey I'm adopted you
        Know. He chose to save her.

VentanaBabe: (9:04 pm ET)
        From man's destruction. Please,
        A war is of a man's
        Disenchanted soul to
        Dwell along a path of
        Sex, but instead come out
        And hunt for more until
        Hoards of women, and their
        Children are at gunpoint
        In front of their cattle,
        In front of their village,
        While a monk burns himself
        Cold. A monk is a man
        That forces the image
        Of Peace into their mind,
        After they have set forth
        Needles tearing angels'
        Wings. All men are guilty,

None innocent. Two men
Of color, two men of
Faiths, set them together
In a pew, in a scorched
Desert. Without women,
The lust for them; one man
Will devour the one
On his other hand's side.
The hand is but a man's
Way of being useful
In this world.

ViceroyElmo: (9:19 pm ET)
    But I am concerned soul—
    Ly for you.

VentanaBabe: (9:22 pm ET)
    Man and Webster, two men
    For which we voice ourselves.
    Language is but man's hearth
    And deceptive pride to keep
    Their mouths at play.

ViceroyElmo: (9:24 pm ET)
    Hold your tongue, for our mouths
    Are not heard in these words
    I type—

VentanaBabe: (9:24 pm ET)
    Ha, they're universal.

ViceroyElmo: (9:25 pm ET)
    Wendy. Is truth, my love
    Universal?

VentanaBabe: (9:26 pm ET)
    If it is not you, then
    Another man will settle
    Down and offer me his
    Hand. But no, not your words.

ViceroyElmo: (9:27 pm ET)
    Damn it. I have met you
    Before in true form, my
    Eyes fixed on your smile.
    It was real, after school,
    After work, practice, I—

VentanaBabe: (9:28 pm ET)
    But who did your laundry?

Who made sure you drove
Home on time— your parents.

ViceroyElmo: (9:29 pm ET)
Baby, I'm 22.
I can give you a liv—
Ing. I can run out nude
And be arrested, and
I don't care if my mom
Is at the country club
Or she is sewing all
Day, and I'm on the T
V. Look can we at least
Get to know each other?

VentanaBabe: (9:30 pm ET)
...

ViceroyElmo: (9:33 pm ET)
I cannot give up. You
Are the only one for
Me, in this Earth, and I
Can't get across. I don't
Have to compare you to
Every single woman
Whose been mistreated or
Loved. I don't have to call
You Ms. Hilton, I don't
Love her. She is not where
I set my eyes upon,
I'll love you always.

VentanaBabe: (9:43 pm ET)
Goodbye Eric, go get
Drunk and forget about
It all.

VentanaBabe Signed off: (9:44 pm ET)

ViceroyElmo: (9:59 pm ET)
Goodbye.

<u>TUESDAY NIGHT</u>

ViceroyElmo: (7:43 pm ET)
Hey Steven!

AnteupBazzooka: (7: 45 pm ET)

Hey Eric, how has school
Been treating you?

VitroyElmo: (7:46 pm ET)
       Pretty cool, but it's now
       Summer so, I am off.
       How is Wendy?

AnteupBazzooka: (7:47 pm ET)
       Always busy. Hey by
       The way— HAPPY B—DAY
       ERIC! I membered cause
       Of the time your doughnuts
       Fell on the street, and you
       Forgot to take your keys
       Out. And then your van reared
       My mom's Lincoln, member?

ViceroyElmo: (7:48 pm ET)
       Ya Ha.

AnteupBazzooka: (7:48 pm ET)
       And it was all your fault.
       And probably Wendy
       Was never the same since
       Then.

ViceroyElmo: (7:49 pm ET)
       Whoa what happened? It's been
       A year, but no one told
       Me if she was not al—
       Right.

AnteupBazzooka: (7:49pm ET)
       Well she had to get stitch—
       Es, and stuff leaked out quick—
       Ly, and she became deaf
       In her left ear.

ViceroyElmo: (7:50 pm ET)
       Man I didn't know. So
       Sorry Steven.

AnteupBazzooka: (7:51 pm ET)
       So you haven't seen her
       At all this year? I thought
       That you were going to
       Marry her two years a—
       Go, in your freshman year.
       Things don't seem to be great

For you.

ViceroyElmo: (7:53 pm ET)
     Ya, you're telling me, Steve.
     It's harsh. Hey how old are
     You? I didn't keep track.

AnteupBazzooka: (7:59 pm ET)
     Sorry, phone rang. Okay
     What?

ViceroyElmo: (8:03 pm ET)
     Your age, take your time, I'm
     Clipping my toenails—sounds
     Just like typing black keys.

AnteupBazzooka: (8:05 pm ET)
     I'm 18, practically
     Legal. But gross man, you
     Must have fungus galore
     In your "corn" fields. Haha
     LOL!

ViceroyElmo: (8:06 pm ET)
     WTF, oh it's all
     Yellow and puss is drip—
     Ping all over the trash
     Basket. And the collie
     Is licking it clean.

AnteupBazzooka: (8:09 pm ET)
     Ew, Ew, LOL!

ViceroyElmo: (8:09 pm ET)
     Hilarious, funny.
     You met any girls yet?
     You broke up with that nerd
     Girl, Cameron, right? Mike's
     Little sister, the Smurf.

AnteupBazzooka: (8: 11 pm ET)
     Ha, we never ever
     Hooked up. Just rumors—zilch.

ViceroyElmo: (8:12 pm ET)
     Life: history is just
     A bunch of distant rumors
     Setup to make a rock,
     A stepping stone in time.
     Surrounded in ripples,

        Presenting costumes of
        Egalitarian
        Looms, but Great Walls bloom for
        No apparent reason.

AnteupBazzooka: (8:13 pm ET)
        Deep shit there. Still on the
        Enchanted smoked leafed wrap?

ViceroyElmo: (8:13 pm ET)
        No, t'was a one-time deal.
        Don't pull the same mistake
        I left behind before
        You.

AnteupBazzooka: (8:14 pm ET)
        Too late Ric. I am doped.

ViceroyElmo: (8:14 pm ET)
        Well fucking get off it!
        Do me a favor. Want
        To put one great rock in
        My life?

AnteupBazzooka: (8:15 pm ET)
        Sure dude, when I have time.

ViceroyElmo: (8:16 pm ET)
        Give it up then!

AnteupBazzooka: (8:18 pm ET)
        How your words stand without
        Definition, because
        They are not given voice.

ViceroyElmo: (8:19 pm ET)
        Voice is directly a
        Mental attribution,
        And you have seen my face
        Before. As I too, can
        Hear you speak, in these words.

AnteupBazzooka: (8:20 pm ET)
        Damn, Shakespeare right? No man,
        I will try, just for you.

ViceroyElmo: (8:25 pm ET)
        Fine, but I'm not trying
        To tuck in your pants for
        You okay. Just finish

                    It. So what has Wendy
                    Been up to?

AnteupBazzooka: (8:27 pm ET)
                    I don't know; ask her. Hey
                    BRB···

AnteupBazzooka: (11:05 pm ET)
                    Hey still there. Wendy's back.
                    She's with some guy named Drew.

ViceroyElmo: (11:20 pm ET)
                    Whoa, hey. Who's the biff lurch?

AnteupBazzooka: (11:21 pm ET)
                    He's kind of a flank, could
                    Be the jeans. He has one
                    Of those puff out butts and—

ViceroyElmo: (11:22 pm ET)
                    Wendy's into assess!
                    Ha!

AnteupBazzooka: (11:25 pm ET)
                    You telling me, Eric.
                    Hefner could easily
                    Confuse him for a straight—
                    Up Playboy bunny with
                    That.

ViceroyElmo: (11:30 pm ET)
                    Ha, ya it's funny. But
                    For me, I mean I love
                    Her. But hey that's life, Steve.

AnteupBazzooka: (11:34 pm ET)
                    Sure is.

ViceroyElmo: (11:40 pm ET)
                    Hey Steve, you remember
                    That spot where we use to
                    Surf? Near Valcona's Cove?
                    Well want to catch some waves
                    At six?

AnteupBazzooka: (11:50 pm ET)
                    In six hours?! Okay,
                    I need to get away from
                    The house in the morning.
                    See you then. Night Eric.

ViceroyElmo: (11: 56 pm ET)
        Night.

AnteupBazzooka Signed Off: (12:00 am ET)

ViceroyElmo Signed Off: (12:00 am ET)

<u>WEDNESDAY NIGHT</u>

ViceroyElmo: (9:26 pm ET)
        Some awesome waves back there.

AnteupBazzooka: (9:27 pm ET)
        Did pretty well yourself.
        Man, what a day. Sorry
        About the board, Eric.

ViceroyElmo: (9:28 pm ET)
        It can be repaired or
        Not. Just have to buy a
        New one. But are you K?

AnteupBazzooka: (9:29 pm ET)
        Just a couple of stitch—
        Es. And no, did not tell
        My family that I
        Was with you, Er Eric.

ViceroyElmo: (9:30 pm ET)
        They didn't think a thing?

AnteupBazzooka: (9:30 pm ET)
        No, not a hint of mind
        Duty, except the bill.

ViceroyElmo: (9:35 pm ET)
        You know why I could
        Not pay. It would be just,
        And unjust as well. For
        A man cannot pay for
        A crime he did commit,
        If the victim does not
        Deliver value. And
        If he didn't commit
        The crime, his fault may be
        His actions are more dis—
        Honest.

AnteupBazzooka: (9:36 pm ET)
                        Either way, you're not at
                        Fault. For I do not want
                        To give you a bad day.

ViceroyElmo: (9: 38 pm ET)
                        But one thing, the one thing—

AnteupBazzooka: (9:39 pm ET)
                        Hey dude we were tired,
                        All beer'd up. My sister
                        And I do it sometimes,
                        Just to kiss her. I mean
                        It was like the moment.

ViceroyElmo: (9:50 pm ET)
                        I was just thinking as
                        Great men do, timely twice.
                        How did it feel, to you?

AnteupBazzooka: (9:55 pm ET)
                        I, I don't want to talk
                        About this, just embarrassed.
                        I mean, now, and then. I—

ViceroyElmo: (9:59 pm ET)
                        Some say alcohol brings
                        The truth of great men, as
                        You were one on your board
                        Today.

AnteupBazzooka: (10:05 pm ET)
                        I guess it felt kind of
                        Good. Just sandy not so
                        Smooth.

ViceroyElmo: (10:06 pm ET)
                        There see, the text does not
                        Hurt or worsen the pain
                        Of our embarrassment.

AnteupBazzooka: (10:10 pm ET)
                        Et tu Eric? How did
                        You feel, not to say that—

ViceroyElmo: (10:11 pm ET)
                        To be up and front, like
                        I said on the shore. I'll
                        Tell you. Steve, I have not

Had sex all year. Damn it,
I guess it's the best next
Replacement, for it all.

AnteupBazzooka: (10:14 pm ET)
So, I don't know this feel.
This feel is not like hung
—Er. To be straight up, I
Think I love you truly.

AnteupBazzooka: (10:25 pm ET)
I mean it. I'm suffer—
Ing already. I love
You. It's not weed, I'm off
It. That kiss, I think I don't
Know.

ViceroyElmo: (10:30 pm ET)
Strong valid words, for a
Man of your age. Because
For you a change happened
Early. As with most men
It happens when they can't
Re—ejaculate well.

AnteupBazzooka: (10:31 pm ET)
No, damn it. I think I
Whole—Heartedly love you.

ViceroyElmo: (10:32 pm ET)
Steve, Steve, I think we should
Talk tonight in person.
Tell your parents something
Else. And meet me by the
Motel on the beach near
The McDonald's.

AnteupBazzooka: (10:34 pm ET)
Anything, anything,
For you my love, Eric.

AnteupBazzooka Signed Off: 10:40 pm ET)

ViceroyElmo: (10:42 pm ET)
Shit.

ViceroyElmo Signed Off: (10:50 pm ET)

<u>THURSDAY NIGHT</u>

AnteupBazzooka: (9:35 pm ET)
> Hey Eric you on now?

AnteupBazzooka: (9: 37 pm ET)
> Hey Eric you there now?

AnteupBazzooka: (9:38 pm ET)
> Eric I fucking need
> To talk to you right now.
> I will then text you, then.
> Sometimes, it takes some time.

AnteupBazzooka: (9:39 pm ET)
> Look I need to talk right
> Now. Please, baby please. I'm
> Crying, and it means a
> Lot of passion.

AnteupBazzooka: (9:40 pm ET)
> Look I'm sorry, damn it.
> I stopped weed and took up
> You— my true addiction.

AnteupBazzooka: (11:35 pm ET)
> I have been sick the whole
> Day. My nose is bleeding.
> But it's love. If a man
> Cannot say love or write
> It, hold it, but show it
> To only be in sole
> Emptiness. Then I can't⋯
> I love you to the break
> And where the great ocean's
> Deepest heart lays, and I
> Will be there waiting.

AnteupBazzooka Signed Off: (12:00 am ET)

<u>FRIDAY NIGHT</u>

ViceroyElmo: (10:33 pm ET)
> Hey Wendy, finally
> Back on. Good to see you.

VentanaBabe: (10:34 pm ET)

Hey it's been quite a day.
You know what, Eric I,
Need to confess something.

ViceroyElmo: (10:34 pm ET)
You do, I'm a waiting···

VentanaBabe: (10:35 pm ET)
Well I thought. And words on
This cannot state my real
Voice about you. I may
Sound like a bitch, or a
Stuck-up. But the other
Night, I meant it with a
Loving sarcasm- truth.
Eric, I didn't want
To tell you this, because
I thought you'd be in pain.
When you hit us by your
Van, I went deaf in one
Ear. Okay Eric, I
Just did not want you to
Feel like you murdered me.

ViceroyElmo: (10: 40 pm ET)
I don't know what to say.
I'm very sorry. For-
Give me. I have a feel-
Ing, is··· what else is wrong?

VentanaBabe: (10:43 pm ET)
Only true love from a
Man can sense the bold heart
Of his love's beholder.
It's my fault, I went with
Another man. It's a
Sign, Eric. I broke up
Yesterday, because I-
I've always loved you. And
It's foolish, I hid from
You, because of this flaw.
But I found the sign that
I had hurt you, if not
All men! I found him, found,
Found, Found, Found, Found, Found him!

VentanaBabe: (10:50 pm ET)
Eric Viceroy, my
Brother is dead.

VeceroyElmo: (10:51 pm ET)
        Oh my God! Oh my God!
        He was, how did this? God!

VentanaBabe: (10:54 pm ET)
        Eric, I was crying.
        I came home⋯

VentanaBabe: (11:23 pm ET)
        I drove home, and the house;
        By the house, on the trail;
        By the trail, to the beach;
        To the waves, to where the
        Morning light first hits our
        Land; His shoes off his feet.
        He was naked. And his
        Shoes neat next to him. His
        Body was sprawled on his back.
        His eyes open, stuck wide,
        Looking into the void
        Of the dark night sky. The
        Knife by his shoes drenched in
        The blood that my mother
        Shared in giving a man
        And a woman a right
        To live. And his pale cool
        Chest. Oh God help me! He
        Carved out a heart like the
        Heart we created, a bold
        Geometric heart through
        His Skin above his real
        Heart that wasn't beating
        Anymore. Like an oak,
        Eric, it was carved in
        Him. And his fist was still
        Tight as if he held the
        Carving Shame. I fell. A
        Heart, like words manifest.

VeceroyElmo: (12:01 am ET)
        I'm here for you always.

VentanaBabe: (12:02 am ET)
        The funeral is at
        Noon.

VentanaBabe Signed Off: (12:30 am ET)

VeceroyElmo Signed Off: (12:31 am ET)

<u>SUNDAY NIGHT</u>

VentanaBabe: (11:00 pm ET)
>> Eric. Are you there? Hey?

ViceroyElmo: (11:01 pm ET)
>> Yes love, I am near you.

VentanaBabe: (11:02 pm ET)
>> Only by two miles.
>> I—

ViceroyElmo: (11:03 pm ET)
>> Ugh, my text mail on my
>> Cell is going off. Sec···

VentanaBabe: (11:04 pm ET)
>> Anything important?

ViceroyElmo: (11:10 pm ET)
>> Nope, only meaningless
>> Words.

— —

HOLD ON! Why did he do that? Was that real? Is this real?

— —

From the Author of

PULCHRITUDE FOR THE MIND

Each click and turn of the clock, the Earth moves in time.
Each orbit carries infinite memories, stars and comets soar.
The days brush the life carrying shore.
The nights cool the stampeded concrete roads.

A baby grows to touch the sky. And the sky picks them up.
And sometimes it's like shopping in a grocery aisle, when it's just
The simple things that mean so much, like life held in a summer's
Day watermelon. Or the first break of dawn, when must's

Will be done again. And in all that chaos, there's sleep.
There's the chance to become part of the poem,
And travel oceans wide, where roots have no end,
And flowers glitter, like new rainbows covering the dome,

    And the Beatles were right. Just imagine, it gets you by.
    But do not void your memories, do not over-criticize,
    Just let your Birds of Paradise under tulip clouds ostracize
    Their enchanted youthful sunsets and turquoise waters.

    Don't let shadows drag you down, because shadows
    Disappear and light is temporary. Lose the age, because
    Time doesn't. Take the Ferris Wheel up, and the long
    Hiking Trails back down. Buy a balloon, keep it close, hold on strong,

    And let go, and watch it soar. Take each smile in stride.
     Give up your chair, walk outside or move it to the porch.
    And in those minutes close your eyes and re-open them.
    Imagine without a question in sight, ignore doubts, the given days' pride.

Just answer in your mind's beauty⋯ Imagine Martin Luther King Jr.,
On the day he was assassinated, he was not, and the man who was
To end his Dreams dropped his weapon and embraced him⋯ Imagine
That the wall to Berlin didn't exist and there was no plight between

Neighboring countries; no conspiracies. And see those Two Towers,
Reflecting the Sun's caring light over the fast-paced, now slow-paced
Eying the moving elevators, and a man enjoying the view with a phone
In Hand looking at the City, accidentally spilling coffee. And someone

Hands him a towel and a kiss. And the war for Jerusalem did not exist, there
Were no car bombs, and the children could run in the street. And Palestinian men
Could love Israel as its Brother. And the Titanic never sank and its crew is sitting on
A sunlit porch watching their grandchildren, spirited and free⋯ The German

Army had refuted to take Hitler's orders, and Adolf Hitler understood and the
Camps never put up to a hose of gas. And your great uncle would be walking
Passed you, telling about how sweet his youth was. And children
Could walk on the street on both sides with their head up, and their

Wings high. And Kennedy wasn't assassinated; he would be with a cane,
Sitting next to the Presidents with a great smile. And life is always entertaining,
And your favorite old shows and plays are being put on like new wallpaper,
And paving their name again. Like the first time you were pushed off on your

Bicycle onto the open road, you were given freedom. Cherish it. And the
Tribes that settlers took from, still exist in their grandest children, and they
Don't have to franchise casinos, they're living just like us, and we share
Endlessly. England and Ireland get along like siblings & there is no protest. Just
care.

And all your children are here. Your whole family is here, even those who
Passed or ran away sit next to you for a warming dinner. And you never
Had a miscarriage, and all your children love you—always. And your veteran
Father lives and is barbequing. And your wife is free of cancer.

And there is no Asthma, no chronic disease, or AIDS, no epidemics.
Your pains from your operations dismiss your body, your limbs are all
In tact. You can see clearly even if your eyes weren't meant to. You can
Hear each splash, hoof, jingle, breeze, violin, and chuckle even if your ears fall

Deaf. You can feel the new rains on the tip of your tongue, the dance of dew
As a new day begins. And there are no traffic lines, no wrecks. No one drinks
To become drunk and loneliness doesn't exist. And your cherished pets those
Living and those who left are all free and being about you. With no thorns a rose

Blooms and its colors match the endless aura of the sky's shades, and there are
No clouds, and rays shine through the trees and skate on the poppies and daffodils
Opening with hummingbirds performing their lovable chore. And war does not
Exist. There was no Depression, no need for supply and demand. For wills

And wants are not of money's bribe, and it matters for the growth and advancement
Of the Population, not for the monies, or a system of such. And a house is always
Waiting in merriment. And your stomach, neck, back, Arthritis pains have left, and
Your numbness gone. Your ears are un-popped, you breathe like the waves

Of shoreful winds. Your skin is free of wrinkles, your hair is free from grays.
Your nails do not ache, your legs do not brake. Your crutches can lean against
The walls. And airplanes never crashed, and Pearl Harbor's Day did not end,
Those sailors are here to stay. And the atomic bomb never became in existence.

And New Orleans never flooded, and those covered bodies removed their veil
And walked down Canal Street to watch fireworks over the River. And War Memorials
Were never constructed. Where the Vietnam Memorial sits, lies a park with all the
Love shared in Vietnam not split but together, and villages sprouting life. And
whales

Swim in pods, like families eating a picnic in the meadow. And they say to stop living
In your <u>Dream World</u>, for that always exists. And there shines no broken
Star, statue, law and symbol. Earth is in abundance. And it was never
Your fault, your pains, your suffers— for fault does not exist as there are
No problems at all. And to consider those great days of the past then,

The great days, the golden days, exist right before you. And life is
Penniless. And let your hates, your sarcasms, your humors, your fears,
Your Losses sift like kettled steam vanquished into a zenith skylight.
And rape is not an act or a word. And desire vanishes. Faith, religions disappear

And life just is, let it be. Be and let the rains drench you, the heat cleanse you,
Feel the spirits of emotion, don't hold back from tears. Free yourself from that
Pained purse of agony. And you will wave to lovers of old. Your husband or wife
Who died stands before you with a bouquet, and it's the most romantic day in your
life.

He or she says words that you can only relate to, and life does not have to
Make sense. And a miracle can fall from the sky at any moment, and the
Waters are cleansed and schools move brilliantly. And to hear a child cry,
Or a plate break is not a threat but an enduring way that life balances. Always try.

And there are no pianos performing their last play, as graduations, weddings,
Birthdays are not celebrated to end, but to begin life anew. And a flag does not

Capture a countries' creation, but its people and its colors are limitless.
And there were no
Genocides, homicides, lines bordering against our interior peace. Let it go. Their

Bodies have voices now and hearts in beating form. And the air is crisp. And there
Are no slaves and hostility, humans were never a trade. Africa is full and blooming,
Elephants in Kenya graze in the fumes of the mudded streams. And glaciers still hold
Firm. And the Grand Canyon dresses in the sunset. And that is where our old

Aged Misery vanishes. In this moment we are human, and keep it, hold it, don't
Let it go. Refuse to give up don't let failure have you. Let friends be friends.
Hold harps and let bells ring. Let the ripples move, and the thunder echo.
And this is where poems, language, life, Earth stand. This is where attrition ends.

With us.   With me.   With You.

&

REFLECTIONS OF THE DREAM PANORAMA

I sit beyond a spare grassed turf,
I've seen my share of blossoms before.
Collapsed at the upheavings of my losses,
Laughed at the evenings of my welcomed charms.
Cried beneath a wet overhang.
Stood up and hid underneath the sands of Mars.
I melted in the trenches of frosted heraldry,
Forged my unintended lies into a subsidiary
Victory. But lost my love, lost my cherished
Phaedrus Drapes, and to my Lyssias my markers.
I spied and spined a forage of oats for the poor.
Yet I did not deliver, I sprinkle to them on high.
My laundry of chlordane, and harm choked
The great and bountiful lionfish who
Paralyzed my freckles to wires extending
Whiskey tapestries and long white chalks.

I captured mind, mine did connect
A tortured soul, a wounded net of frequented
Liberties at stake. Alignment made by
Darting hate. My fireplace is empty its canopy on high.
And one life reflects.

—B–A—C–K––T–O—LIFE.

The World beyond these pages is more than poetry can
Convey at times. And at times poetry can take us where the
World leads us, where time ends, and dreams begin. Where
There is hope, and our realities, and problems end, where
Passion blooms in full and rain can cleanse the fallen day,
And sunsets can edge the wrath of heart, and voices, and perception.

 The World beyond these pages is a struggle, and yet to understand it let
your will guide you, let your persistence pull you through, if you can break
the locks that separate both, then will there be a day when we all
understand.

"In a sense we have come to our nation's capital to cash a check. When the
architects of our republic wrote the magnificent words of the Constitution
and the Declaration of Independence, they were signing a promissory note to
which every American was to fall heir. This note was a promise that all men,
yes, black men as well as white men, would be guaranteed the unalienable
rights of life, liberty, and the pursuit of happiness. (Dr. Rev. Martin Luther
King Jr., 'I Have a Dream')"

The Trails To Attrition

MAKE
LIFE–
POETRY

NOT WAR.

Chapter Two
THE TRAIL OF ACCELERATION

WEAVE

When Victory weaves unto a gentle wake,
And comrades are fictitious as the night is blue,
Tragedy is as suspicious when its unknown laughter quakes,
And waterfalls catch fallen canoes.

When Mourning dims the solemn Star,
And hammocks put their limbs to rest,
Humility assimilates prosperity and chars
Desolated profanity to sour its bolted chest.

When Commodity lures a vacant alley without a price,
And incantations fill the paved spaces incompletely,
Vitality monsters in fevered pity that entices
Nothing to an unlocked hinge screwed so neatly.

– – – – – – – –

PRECISION MAGNET – MOTION FANTASIA

Amore is means for a fiberglass cylinder pumping
At a 200 kilometer heart race,
Driven under distinctive taste.
Marble crack lines grooving deeper along plastic
Hyphenated by the sparkle of blue champagne.

Silent mystic majority of fading vibrato
Waits on a trapezoid tilting balcony,
Not in mere suspicion that dwells
Eight minutes on gold karat pavement, gloved traceless
Scents in inhalation of a peach orange nightshade.

The silver velvet laced rims button each fiber optic
Tire rousing the glitter of the candy
Cane bedazzle on each sky car's
Steel skin. Pacing like piercing breeze clearing jaguars
Gearing streamline claw wavelengths with soul and arrow.

Puddles emitting intrepid aviary scarlet
Attributions casting deceit in midnight
Glamour. Neon yellow bamboo
Remotes the sculptured iced palms as archways to depths
Heightened with edge paving entrapment; dwindling chimes.

With the multitude of an armoire, three mouths open
Side baring, barely entering this entrance
Capitalized by the zircon
Tunnels I venture with coated porpoise ivory,
Reflected off the ethanol stained checkerboard.

Blacked, and opened canopy merged with the sound of Locke's quest,
Curious, I sink into quicksand gossamers.
Satin heels and wheels sing high
Through the granite bell carpeting. Widespread dismay
Collapses as the belle dwells to jump— grasping gown

And rosemary puree disperses through my uncut lungs.
Sprinting as bold pyramid goblets shatter,
Grasping through the lunar's bright reeve,
As jester fangs possess untwined folly, I clutch
The twirl of ribbon holding her from vestibule.

— — — — — — — — — — —

— — — — — — — — — —

THE CATHEDRAL   from *Pulchritude for the Mind*

In the morning the Sun rises in the East.
The tower echoes with seven bell strikes, each with
Its own moment of silence,
The light glides downward into halls and pews,
Shining through stained glass,
Thoughts and memories are welcomed here of the living
And the deceased.
Water near the doors remains still, though air is present.
Some pews tend to creak,
For they are old yet still standing strong,
Other pews, refurbished, maintained and painted hold long.
The colors of each window glitters into the cathedral,
Proving that life is beautiful.
Music in the cathedral is of the voices of the world.
Deep enchanted voices, of the old and young, man and woman,
Mother, and Child, and the Father.
He who watches over the sound is listening.
The guests, who don't try to attend, attend anyway.
The hated, the starving, the weak, and the dying take asylum here.
The happy, the young, the rich, the gallant and dynamic take
Asylum here.

The afternoon comes and the lights settle down,
We are living in the day as the hours continue their course.
The time, the Earth, the ways of life go round.
Clouds and birds flutter by, towards who hold the cathedral in place.

The arms of the cathedral give their support as well,
And give balance and structure in one space.
Footsteps walk along the corridors in the outer wings.
But they do not attend to the main room until the time is right.
Thus they would rather go and do their own things.
Even knowing that the Light is brighter in the main room.
Hence the room of mass is silent, when it could be busy,
Booming with noise, and talk of the days.
But it is sacred, and it is silent, and it is protective,
Its arms cover us and hold its soul and structure in place,
Even in times of darks and grays.
The wood ceiling is the collective of boned ribs of this room,
Every arch holds the body.

The floor is marble, but has blackened spots, and dust that
Doesn't come off.
Reappearing stains that can't seem to be erased stay and last
Until Time's permission grants it.

The Sun begins to set, and the trees outside the cathedral sway tiredly.
Watching the sun pull itself down, bringing its light to other countries,
And other grounds.
Flames in the candleholders shine
Even brighter as the natural light returns.
Each bit of light, the last of the days', bring everlasting crowns
To those who know its ways
And can recreate it for others.
The night opens its doors to its sisters and brothers.
There is Solemn talking, and thinking of the day,
Moments go by, but they have passed long ago.
The present creates an image of tomorrow.
The cathedral does not move, but does let go
Of the ground, and it rises towards the last bit of light,
And follows it to the next day.

AN ALLEGORY OF A RISING NATION

At restless ease I watch the delay
Between each winded chime.
Gathered between the footsteps,
The transformation of the fluorescent faces;
The cellular motivations that
Connect us in single
Sympathy of our own kind.
This visual is heard through thine departed
Eyes.

Have I touched those other hands before?
Mentioned to a hot brunette
The passions that my bleeding
Heart could at least give out, unyielding wild
Anxiety that I felt. Could not
Reach her soul as I did
Unveil my darkest method
By bluntly emphasizing my biting heart
Torn.

The time lapsed her, but then others broke
From upon the conceit,
Metabolic romantics,
Who for I entrusted my liberty; youth.
The openness of air between first breath
And edging immortal
Mindset weakened under
Worlds of antipathy tortured my freedom's
Start.

I gave, I gave ages everything
Hence Aphrodite could
Not, but oh regret begs her
That I need her, yet purpose unreasoned paths,
Nonsensical, are treachery that
I; her⋯ I drain without
The cyclical expected
Lips, who Shelley well-deserved, garnish through my
Thirst.

Never a romance, Napoleon
Triumphs in history.
My impaired tactics nimbly
Undone, as I rape my eyes from ever left
To see that dawn's grace was not to be.
Journeyed from un-wanting
Hands, my family, a love not
At one the narcissist desires; but
Here.

What a family has, the latter to
An orphan who needs it.
Due, with nobility gives
Me a pleasure for my able eye stems, who watch
With wagging tongues. He is a man; lacks
The guilt, but holds the scorn.
I sheath, as he's brought stripped
Like a fallen angel. Innocently over-
Touched.

My hands drip with all the blood vanquished
From my feeble attempts,
As my liberty is won,
Psychotically with tears on all faiths; I tremble.
He smiles, and feeds on me, but he
Knows nothing of my real
Lustful perception, with the
Consequence he provides my longing heart to
Kill.

Oh Adieu, farewell innocent lame
Falsehood underneath the
Standards, etiquettes which
Do not match internal boundaries of my
Intricate judgment, passive towards the
Morality direct
By the most ethical priests.
And I, eye of the new frontier to pillage
Tame.

Set by foot, one thousand knaves, knights, knives
And all your wits, lack guilt
Until your own gold decays. I
Urinate on grounds that once kindled kindness
By guided children splashing glory,
Naked and unclothed in the
Filth, whose stench I witness fall
On my hands. I back away, douse the landfilled
Harbour.

The banner waves as orphans come
And kneel underneath my mane.
I separate them like the
Orphan whose life went contained behind the bright
Fluorescent signs··· Now I'm older, watched
Those protestors, and the
Rioters, who "figured" it
Before the people do. I laugh because I
Knew.
– – – – – – –

You always mention what's wrong– what is really going on?

Come on enjoy the text, keep trying things might get better– one day.

A man on a red eye flight takes not his pity in society, but dwells on
The dream in motion alongside motion's parallel.

–   - - - -

SOARING BY WATER'S EDGE

Silence breaches the Eastern Seaboard,
Tides wage evenly upon the sands' mast,
And air sweeps you like a fallen leaf towards
The tip of Florida, and the tanners going to baste
In the morning sun.

The warm ocean glitters in its green
And from sweet white sand, to swamp land, the exhale
Of the waves pave an even glide between
Palms and evergreens, that hold swinging hammocks. The wind's gale
Brushes you easily.

And the gale heaves up a heap of air,
You land along the open Gulf and brush
Passed Cape Sable, then up near Fort Myers.
Hovering along the white hard—sanded coast, the winds push
Passed flamingo pinks.

With dazzling vivacity, turquoise
Clear aqua blankets paved, yet uncharted.
Not a cloud in the world it seems. Seagull noise,
With Caribbean vibes begin to serve guests. Time started
For, yet, once again.

Beach villas, peach and stucco side palms,
Two former spring breakers from '52
Bring their grandchild for pails and the calm
Building of temporary homes that die underneath two
Sweeps on the beach shore.

The child smirks and continues her
Construction again, and the couple watch
The early risen men with their hooks, fishers,
Who returned with a smile because nothing gained, or caught.
Always tomorrow.

Dolphins reflecting the simmering
Sun's early orange, shaded by lenses,
Do the Butterfly. Swimmers glimmering
Adjacently in beach pools ease their eager—stressed senses,
Loved by our Nature.

A melodic gust lures us over
The condos carrying the view passed one
Coast and the highways bridge new commuters

To more scenic sights passed evergreens uncut, with not one
Separated hoard.

And herons take flights. Over spread exits,
With Cracker Barrels, Texaco stations,
Highway lighting turning off, the thickets
And Algae covered swamps hum with crickets. Some sensations
Of sulfur's strong bite.

The sting hastens as you reach the Pine
Island Sound. Nestled in a pristine view
Of the dark green waters, docks, otters, fine
Aquatic crafts. More advanced than the Calusas' canoe—
Which guided hunters.

To the Cayo Coast, West of the Sound
Lies a secluded beach with some lightning
Struck limbs of palm and evergreen abound
The hard gray and white sand combed by flaking waves tightening,
To get only so close.

A Floridian with a sweat—stained
Polo shirt with the scent of vanilla
Deodorant takes your hand. You are drained
By the humidity. Here's some sweet tea, with an umbrella.
On his Carver yacht.

He knows you're a visitor, says relax,
And you're off the port in no time. Gliding,
Steadfast, you finish your glass and he asks
You where you're from. He tells you his life and dreams while driving
The sky's reflection.

He slows down at the wake of Charlotte
Harbor to refill the gasoline tank.
He waves to his wife and children, scarlet
Colored bags are in their arms, walking to the yacht. You yank
Them hospitably

Up on the boat. But you want off, his
Wife urges you to stay on because they're
Also headed to Biloxi. In agreement with
Her she shakes your hand, gets up, and she goes arranging their
Picnic with crawfish.

New to crawfish? The glamorous bright
Red delights boiled towards mouth—watering
Amazement? First take the body from plight
Of not being eaten. Break at mid; eat meat; start sucking
The brains from the head!

She knew that from having been raised in
Lafayette, Louisiana. The town
Known as Acadiana, with Cajun,
Creole cuisine, and where the state's beat, Zydeco was found,
And other lagniappes.

The husband finished filling up, and
One of the kids pointed to a bobbing
Manatee, which had propeller scars and
With a silent peek to the surface, she began dropping
As the engine raged.

She also unveiled her basket of
Sweet potato fries with a honey dip.
And watching the sun now fit in gear above,
Charlotte Harbor began to open shop, shutters, to sip
It's mid-morning cup.

As leaving the port the fumes gallop
Of salt, oil, and pineapple and citrus,
And the gallery of named boats elope
With a bottle of champagne, the Esmeralda, Marcus,
The Jolly Roger,

The Love Boat #9, St. Claire Two,
Big Black Betty, Orca Orca, Georgia,
Helen, Paris-France, Tally Ho, Por Tu,
Ahab's Wife's Boat, Ketchup and Mustard, The Loch Ness Mama,
Cupid's Winged Arrow.

Two pelicans drop like pterodactyls
Jet on their prey, and glide in victory,
With specks of drops from their wings, like Dactyls
With sparks from molding a great wheel in metallurgy.
Then digest at port.

The port veers out of view, with the coast
Of Sarasota with its beaches and
Evergreens and ivies, Orange Cosmos,
Dazzling red hibiscus, a Florida panther that stands
Eying through the trees.

An empty old oak lifeguard tower,
Creaks as the waves pave into still sparkles.
What's this? There injects a colored clover
Rotund fin that slaps onto the surface, with gleaming shells,
Mothers are ready.

The sea terrapin waddle in a

Brittle pace, with each smack and pull, no steps
Or stairs, just survival. And trailing the
Mineral sugar briskly like snow angels, are bereft
As they'll leave them behind.

His wife while cleaning up the lunch drew
Up on her early rise activity
With the kids called geocaching; A clue,
And a GPS device is the only guide— solely
To find the treasure.

One of the children portrayed this game
As if they were a gang of Cutthroats on
A treacherous journey to find the same
Aztec jewels and galley as Jean Lafitte may have hidden,
In open beauty.

Jean Lafitte, the Buccaneer, the Gent
Of Fortune, the important man of New
Orleans. Blacksmith, and debonair agent
For the female spectacle, desire. Yet for he too
Was a Patriot.

The treasure they uncovered was three gray
Shirts with Eco—Tourism America
Ironed on the surface. It was really
Worth the price for the experience. They even got a
Coupon to return.

Two wave runners zoom on by with four
Frenzied young women waving and giggling.
Of course everyone smiles and waves pour
Out like banners in the wind from your sticky hand jiggling
As the yacht bounces.

A film of sea breeze hits your forehead,
And trickles onto your Hawaiian shirt,
With Magnolias and Sailboats instead
Of blue orchids and oceans of reefs and Hammerheads worth
Another voyage.

Like a new frame placed in the Louvre,
The Keys unlock into view starting with
Manasota with soft plucked plush swept shores,
Opened back to maroon and purple, cream beach homes, equipped
With some dish networks.

With gated pools sitting next to white
Catamarans, beach balls, blue cabanas,
And a barely flickering, holding tight

Sunfish sail. A man in Sunday clothes holds a banana,
While playing a flute.

Then edging passed Manasota there
Breathes Venice with the rows of beach resorts,
With balconies holding wet towels, over
A tranquil paradise of beachfront cafes, with all sorts
Of playful venues.

A cloud passes overhead briefly
Shading your warm skin—with humid drew drops,
With a glazed cool joust, but convectional glee
Builds back into the heat, and his wife with the blender, pops
A fresh fruit cooler

And mixes it with rum and ice. Then
A salmon pink, neon green, parasail
Begins to ascend as the view glistens
With two international tourists, who both laugh and yell,
And the children laugh.

And with a streamlined exchange en route,
Manasota fades off, with Casey Key
In its solitude and a parachute
Awaiting to take a visitor unsuspectingly—
The yacht yields towards shore.

The children politely offer you
First turn to get a new glimpse in the chute.
Not that sure what you are getting into,
You are strapped in a harness—chair connecting to the chute,
In front, the steel cord.

White sand below the palm of your foot
Brushes away with a light tickle feel,
The children and the mother smile, put—
—ting your glass safely on the yacht. The polo shirt man reels
You in for safety.

He cranks up the motor of this red
Boat with yellow words: "The Great Wanderer,"
You leg your way onto the edge with threads
Of the blue chute behind you, and the boat excels faster
Than you expected.

A burst of wind pillows your face and
Body. And he nods and lets the reel out,
And the air jets, zigzags through each nail and
Limb. And the ground is not with or without
Its laced gravity.

But you rise passed the occasion, just
In five seconds you are at 50 feet,
Then at one hundred, then two. He adjusts
The line, and you are winged again. The line and chute, then meet
Their ends and vanish.

And you descend through a cloud like the
First drop of a brewing storm landing in
Clearwater as the pearl of light forms a
Triangular prism of violet and marigold thin
Rays of the low noon.

Tikki flames shine on Caladesi,
Where dwindling pass the puff of the night's heat,
A nervous young man looks at her true eyes.
And kneels with the setting sun. And takes out from a rose sheet,
What sparked great Dactyls.

And with a slow kiss the soar raises
You over into the tops of clouds beyond
The constellations, and you are in paced
Appreciation as you touch the sand again out on
The white sanded turf.

This is Panama City Beach and
The midnight stars are glowing on an F-
15 Jet cruising passed the freckles and
The heart-pumping neon, giant fiberglass. High sounds deaf
The passive party.

And just-married or the completely
Free step up a bar, get soaked in chlorine,
Or high bottled brewskies, with extremely
Over-flowing pools of love. A newlywed feels just fine
To get ten tattoos.

A black light club strikes a soul bit tone,
And arms move like flames on red monarch wings.
Just lick the air and it isn't the zone
For minds stuck on fishhooks, nooks and crannies. Fashioned on things,
Irrelevant dreams.

A drunken boogie boarder is flung
Off his board in a two-foot wave onto
Half-lit bikini smoking space outs. Who hung
Out with the wrong crowd the night before. That's okay you two
Can come chill with us.

They place their hands on your back, you're not

Too comfortable, but they certainly
Are. But damn, their parents pull them, unknot
Them from you, because they had school to go to. But really
The night is all heat.

Just think if you weren't there, and wheels
Touch Down from a two—hour flight from the Fort
Myers International. It still feels
Humid, and you see a console of some migratory
Flocks. You're in Biloxi.

—   — — — — —

YOUNG LOVE

    I shut the car door, and the Mazda hits rock bottom.
    Seven stories below. I turn to you and follow through
    Like a pitchfork evacuating through tangled kelp.
    The flares and clinking axes tap our windows,
    Now is not the time to call for help.
    The engine smashes, the wires tangle around our legs,
    Everything is tempting to stop us now, the air bags break.
    The wipers start working at 4,000 feet, and it just keeps
    Getting deeper.

    Nothing rhymes, nothing seems the same.
    The glass bursts, you wonder how I got you into this mess,
    I press the acceleration in rage and plunder.
    You try to escape but you're caught in stress
    Upon the Velcro of the car window mirrors.
    At 12,000 feet it is unbearable to breathe in each other's
    Mouth, but it's working···It's working. Hold on, 8 seconds.
    One of the wheels loses their tires, and we begin to twirl.
    Capacity has reached its limit, passed its limit—and

We are fully immersed in quick sand, in clam's mouth,
   And weeping pearls. We descend; gravel and dust
Whiskers our faces. You call a friend; but your battery has died,
    And there's no escape, as we are hit dead on by a submarine.
      Of ignorance, you say "Hey watch it Asshole!"
    I see your anger, and suddenly the ignition turns on,
      The lights are getting brighter, and brighter,
      And suddenly we're almost there, I think.

      We separate for a bit as we hit a land mine.
      We wake up and bob to the surface.

THE MINNESOTA TOUR

THE GENERAL PROLOGUE

Here embarks the Book of the Minnesota Tour.

After the bend of the quarter of a
Fiscal Year, April's Tax had smooth'ed fray,
A dawning of bold reminiscent plans,
Had yielded wide, for strong social demands.
As Aires lays his able flames to rest
With his trimmed lasso round Taurus' crest,
Vigor remains an altered ego, as
Children loft inside at watching time pass.
As the air for their breath is monitored,
Hence another bill, another source lost,
A balloon in cost ascends despair; tossed.
Honest first is yet a brash ridicule
For Scottish hunt, and seize the gowk and bull,
But if one is to lose grip on what
Is false, what is true, then they are well—put
As fool of spring and loss of truth's meaning.
For as facetious men, who are weening
On the topic brought by Eve's fallacy
On his own minute fault line (its lacey
Unabridged course) men choose to take Earth's crust.
Hills of lavender aster become dust,
Daffodils in Apollo's golden rays tracked
Into Pluto's follicles along cracked
And narrow edges of love—struck Gaia,
Settled between the prisms of Maya.

   As Nelson bloomed in nineteen—seventy
That Earth is but a gourmet brevity
Settled as the protégé of printed
Touch, disregard in the least, hinted,
As left to perish by the wrathful nerves
Of man's dominance. Men made unjust swerves
To market their success, but led away
To drive excess—led a false unpaved way
Channeled to clandestine souls of the lay.

   Easter given name by graced Eostre
Who the Sax rejoiced by Bede's bistre—
Clear non—cryptic words. It was said that she

Divine, saw a distressed girl, who barely
Glad, mattered only toward a paralyzed
Frozen winged aviary hurdle stylized
In Frost's yule of solemn episteme.
Eostre despaired in dichotomy
Of loss and rebirth; transformed the lamed bird
To a snow hare who laid eggs of closed surd—
By her reaction. Let alone then, the
Hare became crème, mocha, coco, of a
Plastic–cased display paved in Earth's surface
Above the plastered pink chicks in a case
Of marshmallow delights. While tractors rode
Lover's lane, and rabbit lay, to corrode
Where betwixt a heart could have engulfed true
Pain of Cupid's amorous arrow crew
Drawn back, sprinting into meadows and stay
Harpooned in the mind; thus, to get away.

    Traveling in lasting Minnesota
From New London to Alexandria,
Routing on the verdant Glacial Ridge Trail,
A bright blue tour bus carries several
Citizens and one immigrant waiting
To see their money's worth, while debating
If romantic imagery has become
Faded lust, just another Feng Shui phylum
That re–instates a human pleasure. But
They came to forget temporary glut,
To see what else is to be remembered.

    In the front seat sat an AIRLINE PILOT
Garnished in a fuchsia and violet
Polo shirt with plaid shorts, sitting cross–legged,
With a silver karat Rolex that pegged
Into his sweaty unshaven arm on
The green arm rest. His crew cut made salon
Perfection seem cut and dry. Scrimmaged down
Underneath his Roman nose was a frown
Of a stiff chunky mustache that had hooks
On both wings. His clothes always ironed. Nooks
And Crannies of his daily life measured
As firm as the buckle he so treasured
From a fellow militant friend in the
Trench called Nam, and had golden horns on a
Desert drenched bull skull; a bovine price left
Unspoken, chewed and fixed, a life bereft
Of a vengeance now controlled by signals
Blinking in the morning. Diagonals
Of grazing hands that direct sanity
Into the appropriate fanged vanity

Of Plot A, Runway B, Gate thirty—two.
He has traveled the world, and though he too
Feels his edged martyrdom towards a lost cause,
He feels there may be life without a pause
If people fly—high – like his son—in—law.

Both from San Francisco, though his son saw
Only in Californian eyes. His son
Was a FLIGHT ATTENDANT, and was Asian
Like his mother who was at home washing
China and assorted bone plates, coshing
Out the smudged stains surpassed in their homeland.
He wore about his skin—tight soy green and
Spring blue tank, a string with a dried flounder
Covered in red glitter from a bunder
Merchant in Beijing. He wore two fake pearl
Earrings, and his lips of sparkle and swirl,
Refracted through his scented potpourri
Cologne. His serving fingers, no hurry,
Patted his guava—smoothened—glossed hair as
When he wiped a spittle from a babe's gas,
And was thanked upon with a friendly wink.
He wasn't eying the verdant distinct
Flora and woods on the road, but how to
Emulate the ANCHORWOMAN'S hairdo.

Her extensions curled and broadcasted her
Goopy eye—liner bogginess over
Perplexed stainless steel gritting headgear. CLANK!
Each rubble thrift layer, fired a blank
In bounty of the springing tires. She
Wore her high school jeans, ten years since, would be
Years of just crèmes of suits embroidered
Skirts and Faberge tipped ink pens conferred
Near blinking screens and overfilled coffee
Mugs. Hers, white, said: "I Heart Salt Lake City."
Of hearts she delivered to more than one,
Her husband, her mic, her waved cue to run
Down cards, and the red lit blinking lenses,
She had to be with Beth to build fences;
Wash the carpet and his briefs with April;
And get ready for her husband's new girl,
His fourth, like a sister she guessed. But with
April and Beth they drew tears as if pith
Of noble woo had no sole defining
Momentum laid by matching crystal bands
Another clunk! She put her jaw in her hands.

Looking through all the windows to get a
Better view, the CROSSING GUARD, edged in the

Aisle way like a hermit crab checking
The outside presence of bleak life's infecting
Enigmatic possibilities veiled.
His alligator eye patch strapped on held
A blank veracity to the eye that
Matched his sharp turquoise penetrating cat—
Optic bulb in orbit to let pass those
Ready body systems verging where goes
Time, between stops, breaks and whistles blown loud;
Nearing his old age, no tenure, but proud
To be going, walking. Thus he sat and
Observed his opened window at command
Of his own hands— directions not for those
Of others. He plucked his gray hairy nose.
His home was of the Cleveland *Indians*—
Of such a word, justly, Americans.

     Glancing off the thermometer sat one
Gender—less state and plate PLASTIC SURGEON
Who was chewing on his two value meals,
Burping between each slurp, who after keels
To reveal half his back edging over
His cushioned pungent oozing seat cover.
This was his far—out vacation from the
City of Minneapolis to a
Natural experience on vista
Of a safari of wonders. Missed the
Train, but took a cab all the way. Unlike
His clients, nature didn't need planned pike
To disassemble branch with silicon
Temporary beauty. Already gone.

     In hungered swelling eyes sat a donut—
Wielding stomached POLICEMAN who put
His belt at one notch instead of two, like
Normal. He wobbled to and fro for wike
Of a juicy mustard drenched beef soaring
In a field of mayo—ketchup pouring
Like a winged Pegasus in stampede of
Many collapsed in a bun of hot love.
His Cirque du Soleil "O" was covered with
Dried pink Slurpee. His tongue hunger a myth—
Tormented desire spilled below the belt,
From his inner growls, passed his badge he felt
His handcuffs, and the waistband of a dame
He met in the Mirage of Vegas fame
Of triple—sevens and X's. His tear—
Drenched eyes with his drool, found a leather rear.

     The elder STRIPPER sat in yellow hide

Though passed her torched pink stilettos drove road—wide
Stretch marks within an Everest jacket
Sealed tight about two cantaloupe packet
Conundrums. Her multi—colored finger
Nails shelled a long, hardened dinger—
Shaped Clorox pen wiping away at a
Lipstick stain on her lower container
Pocket. Her duck—billed brass cane was caged near
Withered spinach—sandaled toes of nails shear
In a jam of sparkling psoriasis.
Her moonlit raw umber dialysis
Of skin and brasserie tan line jiggled
At the potholed gallop hop and giggled
Agility of the tight shocks. She was bald
And hid her scalp under a franchise called
The Kansas City Chiefs, KCMO.
She had a green wig, but carried it low.

    Watching with his face constrained sat the laugh,
The COMEDIAN of Bronx. A giraffe
In making long—necked overdosed edged jabs
In front of gum greased glazed gray blue brick slabs,
Extending his three—fingered hand to make fun
With a Taurus PT1911
Lurking behind in his unzipped pocket.
Wearing a black button down, a locket
Round his pale bony Medusa tattoo
Whose snakes were impaled with plastic sphere—blue
Rings in his breast biters which were like hard
Frozen strawberries. His nails nice and charred
With piercings in them. His jeans had not been
Washed in two weeks and carried a rich keen
Crotch aroma. His pink Mohawk was his
Enthusiasm in deep—charted—bliss—
Next to a splattered birthmark chiseled on
His smooth snow hued scalp. However Gaston
Leroux would not, could not plaster the masked
Rubix—perplexed torment jumbling throb axed
Circling his shaded eight ball eyes. In awe,
Looked on a TAX AUDITOR, who so saw
In him his youthful rebel self displayed.

    Through his early baby booming light grayed
Curling hair in his benzene—fumed mind drew
The days when his friends ventured up on to
Rock Creek Park, near Woodley Park Zoo and in
A legs akimbo circle would roll up some twin
Mary Janes, and think about a blue—eyed broad
Wearing a clear gypsy skirt. Then her bod
Swayed. Her long silk black Janis Joplin hair

Carried groovy psychedelic vibes. Bare
Necessities of life; but then he'd wake
Up with a bordello scent and great ache
In the Sigma Epsilon Alpha Pi
House, as stringently soiled and dirty,
Staring at a sign that said "We all made
Ahava with you Lester!" then he'd fade.
His navy wool socks added fluff to his
Maroon beach sandals. And up above this
Had looms of fast food meals combusted in
Wandering gyrating fat limbs. His thin
Days seemed viable in his mind with his
Fifteen daily Nat Shermans. Back to his biz,
With his long nose inhaling numbers on
Ledged sheets, not linen sheets. His wife a non—
Janis Joplin; his children—spoiled brats.

    A HOUSEWIFE then offered some chopped carrots
From her well—kept Tupperware on a free
Seat near the window of still and blurry
Fluttering trees, and briefly, a rippling
Meandering creek. A brilliant tripling
Gander of loons with spotted wings glided
As if Irish violins abided
By the drawn out labor of a bagpipe
Yet conversing to make life a calm wipe
Of a gentle offering of peace and
She placed, with a smile, it in his hand.
He took it brashly and chucked it at the
TELEMARKETER'S head. In response a
Cell phone was dropped from his hand and shattered
Its screen on the carpeted floor. Battered
And bruised the telemarketer turned his
Head to the housewife; she was in a tizz.
And sprung up not his index, and she flew
Into sobs, as she had to deal with, too,
Arnold living in her Sacramento.

    Yet the culprit was not incognito
To the broken phone. The T—marketer
Then picked from his seven bags another
Cell phone to draw. Then his swab—cleaned Persian
Ears began to satellite coercion.
He continued to listen to an open
Seminar on speaking English. He then
Took out a dictionary, kissed it and
Turned to C, to R, confused, turned to N;
Thus, finally found A. He kissed the page.
He took out a pen from his buttoned sage—
Colored, "God Bless America" long—sleeve

Shirt to mark the many words and the leaves.
His shirt tucked into red, white and blue shorts.
He liked Michigan, and USA sports
Were not his cup of tea. He married there.

    A peach INTERIOR DECORATOR
With rosy red hair, giggly dimples, a
Hidden plump nose, two Bullfrog eyes, a fey
Odd mouth that had two gold male teeth attached
With lasers for her curved buckteeth. A patched
Italian tablecloth served as her dress,
Stitched towels paved her thorax to then press
On her roasted dough and inflating whiteheads.
She was reading *Living*, and the sweet breads
Martha was baking looked scrumptious. She was
From the land of the famous horns—on gaz—
Fastest animal in the USA,
The pronghorn in Wyoming. Every day
She would rearrange the furniture so
The pronghorn could pick up a bite and go
Out to Nature. In the 30s they were
Shipped to Germany by blimp, and were sure
To spread more than what was needed, it seemed.

    Sleeping next to the red gelatin, beamed
Her teenage—old nephew from Manchester—
In New Hampshire. He was so much thinner—
So thin that as he was sleeping his pants
Would sift lower to second layer pants.
He was a willing CONSTRUCTION WORKER.
With the sun barring on his grand slumber
He put his beanie over his dot eyes.

    Stringing a ukulele with two sighs,
Bold barge—built bronze hands whipped each aluminum
String round the tuners. He began to drum
The bridge, performing Chopsticks. Adding M—
P3s to his ears, his right hand played them—
Or so the BODYBUILDER thought and
Was just striking the strings like waves on land.
His orchid pants were about to burst open.
His eruptive quads with a tsunami pen
Could add a domino effect to the
Tour bus. Fortunately he was on a
Rare bottle of Paxil that kept him "strong".
His top was more Kalua pork than tong.
On his drum was Kiwila's shell, his ol'
Sea turtle that he sat on. Its green soul
Was in merry lani. He was also
A Diabetic from the town, Hilo.

Fogging up the black window rained black curls,
With the armrest raised, her lips drew hot swirls
Around the CASINO RESORT OWNER'S
Dice! She, the fast salsa calor puller,
O' the bella—ILLEGAL IMMIGRANT.
Her Tijuana blazed sangre vagrant—
Passed borders wide, her legs like twin cacti,
O' the margarita drenched in sky dye,
And where it aches she'll make it rain cold cells,
And where it bakes, her skin drives caramels.
Where sol and luna intercourse lays her
Velvet lasso, played round your bold lure.
And by that time fall will have cojones
As the zorro has just sniffed her lonely's—
He goes cadaver to days of the dead,
She takes it all with some serious head.

The sweaty resort owner is even
Native American and her heaven's
Gate outdoes the stellar divas, he can't
Compare his own workers at all or chant
A soaked cloud amor as her grappling hook
Draws tangled Old Glory from his fly. Look
She replaced apple pie with tortillas;
Plus Southern Baptist conservatistas—
Especially the innocent Book ladies—
Would love to cross their tongues on her lovely
Daiquiri lips and suckle. He is not
To go to his wife in NM; he's bought
An entrada por todos pescados
Pobres to escape the labor of those
American women. O' the graced bell
That she so strikes unlike Uncle Sam's taxed hell.

The SALSA CHOREOGRAPHER observed.
Her fingers on her all red striped preserved
Puma sweat clothing and Adidas sneakers
Watching the rolling, clinking like beakers
Tossing about a lab of dance and prance.
She fixed her orange beret, took her glance
Off the burrow duet onto her black
Satin handkerchief, and her nose a clack
Of Valencia vigor performed a trot
With high sorpresa, quick snow—white phlegm shot
And speckled her purple—star—shaped visors.
She took them off to reveal her blind cores
In a sight passed the words of poetry.
She wiped them, and put them back merrily.

Her comrade lover the MADAM OF THE
COUNTRY CLUB patted her mucus with a
Purell Wipe. The madam with her ninety—
Year old lips approached her cheek as if she
Was attempting to set her car parked with
Halts and screeches. Like a spongy wet lith
Her die—hard bridge—face—lips merged a suction
That drew out TPs of prune juice auction—
Bidding the longest to stay on her frost
White—twenty—five—year—old cheeks. Her eyes crossed
Up to her visors and put them on right.
She fibbed she was sixty to add a bite,
But the 25 thought she was thirty.
Madam wore a full gray gown all perky,
With two sets of sky blue spandex stockings
With varicose veins bulging and hocking
Out of the attached meat her porcelain
Could carry. Her hair bun less like a crane,
But ladybug—like with white spots on a
Gray shell. From her throbbed kiss, a stare from the
BARBER sliced in suspicion. Madam was
From the grand Catskills. He ignored the fuzz.

His sharp eyes clipped in a blink back to his
Seat, and the turned off TVs, and what is
Going on in the paper, and the clear
Yet bird pooped window, and his cramping rear.
Sides himself he noticed the other dark
Skin tourists: the stripper, who was a lark;
The flight attendant rubbing his firm knees;
The rich PRES. OF A RECORD COMPANY;
& the flamboyant PEDIATRICIAN.
He was from Saint Louis; Missourian
By birth, and his job at the Supercuts—
Whites were a major part of the gamut.
O' fro and the two "mergers" in the back.
Caramels in a fun—sized space: compact.

The FISHERMAN from Coos Bay, Oregon
Sat humbled with his greasy gelled beard on
The edge holding a fresh clipped spine with a
Straw—tube spar, and taped it to the spine's gray
Slits. The heaviest spine he caught was of
A Chinook salmon that weighed way above
Scale; One—hundred—thirty pounds! He gave it
All to charity. He ran a red bit
Of thick yarn from each pointed spar—spine tip
And knotted firmly. He recalled his lip
Dried in the frost of that Pacific night,
And his wife nestled in his arms as bright

As a golden poppy. Rain, sweat and tears
Beat against the main sails like the clunker
Feel of each shocked bounce. He laid out her dress
She wore that night, and clipped it, took a rest,
And thought of how the boom slammed her head twice,
And her foot caught in the line. She bled thrice
While laying her head at bay and the tempest
Waves, and whipping rain pouring down. The best
Catch was on the line, one hard to reel. A
Choice not taken—could not have. For then the
Waves ceased, and her last words were: "Get that Fish!"
He fought the Sea of Deception to dish
And wager a three—hour pull to then
Achieve a last wish; thus he said, "Amen."
He finished sewing, and tied the bridles
With the flying line, and the reel. Caudles
He gave to her injured body did not
Soothe, and could only hold her hand in hot
Misery. He finished the kite, and looked
Out at the peace blue light called sky, hooked
With dreams, love, and life's uncharted nature.

    Teary, sat the speechless SOCIAL WORKER
From Des Moines, Iowa, at watching this
Kite form. She had white long hair. With a hiss,
She realized his to—go oxygen tank
Required a refill. He gave her thanks.
She was wearing her turquoise Peace Corps shirt
That had bleach stains on it. Her suburban hurt
Neck needed Banana Boat, but she was
Use to it. Her work in Zambia caused
Her pain—resistance to build. Though she seemed
To want to leave this paced life of well—deemed
Good for love, for an inexperienced
Opposite transaction of the line spliced
In those basic steps: birth, life, love, and death.
Life's line lacks a ruler she thought; the breath
Is to survive—she figured on birth. There's
A God, social help, parallels, and cares,
And when life is empty, there are great needs.

    A man with a bow of blue mopped hair with beads
Of holographic shades perched over to
Watch a colorful Tetris take form. "Oooo,"
He gasped. He was Canadian from the
Island above Washington of such a
Grand British, and stunning carved totem pole
Venue: Victoria. He became whole
When feeling majestic in lines than lives.
He practiced back and forth with falls and dives,

Twists and turns, and landing that perfect grasp—
Even when he was drunk, making girls gasp.
He became the TRAPEZE ARTIST. Under
His blue beading Bob Marley hair plunder
Were a set of green cross—eyes. He giggled
At the game play, and his round ears wiggled.

The PRESIDENT OF THE RECORD CO. sat
Wide in espresso corduroy slacks at
The second to last row with his marble
Black shades, deceived his spiced mood in garble
Mixed in with his pure sepia soft skin shrine
And white gold grin. Dollar—wise, he was fine.
But his wife is at home in labor to
One of his own clients' kids. One eye blue,
And the other brown, his hair was dyed blond.
He met her when falling into a pond.

Across him, checking his own pulse in his
Own boredom sat the doctor in drained list—
Less lethargy. The PEDIATRICIAN'S
Stress dwindled in outmoded expression
As he looked out the window at a blue
Jay. But felt his groin pang because of two
Children that delivered great reflexes
To his PhD Johnny T. Texas—
That's what he called it in Abercrombie,
North Dakota where he worked. Like a bee
He'd check children and their problems day by
Day. He was from Pakistan, and asked why
They called him a true blue North Dakotan.
The Record Co. Pres. Traveled from London.

With running clipping stampede of fingers
Sat the AUTOCAD ARTIST with zingers
Being thrown at his huddled position
In symmetrical and formed composition
Planning out rooftops built over pansies.
He designed what came to people's fancies.
One client wanted to balance their chi
And their yin and yang better, be happy
With their atmosphere, so he designed a
Stainless—steel plate gourd—shaped tower by foyer
Over stork nests and newborn baby birds.
The Cat 5 pillaged and plowed, with their words
Becoming squished entrails on vinyl sharp wheels.
He paints what his client wishes to steal.
His brush drags from Chicago, Illinois
And nature cannot take on art's convoy.

        Sipping seltzer, the INSURANCE AGENT
Withdrew Yellow rimmed teeth, two buck teeth bent
Underneath the quills of a sharp pierced gray
And red mustache over chapped lips. As a cray
Chewing on the low tide, he sips the
Last froth and douses his lips in licks. A
Black plastic rosary tangles out on
His plush perspiration double—chin. Blond
Dyed hair in a scrunchie leaks down his curved
Osteoporosis spine. He so serves
Across a Cross of different beams set
In flames against Butler's Act that beget
All men to dream—more than they should—he choked
In thought, looked out at God's landscape and poked
At a crisp stream, and remembered his white
Wedding. Then in finding his wife in light
Scarred youth skin, the day after, he who told
Her he'd always be there, found her drowned cold
In the Congaree River. His good friend,
The police chief, also her youth boyfriend
Who loved her from pigskin, to the diner,
Informed him about the "real" purloiner—
"Them blacks outside Charleston." He so joined
For the assurance of others and groined
In shaky hinges, doomsday rituals,
And ceased his cap and gown in mutual
Solemnity in a vault with his wife's
Ashes. Though during his just—wed love life's
Funeral, his friend never came—her friend
Was but humming, sewing his sheets to lend
To his infrastructure of followers—
Who made status as top insurer.

        Applying on Avon blush with wobbly
Hands and an open purse dropping hobbly
Scampering cosmetic items down the
Bus, the FURNITURE SALESWOMAN gives a
Nudge to her husband, the USED CAR DEALER
To obtain her mints and tampons for her.
Her husband with black hair in pale white skin,
Was sunburned, ignored her and scratched his chin,
And she let out a scowl, bent over in
Her blue tennis skirt, and very foreign
Fashion to her civil view, got on all
Fours just like an armoire, on the bruised balls
Of her palms—forgetting she didn't wear
Her G—string, and her spouse started to care
And sat her back up, and picked them up. She
Was from Sweden with her deep blond wavy
Bouquet on her head watching to savvy

Her husband's crack wiggling down the aisle.
They're from Florida— Amelia Isle.

    And there sat the HISTORIAN without
A concern for the present clanks and pouts,
Who knows that there will come a time, as he
States, time will be time once again. Airy
Vents gallop and pace fast through his hairy
Uncut display like palm leaves of curly
Stems hedged over in solid white pearly
Shades. He was skimming Chaucer's "The Legend
Of Good Women." A kilt that he mended
Wrapped around his almost anorexic
Waist. He was also from Boston. And havoc
Was about to go underway when the
Plastic Surgeon's ketchup burst and sprayed a
Stanza on one of his pages, when the

The—
Bus halted. The DRIVER got up in an
Abrupt way. She was in an American
Yellow star costume with her gray curls out
And getting caught on the fuzzy cloth clout.

    She had forgot to refill the gas, and
The sole option was to wait for the band
Of the next bus to pick them up in six
Hours. Nor did their trendy cell phones pick
Up any signals. A problem that one
Can only dream just for the sake of fun.

    Then I, AMANDA SKYMETER trying
My new McLaren F—1, drove frying
At a ricocheting torched speed of two
Hundred—thirty—nine mph. A blue
Stopped bus appeared up ahead, with a group
That could match an asylum or a crazed troop
Of circus performers. So me and my
Estrogen ways, decided to stop by
To survey the matter, and smoothed to a
Streamlined stop. The red doors unhatched to muh
Cockpit, and unfastened my yellow belt.
I got out in tight bootleg jeans and felt
The spring breeze gliding—O! I quickly zipped
My fly. My sports bra seemed okay. I lipped
Because there were some old gray geezers so
I wore my geeky glasses and my toes
Received some purple socks in my Vans shoes.
They seemed like they caught a bad case of blues
Until I strutted towards them and saw some

Bizarre trench coat smiles. The land of bums—
O' be tidy in your manners I thought.
Then a spank retaliated by not
A man but the blind Choreographer
Searching for her dear old wrinkled lover.
Confused, a shooting star sped up to me—
The driver, who explained it all briefly.
Looking around it reminded me of
My trip to Namibia with my love,
Where Baboons attacked and plundered our camp,
One of them took my wedding ring, that tramp—
And we broke up after our trip. So my
Solution to help out would be to try
And take one of the people who needed
Assisstance right away. Who I heeded
To most was the fisherman and his kite.
The barber said I chose him as a white,
And they argued against me with petty
Racial comments ending with white pretty
Women can't make the best choices.
And I lost my care in the cruel voices.
So I began back to my cloud hue car
When suddenly shot back the happy star.

The Driver said that we should have a tale
Contest. They all booed, even the fat pale
Plastic Surgeon threw his fries at her fluff
And caused a stellar stain to her bright puff
Her anger beamed out of the great cosmos,
"Fucking agree or wait!" like some sumos
Ready to plow weak squid—eating—children—
Even the air tank seemed stuck, they listened
Attentively. She stated she would be the
Judge. And the seat goes to the winner, a
Story—teller that will thus make her want
To have a reason to live, without a flaunt,
Or ostracizing who is of great wealth.
They began: O' at least I have good health!

— — — — — — — — —

HISS AND SPRAY   From *Pulchritude for the Mind*

The man in jeans loose and free
Removes the can from his back pocket,
Shaking it with glee,
He opens the top and looks both ways,

Before performing his choice.
He begins to wonder from an odd daze,
Ponder, and plot and plan ahead.
He shakes the can and pops the top,
Looks the context, and starts in the red,
Slowly, then quickly, like a python moving to and fro in the fields.

Over the bricks and concrete walls.
Under the sun and over windows,
Spraying yet quiet in the echoing halls.

The words he sprays do not define him,
They define who he is at present,
The pictures, both grotesque and shocking,
He is neither and does not resent.
It is simply art, yet illegal.
Simply it is sewing with a knife instead of a needle.
An image can be blunt but expressive, not regal,
Nor dignified, nor solid,
No boundaries are implied.
But the line has crossed the boundaries, as the overseers notify.

The police pull by and grab the man
Whose alibi is he did no harm.
A fault is always taken into one's hand,
Never given, but accepted, and is caused from a source.
The security pointed and proved him wrong.
Displaying the can eye to eye with force.
Red liquid dripped from the can, right onto the navy blue cop shirt.

The man was locked away for about five years.
A Spray can for art, is not to be piled in the dirt.
Though illegal, law is our boundaries and fears.
That we can only romanticize but never rise above.
The only result would be a graffiti of tears.

— — — — — — — — — — — —

PURE TROPICS   From *Pulchritude for the Mind*

Nestling in the low sunsets,
I lay on the hammock
Watching the glistening purple, peach,
And Flamingo Pink
Resting on the waving water.

I tilt my hat to see the sky.
Like pteranodons fluttering up above,
Come pelicans and herons gliding through the sun.

I take a look around and see the banana trees,
The palms and the tall grass on the sand's surface,
The Hibiscus and the Birds of Paradise;
A painter's collaboration of different colors that makes
An island beautiful.

I hear the playing of steel drums,
The beat that travels in my mind when off the hammock
And into my sandals, touching the soft sand—
Moist yet dry, and life walks upon it.

I look at the valiant sun going down,
And to my surprise, bursting out of the water are two porpoises
And a flock of great and harmoniously beautiful aviaries on their way,
With the pulchritude of butterflies in rich gradients passing by,
Nothing else can hold the same degree of beauty.

There is one thing I can compare Earth's great beauty—
A creation of the Earth whose beauty like the glistening sea
Reflects on all of life, and whose joy is like orcas and dolphins
Jumping in delight.

She walks now and matching with the Sun,
Holds a red hibiscus in her hair and wears rich colors.
Treading in the sand, she walks in grace.

For I do not deserve this tropical masterpiece,
She has chosen in me—yet my awe is still endless
As the waves rush against the shore.

Chapter Three
THE TRAIL OF MYTHOLOGY

神話

THE
HUMAN
TRIGGER

PART I

ORIGIN
TO
THE END

Man was given form to love and cherish
Woman was given form to love and hold.

A carbonated clause carries killer conniving
Thirst theories, thinly thumpered thoughts.
Dressed down dark dwelling devils dueling
For fevered frenzy, formulated functions for
Listing lustful ludicrous listless love loss less
Idolizing idiosyncrasies, isomers iconic if I
Perchance perhaps prefer proportionate
Time to twist, tying tight twin tightrope twos
Over out on our orange Optima operating
Buttons between buried barking bass by
Scissors sipping soul-struck symphonies
Echoing epidemics enduring educational
Anagrams. After an altered accusation allowing
Sin's sly self sips slung slightly snug smoking,
Most mesmerizing. My mental morgue mortality
Philosophizes physical pharynx's photolysis.
She sure ships shots shrinking shorn sheets
Gouging, gushing, glistening, giving ghost
Howls. Hushed. Horrifying haberdasher hands
Unhinge, undo, undress, unbuckle, unclip, unzip
Zippers—Zoned. Zu. Zoological zephyrs zap zeppelin
Spurring spermaceti sparkling spurts spinning,
Upping upon upholstery upside, upheavals
Jousting, jocular jostling jots. Jobs jolt
Alarmed apparatuses awaiting autumn and
Living like lone lovers left-over.

It was the twelfth.
And she left me for one.
I could not keep two.
And seven before could
Have opened my doors
To more. But I wanted
To love. I perplexed my
Findings. Searched in all
Sorts. Inked my quill by
Dipping in running jets.
My handles over-oiled,
And no man deserves
A loss such as one of love.

A man was structured to work the fields
A woman was placed in the domestic zone, but not now, not now.

A stapler side steering sinks strong snarling
Teeth troughs tearing, ten times, to test
My mnemonic missile mycology. Mercy's

Nameless nuance nudges knocking nothing
Out: opiate optical ontological objects objectifying.
Worldly worthless wanton women wishing what
I import, in intricate isolated isotopic interests,
Stimulating style; strung stamina stringently stuck.
Hate hinges hierarchy's hypocritical highness historically
Speaking, sporting speech spontaneous specification
Sanctifying sarcastic survey— Suppressing subtle sudden
Gestures genuinely gregarious. Gyroscopes jarring
Earnest elisions emitting entropy, editing edible
Time to tool. —To touch. — To trip, to tons toppled tearing
My mirth. Majestically muscled mused mourned meaningless
Ringed rhinoceros raped, roaring, ripping riptides raging river Rio
Grande. Grown green grass groups —grin grabbing great—
Chunks. Choosing choice chronically chastised.

I am fired.
I lose my job.
By a wanton woman.
I ignite my cards, I break the bars.
I crush the chair, my house evicts.
My car is robbed, my dog dies of ticks.
Drawers devour my domestic items,
Windows wink and sink in suicide.
As I bat each one, the neighbors ring.
I answer— no one's home, the sirens ring.
I pour out Crisco, to the oven on fry,
Act as if I am frying chicken, but I dice
An outlet open. I stand my dominoes
On end. Cat the sofas, and the curtains.
Dog her white pearl bracelets into
Pouting puffed kernels collecting countless
Fumes on board the skillet.
These empty vases are gargoyles ready
For the Break—I slam each one with ounces
Of Hate! I crack my neck, I wring the chandelier
Of its spine. I'm not fine. I'm not fine. I'm not myself— I should—
Take apart it all. I take the skillet and break its fall
On a twin bed, plaid soul'd—Fluffy!
A foamed cottoned unstitched renegade evolving
Sludged blooded and garnished lava larvae—ing lasting
Lashing long lustful loops lost lingers lovingly
On my soul and my youthful wronged bringings.
The sirens extend to my Calypsos, seven years
Of often overdosed audacity honestly awe—
Scraping, boulders obliterating, pipes unscrewing.
Rivets riveting, ribbits rioting, rumbling remorseless.
I rake open the carpets to reveal its naked wood.
The doorbell rings, my knife drawer open. I open it.
I rage and yell through tongue—wielding breast, and through her I stood.

A young one, offering cookies, and falling back on her wagon.
A Father escaping a van in violent vortex vicinities verisimilitude

Of thunderous throat thrashed thought thorps. My shakes
Become primeval; I take Evil, medieval, upheaval,
Grasp onto my victorious elemental gear. I level
At my defense at this polo shirt, tubby—faced hair—curled

Encore for my opening act.
Nothing up my sleeves, I'm not in tact.
I pull my spear dripping with soiled fat,
And get ready for another warthog. My top hat
Is thrown aside, and my whip to tame
This arcane to be cadaver, on the verge of the same
Juxtaposition of men and their lovers. I ready
Cannons at hand. He stops at the stairs, steady.
Make your choice windbag, which wish had I to offer?
He takes out a gold—chipped radioactive clipped Asian fingered
Plastic talkie. I do not linger.
I grasp my knife and my treble did raise into his follicles,
And his phone did wring. More obstacles.

My house grew into a marigold of flame and obtuse
Calamity.

A house was structured for a place to live.
A man was made to make shelter for his body, not to destroy it.

Roof red ready remoulade reining, raining, writhing
Contrasts coppered coupled canopies; conquered compositions
Destroyed. Disassembling dismal dichotomies disperse down
Troubled Tintern, tinder, tender, topless trajectory tossed.
Grains giving great gout—gashing gorges gored gruesomely; glamour
Star stripped sewn sulking sovereignty. Sordid swelling, squalid squalls.
Doors donate despair, dividing delinquent doorknobs, deranged.
Fierce flames fold, frolic, ferment framing far far forever—filled fears.
Crackling, cackling, corroding, colliding, collapsing, corrugating, crusted.

Bridging on this tormented outcome, I wait
As the flame approaches me distilling, engulfing
My body. And in that moment I dispel
Discord from the youth's tear—drenched foaming
Skull, and the van driver probably her father still
Reaching. Still reaching. My heel as a javelin
Incorporating his facetious soul to grasp away at what was
Never caught. My cortex unhinges, and Prometheus's
Gift drifts, lifts, swifts, sifts, thrifts, rifts nifty
As a boa constrictor tightening the core of my bones.
I kneel. Covered by the Sea's opposite as there is no
Sun. Galileo cannot contrast this awesome flame to
Any comet, star, or black holed galaxy. For
There is no sky, no ground, nor limbs, not bound.
And I am tired. My yawn collapses into the kaleidoscope
Of entropy. My labyrinths lay in front of me,
And I am long behind the entrance, melting like
Seesaws touching the fallen branches without a fulcrum.

By branch, by branch twilled twig, ivy twisting my venomous
Voluptuous voracity vindicating veritas vergo, venor!
My Socrates I take his paled rotting fleshed held cut and sip
Each reason, archetype unchained rhetoric, my Aristotle emptied,
Raising my dagger to brush against the early fangs of Hell, I grip
Rip, tear. Strip, struggle abuse my wooly pubic flossed organs,
Jupiter cannot have intercourse no more. I lip.
Losing love, losing lore loaves life long lulls; lush loud, loathe lonely.

But all is not an end, all is not at end, end is only
To commit oneself to failure, to lie along a stream uncharted
Without a constellation voyage. My symmetrical star starts, that parted
Before in orbit like meteors hitting a China warehouse in mid Beijing,
Sizzling great violet nectar drilling into my dilations, and lashes being
Transformed into great hippopotamus whisker lashes.
My cancerous fleshed out burns in all degrees succumb to ashes
Instead of peeling, or pitter-pattering into the cracking song
Of a Pharaoh's army demolished with two oceans becoming a pronged
One. And with the point of his fat drenched goatee my skull ejaculates
Three large antlered horns made of my baking muscle that calculates
A substance harder than any calcium transformation of skeleton.
Standing strand-curved like a sweet, platinum smelt fleur de lis, undone
The hairs on my head sift into my skin, and I can feel them coil up, curl
And knot up and down my spine. My skin unthreads unveils, unshades, hurls
Peripheral volitions, and I spell into contortions, conversions, and
convolutions.

I become a Bunraku and the claws and talons maw their way in my
Bodily connection. My ribs, my ribs, my ribs extend bended into fully
Cylindrical like wire coat hangers, elastically enhanced and comb
Their way like a mixer leaking thick yeasted batter, dripping slime foam—
Bashing, and crunching igniting a punch through my nipples, my shoulders
Flap back and my arms graze aloft, lofted, lamed, lignified as boulders
Become gravel, and pour back behind me swinging. All my blood drips
And gathers, swims and lathers into my clear fingered and toed shell lips
Like rubbered hands squeezing the non-fertile bovine utter for whatever
Remains; reminiscent ragged rousing roots rushed wrongful wriggles.
Coagulating and formatting into leaking habergeons of brutal tyranny.
My now exterior ribs stretch like Ziploc combustions and pairingly
Swallow and glass each bone into a vase sealed of its own. I am breasted
Shield. Each court and sprinkle of my spine sperms needles golden pressed
And exteriorly acupunctured in the husbandry of bushels.
My gums, my cartilage, my fat becomes as black as the coal that rustles
Beneath thy Earth surface.

The scratching behind my hula skirt lashed sockets begins to quake,
Mucus and tears bag out like wrapping paper being disposed
In shuddered plastic bags.

Eyes of man were constructed to see and interpret life around him.
Eyes were not made to be used for harm or to be annihilated.

Purple perished poring pornographic porpoises pouring puny

Green grasses, gray galoshes, gold glimmering goldfish, guppies;
Orange orangutans, ochre offered orchards of olives, orchids;
Periwinkle parrots, pastel pink Porsches, pumpkin parades;
Royal red rose rhinoceroses rumbling russet rust rushes rambling;
Saffron cities, submerged sultry sangria salmons, silver stuffed sepia;
Tumultuous tan transforming terra turquoise to teal to taupe to tenné;
Musty magenta milled mustards muzzling maroon mentioning mauve;
Lemon-limes' lying lavender listens like lilac linen lore;
Khaki creamy corrals capering corn, carrots carrying crimson cardinals,
Chafing chartreuse, charmed chestnut, choking chocolates charred;
Bronze built barges, bright browned brass, burgundy bushed buff bistre;
Athenian azure, African amaranth, Arcadian ambered asparagus, amethyst;
Dark denim doesn't dodge dark, doesn't dodge dark darks, doesn't dodge darts;
Fuchsia fantasies for feverish flax ferns find fornicating feminine floras
fun;
Eggplants eructate, emerald ephemeral esophagus elusions, erupt endlessly;
Helen's harmonious heliotrope hurries hushed hushing his howls,
Indentured indigo indignation interferes ivory inducing individuals;
Jaded justice jaguars juxtapose justly just jade gems;
Ultimatum: ultramarine.
As the sky is alive, then time is still moving.

My jaw's last rose cheek variation evaluates the humility
Of being descried dehumanity, dressed down duffed dignity demarcated,
And sinks into a leaking, dripping stemmed steaming acidity,
As the reds melt up to where my closed eyes were last, but not exonerated.
And every string holding them in concludes like a coaster on ascent
To a falling plunge, and my last brown halo around my pupil
Fades away like the clockwise contortion of counterclockwise corks
repenting,
And retreating into the expanding white bulbs. And on the bulbs drilled
Fault lines jag, and cipher rich Richter red cracks only the last struggling
Heart monitor can display. And the divorced nailed hand has the kill

As she rips out the cords and the surge protector, giving one to one-hit
shock.
Then through— two flaming skull coal burning black craters grab man's
wondered
Mystery. Two ruby red pyramids constructed of last real muscle enclose
The eclipse into prisms of misery and I—eyes can see all ends to ripping tip.
I down-lock.
I'm plundered.
My mind torose;
My sight beams like beams onboard a cargo ship.

For reasons historically etched makes the every man wonder why
A pharaoh is wrapped and mummified
Into four collapsed triangles holding onto squared opportune Earth,
And why the paint and glyphs, the dyes and myths are inside as mirth?
An eyeball works as such, though with these pyramids I view across
Vernacular, verified violet vortexes grooming with evasive vanguard.

The eye of I, man's self, soul, body and mind, the enigmatic mixture,

His fixture, his storage, to flourish, to nourish, and to twice explore
His boundaries, his foundries centralizing spherical sight.
This is the eye.

As I sit before these time wielding flames, exhausting, burning in passion,
I see where time left us off to on our on—purpose paradigm.

I will tell but a tale, a lib or a fake, but a jab nonetheless how
People destroyed people, and by the eye of Heaven, hath
Heaven more than one. The tale of construct, destruct, embodied
By the human contemplative corrupt
And the dripping desire, of seven lost hates.

The Tale of the Human Trigger.

Before the age of Creation, formatted the age of the Eye,
Humans lived on a grouped continent shaped like the ring and the pupil.
And surrounding this great green ring with a perfect inner—ellipse of black
sand
Grew the great Seas of Silica which composed the rest of the Eye,
Or Earth.

There was only one time zone, one day and one night.
These sifting time transitions were referred to as light
Light Dark, and Light Bright. But no in between,
And nonetheless only two seasons
Of Earth.

The purpose of the eye leads this culture on course,
To see, view then is to be. Through the eye all is seen, as
There were no clouds in sight. At light dark all the stars and the Clear
Lunar system with its meteor orbits played petty mobile forced delight
Above the Earth in dark light.

But by bright light the sun would be clear red, and its rays
Quite direct. During the day they would enter the Silica Caverns
To pale out their water from the dripping crystals and eat off
The fatted leave trees of a rich vitamin sugar foam. These rays
Ended when the blank black sands grew frost.

The need to stand would not be unless by our eyes,
The need to sit would not be unless to rest our eyes,
Our body was composed to situate our eyes, as
We see out of only our eyes from our mind,
As Earth, as Eye is seen out of eyes.

The human balance is brought by the eye, the eye delivers
Language and manages the line of bodily functions,
The human trigger is the eye not the heart; eye and mind,
Eye and self. None in the age were blind or disabled,
And life seemed abundant on Earth.

Clothing was visual—based, the earliest Egyptians for example

Painted around their eye to indicate its presence, and pharaohs
Had the benefit of the glued beard as it gave their tired eyes a pivot,
While we today rest our head in our sweaty palms,
And to cry was a plus as it healed both your eyes and praised the Eye.

Clothing and loose tunics were brought about to garter the
Eye with the mental shield that its body was protected from weeds,
And venomous plants, but none too many animals, as the main mainly man
And Mammal & Bird and reptile and all lived according to one time zone. The
Earth seemingly one.

But there still lived hate and fear, and confusion. But no war.
For example those animals carrying the same eye of humanity
Were of no threat, but cats, and reptiles were due in that aspect,
To die by the hands of our then lengthened yellow nails and be
Broken and drained into a suitable drink tiring the eye from the Sun's heat.

To appease the eye of men, women were selected and married,
But women also helped build the eye of confidence in men working
In the fields until their children were fully mature. But no one touched
The black sand as that was the pupil of the eye. They had learned this
By one who lost their eyes due to its encounter and was impaled on Silica.

Early mathematicians studied two frames— the light and the night,
Light bright and Light dark. With spiked spheres carved from the trees,
They traced in the sand where night and day truly began. They were Not
The first to calculate time, as to be born—
Time is but your instinct.

To sleep and dream the eye imitates the sky, to wake and walk
The eye imitates the sky, and through the eye of eye, that I began to form.
They began to wonder in deep, deep thought —if there were eyes beyond,
And that the stars, planets, moon and sun were of the eye as well.
Striking on heaven, striking on high, the whimsical, the struggle—the bell.

And humans began to feel lonely as I once did, now being strung in
What could have been my white winged fate. The men and women of
Health would take the dead—those flung into the one pink foam lake and sunk,
and
Would remove their eyes and examine them as they did with other mammals,
Except felines, and reptiles.

And in time they withdrew, but not in the same terms in anatomy:
It was said the eye carried the traits of the Eye, and shared the same
dichotomy.
The same fraction to ratio comparison of Silica Seas and land,
With silent untouched black sand which is peered through,
And with avoidance not touched.

The Cornea the five—layered constructive composition
Was the atmosphere, the Silica Seas and of the land which was the habitation
For dwellers of the Eye. The pupil was the bland dark sanded circular part.
The landscape was the verdant and turquoise glimmered iris.

But the Silica Seas went deeper than expected and were then the Sclera.

Not too sure on the nerves and other materials, they made the assumption
That it was a match. But they predicted the core of the Eye was of a mind too.
The Vitreous gel that gives the eye its round vivacity was to
Be considered what that reddish—pink frothed lake appeared to be.
But, keep in mental diagram the water was crimson red.

Then one day, a full day as when a day came it was noticed by all,
The mathematicians drew a scale of a pyramid imitating the Sun's
Rays on the green sand (as it was turquoise of course), and bounced the ball
Of mind's curiosity played by eyes captivity capering casual crusade in
Quest for invention, exploration and the eye of success.

The first pyramid was built out of green mud hardened with the
Blood red water to make a browned brick. It was round but with
A point matching that of the diagram, and many believed it was
The eye for other eyes to view them, so that they would not be lonely
No more. They built more only on the outer iris rim until there were six.

The interiors had drawings like that picked up from a human eye, they
Believed, and were fed into there. They found too about mirrors, and
How they reflected and carried light elsewhere. One day of days when
All would notice, they built a great cylinder mirror, and there were
Mirror rocks in abundance in the Silica Seas.

Though it was not a smooth mirror it gave almost lucidity, and with this
The eye became an addict. The humans came in numbers to seem themselves
In form, and face, with leg and grace, even nudity on public display,
It became a festival at bay. But then a noticeable day came, a day
When chaos erupted.

The mirror's stand, two turquoise boulders lost balance, and the mirror
Rolled down and scraped into the black sand. Immediately lightening
Struck and the rains came down. Humanity screamed and ran to their pyramids
For a home, a shelter, a first retreat from it all.

And after the storm and the light night, they came and saw
The most glorious ethereal phenomenal sight, the first rainbow
Peering out from the resting mirror on the pupil into the sky.
But they saw some of Silica Seas had been damaged with long
Crack lines extending and bending down endless ways.

Some of the red waters had wiped onto the turquoise and it
Had become mudded overnight. But this clear substance of water
Had made some of the sands mildew and yellowish green,
And some of the other plants were enrooted, uplifted, uprooted and
Thrown into the orange red cracks in the Silica Seas.

But despite the problems and debris, the humans were fascinated to
Twice explore. They threw objects, and even animals, and sometimes
Bad children in, to watch the lightning and rains and hear thunder boom,

And they would walk out in the rain, some struck by lightning,
Others would laugh until they realized they had lost a sister or mother.

And three gray clouds would appear in the light bright day from that
Point on, and consecutively on the third day of three, the clouds were
blinking,
And would pour and defecate a chronic tempest, and the people would
celebrate.
Some realized they too could reflect the rainbow and unbroken light
From the mirror to their mirror rocks. And then came

The hexagram of mirrors retracting and reflecting light in brilliant
Measures. In the sunse— now more purple with the, now, twelve clouds,
Rainbows would dance and fill the continent and beam into the sky.
Then one day, a person to cause the rainbowed—ballet spectacle, a child who
refused
To be the one to be thrown at the great pupil, grabbed his mother's leg.

She tripped and fell back into the sand, grasping to get up with the rain
Pouring hard on her face. She grabbed a mineral from the sand that ignited
A red gushing geyser: a handful of gold. And with interest and risk
Began a great bloody dig. The men would come home drenched in
Red water, and the women would take their clothes off so

They could stand and run naked in the rain and return home.
The women began to undertake the knowledge of the wash,
Realizing, initializing that clothes washed were best without a body.
But did you realize that the humans themselves were also green,
Yet different shades because no two men or women were alike in color.
Burnett's Green Giants in motion, but not tall, three to four feet,
And by feet in measurement. Maybe Burnett was there when humans
Looked to the stars being the one who instead raised his hand.
But their bodily pod was not a sliced cabbaged horseradish display,
Humans realized they too matched their red waters' substance.

The green humans however all had the same color eye that matched the
Eye. The felines and reptiles however did not, and their irises were not
Always green, but also red, blue, orange or even purple. The only un—
Green greenness besides dried bricks and mildewed sand was the great
Rickety vehement barks of trees with circular leaves and red flora

That browned by sipping the red aquatica running beneath in
The Silica Seas. There were more minerals than just gold— copper
Silver, zinc, bits of pure tellurium, and veins of platinum ore,
Were torn, tapered, twisted, tortuously taken from the gushed
Pupil. That by the rains, the gushed red water draped into the iris and
browned.

Soon there were hundreds of clouds covering the pupil and the iris,
And the people. And the plants were over abundant too, adding
Even a festive décor to the now several dried pyramids. Leaf tunics
Were in abundance, and life's reproductivity was high. Humans did not
Have teeth and used their nails to rip into their leafy or silica intake

Before swallowing. However they had very roughed bone, like
Those of toothless giants roaming the seas of our days that are
Hunted by the loving—eyed beings, raping the world of its wonderfuls
And bewilderments. But there is great reason for this unreasonable
Act that will play out, as time and curious eyes need knowledge.

Then you will learn the ways of man's mind soon, and like my own,
Was one at fault as well. I was a witness, a follower, believed I was
Indifferent to their cause and lived on my own path, but hath I
Known that all trails have a similar route, and all the trails ended
With the result of this truth, had I but lived to tell the tale, as I do now···

The gray spreading clouds became what is known today as the Stratus,
And showers would come twice a day, and people became lazy and
Yielded to farm up and pick the plump leaves for the present day, as
The "agriculture" came to them, and literally through the empty opened
Outlet roofed holing of their pyramids, so much that they ate when they
woke.

There was no worry if the animals got to some of their leafed crops,
And women lost their sense of training young men how to work,
And both became lazy and pranced in dilly dally with the rainbows,
And the patched blue sky, and now the more carrot red sun peering
Through the clouds to make stronger shadows. The shadows made
Animals more lazy as they would migrate towards them during
The radiantly, though not at all, blazing heat days.

One day of the days now to come, two boys who would have
Been working were tossing a gold pebble back and forth.
They passed at forth and back, back and forth while walking
And jumping through the ivy of crops. At one point one of
The boys jumped on one side of the reflected mirrors, reflecting

The light of the great mirror (standing near the pupil), displaying a
Rainbow light, and threw it in the ray. As it passed through the
Beam colors spurted upwards as did the light for a brief second,
As time was not measured in units back then; probably a "wink.
They both stopped and repeated the action, and the light refracted

Again. They continued playing with this deflection, not knowing
Exactly what it meant. It was near sunset when four mathematicians
Were drawing on two dead browned plants where the sun had
Left its last rays, and noticed the playful duet and majestic sparkle.
They picked up their turquoise sticks and hurried, and the people

Did marvel and gather to see this amazement. The following day,
The metals that were discovered all along the iris's great hexagram
Of pyramids able to reflect light from the great mirror to their mirrors,
Were then piled between the existing rays of light, creating six
Large piles. The piles were however moved to refract light from

The corners of the hexagram—where in turn the piles reflected off

Distant piles across the pupil. Three lines crossed over the black
Sanded circle that spread an almost a year—apart walk from one side
To the other. However every other year, the humans would meet together
As they did for each miracle and way of knowledge to bring

Their "eye—deas" before them. The men continued their dig. The
Women continued their wash and relaxation. And the children
Would play around near the beams. And at sunset, the people
Would watch the light and the rainbows fade away as if the theatre
Had closed its curtains when time least expected it, and they wanted

More. And at the brink of morning all would stand align to the mirrors
To watch the Sun's ray touch upon the great mirror's surface, and in
Reply would bounce to the other spokes, whose spokes would draw lines
From the piles. Immediately, the Men of the Morning as they were called
Would get ready after the light spectacle and jump into the pupil causing

The initial storm. Men, not of the morning would run with their sticks and
Great sharp turquoise tools and leaf sacks to begin the dig.
It was a "rush", and men who survived came home as if relieved of their
Worries and to find the women ready to express how they felt— this New
Stronger love of companionship. At almost light dark's end, the dead

Would be picked up and thrown into the frothed red water. This cycle
Continued every day for years on end. Finally it came, the solar eclipse
That happened for one month every fifty years because of the far—out
Orbit of the pale moon, which I will explain as you astrologians,
Astronomers, ecologists, mathematicians, scientists are all biting

Your tongues at this point in time to these words in disbelief— but
A *wonder* that these green men and women felt too with light. The Moon
As you may recall, but are too perplexed to look back through the text,
Had an orbit of meteors around it of all sizes, but sizes less abominably
Gigantic to that of the Eye's pupil. The Moon itself had at that time,

Ages ago, an only one color, light gray body, lighter than all the stratus
combined.
But not as light, as bright or as white as the Silica Seas. There were no
textures,
On the surface of the moon, and it was as smooth as the sanded pupil before
It was excavated. They all waited in the one area of miracles at the area that
Would become Egypt ages ahead. As the occultation began, the orangutan

Crimson'd sun, and smooth lunar presence with its silent continuous orbit
Of the meteors of its belt began to intersect. Though the relationship to the
Sun and the moon was much more of a periapsis, in that its distance from
The orbital connect was much closer in range than that of the apoapsis from
The Eye to the Moon. As you men and women of science are jotting and

Scratching your bitter soul—struck creative interest, you can apply that
This eclipse was an annular one in that the moon even though, t'was
Much closer in comparison to the Sun, it still—it still was and is much
smaller,

And was but a black mark before the sun. But also a very radiant one too.
As the eclipse began, the rays of even brighter light came down and ignited

The divided hexagram, and there were no rainbows just very high light
Wavelengths being reflected. However several people, primarily the
Men of the Morning who, just a small distance away from the great
Mirror, who were getting ready for their sprint, were instantaneously
Blinded. Then two of the piles overheated, sparked, bringing the first flames.

The rain however was on high alert and the gold was cooled and
The People who could see, and see the flames that emerged from
This and the extinguishing, eyed in deep wonder. They decided to
Quickly put down their mirrors and the great mirror by force.
And the month of wonderment grew.

After the annular eclipse came, they set their lives back up again,
However they noticed the burned and charcoal marks left by
The metals. And during this fifty year transition, the mathematicians
Put together the brink of human sin—a "great plan". During this planning of
sorts,
And since the first flames, they noticed that their atmosphere

Appeared apparently like a thick layer of glass now visible over the
Thousands of Stratus clouds. The plan was started by a great wall,
As doth all man's failures dost beginneth. The wall was compiled of
Bricks of the dried brown mud surrounding the pupil, with six bridges—
Of the long turquoise trees and vines that grew up to the same height of the
pupil's

Highest point or its center. Thus the trees could meet the radius, and
Were conjoined to make a six—part bridge without touching the base of the
pupil.
And with the bridge creation they found the trees to be really tact for

Building, and could hold the metals brilliantly without error. With the
Turquoise wood, they hinged it with the vines they used to create the
pyramids.

The women went back to work in making the great carrier basket.
It was also composed of the turquoise wood and vine. In addition
It had mudded walls inside and the height was twice the height
Of a single created pyramid. All the metals were placed in the basket.

Over a million, each several hundred miles in length, lime green
Vines, the most dense and flexible ones were attached all along the
Rims of this great bucket—like basket. At this moment of tightening
The grip of the metals and their basket, the great mirror was placed
Above the shiny ores. The other mirror rocks were placed on top of

The great mud walls— yet were tilted facing upwards. All were at
The same degree. In the fortieth year the vines were tied and extended
Firmly to all the Iris pyramids placing the 40—ton basket with the great
mirror.

Solely a meter from the pupil's center hump. One could imagine this as
A large circular wall, like an over-artistic prison, but instead of a Crow's

Nest with spotlights and watch lights grooving the area on patrol,
There were the slanted six hexagram and smaller mirror rocks reflecting
Their light towards the basket. The vines were above the mirror rocks as
they
Extended from the tops of the pyramids, with also the now pyramid-
Colonies as the population had expanded terrifically to 8 billion.

The purpose of this test was of a revenge and a reflection. They
Saw the eclipse as that of a malevolent eye lashing a renegade of rays
Towards the Earth to blind men as it had proven from the previous annular
Eclipse. They also for the last ten years before the eclipse with the
Invention on its heels of great delivery, refrained from making anymore

Rain, and some of the clouds vanished, though the majority remained.
During this rough transition, they had to function again for farming,
Though most refuted to return to that system, and primarily the
Women had to farm while the men sat around with the mathematicians
To stare in composure, laud, accolade, praise, accord and enjoyment

At the great work of art they created; and in being of course thought
It was much fool-proof, as false-proof, for it had not been Disapproved
Or had it been proven proof-less prior to partaking primordial formation.
Though the women were responsible for the basket, and weaving the
Vines appropriately, the representation of praise from the population

Was to the men, mainly those of- that of science, so you science readers
Can go back to feeling that you're special and needed in the world
When reading this. I will present to you the engraving, that you never
Really knew why you had in your mind, lurking in your imagery of
Evil. And why this "it" appears in our representations of the wronged.

Have you ever wondered why a man uses symbols, categorizes
Thoughts with imagery, and designates his entire life to go back
To whatever these made-up symbols have to really offer? And oh
When he or she gets there, he or she thinks they've found all, and
In the harsh misery of it, no one believes them, and those that think

They do, secretly acknowledge how invalid truth plays on them.
Now all you theologians and devout worshippers may be at a
State of great malevolence-as was I, as was I. And I too matched
The symbols, the enchanted kiss with musical chimes, the metaphors,
The science-fiction; yes our works do something-but not to create-

Aw there's the word create- a path leading to a symbol or more,
But to accomplish a step or action, or proof, or reason. That is not to say
That there is not a "God" or whatever you may call the being who
Created a system of Eyes and their cultures, it is to instate that one who
Forges, and becomes a path-wielder, may very well be a pyramid dweller.

As you shall see being performed for you the acts of Man's Original Wrongful

Act, if you shall call it not an act, or a fault, being devout as you say,
Call it Sin. Apply the first name Adam, maybe create a myth—but woe; whoa
We shall not embark there quite yet as I have exhausted my tale, in my
Soul's eternal argument, thus now in yourself reconcile, prior thoughts

Contempt. Open through your condemnations, and in hearing this—you
Must let your eye be opened to feel it and your body will recall it all. I
Am not to give thou a warning, as that is of our creation. I am to explicate,
As through these pyramid eyes, I see your nervous hands and beating
Heart. Your parched dried lips, and the brain formation in your skull.

I will tell you what happens in whole. As the day embarked, the day of
Days when the 8.3 billion stood over—crowded in the place of miracles.
There came the light gray moon and shimmering wooly orange Sun
Waiting as if watching, watching as if waiting for the public bus
In the early morning hour alone on a silent street called home, called Earth.

And it was a great picnic of such. Though with less rain in those ten years,
They ate enough to live, though the majority of the population, overweight.
Now what I didn't really mention before was that the vines holding
The bucket were braided as ropes—thus giving room, for the mirror rocks'
Reflection to follow into the lead of the great one on top of the bucket.

But keep in mind the mirror rocks too were slanted to carry the Sunrays, too.
It began. The occultation emerged and a shadow covered a minor portion of
The iris, where no one was. Children in anticipation yelled in happiness for
The reason of only to display how they felt. And it was silent. Immediately
Like a running zephyr full blown into the great Mirror, the sun light shot in.

And in addition the mirror rocks also shot back at the great rock their light

Too. And rainbows bloomed from the great mirror into the sky. And it was
Beautiful. Like our fireworks, or turning on the switch of putting out a
Christmas light display and watching it light up for the world to see. It
Was the symbol of Love. It was the symbol of Desire, what we still long for.

And in that moment, men kissed women, men embraced men, and children
Loved each other. Some of the infants cried but they calmed down in minutes.
And the animals were silent, completely. And the only noise that began to
Ascend in volume was a light sizzling like that of heat on a skillet.
The bucket began displaying steam that gave the rainbow shimmers;

Ambience. And then the turquoise bucket sparked. The metals were
Heating. One mathematician moved forward as if to attempt to
Run to the wall, but his wife blocked him. The bucket caught fire, and
The retracting rainbow became more yellowish green. Smoke quickly
Rose up and drenched the ray with rising puffs. It was the smell

Of a mountain of flame. Some people ran towards other forests. But
Most stayed and watched the spectacle in awe. The cackling and
Crackling. Soon the vines were receiving their first flames. Surprisingly
The vines held much stronger even as the wood of the bucket was
Crumbling in their wrapped reach (a holder for the bucket).

Smoke was pillaging the people's view and they realized they
Could not breathe it as a few had died from choking, and the people
Ran back a ways until they thought it was safe. Like flames crumpling
On thick redwood logs with an amplified vortex echoed throughout the
Whole iris. People did not know what to do. They felt useless, and

They just watched. The large vine ropes within several hours were
Charring and dripping with their red water, becoming blacker.
And their black was like a gooping tar—deranged wet concrete,
Spilling wreckage from a falling highway bridge pillaged by
Unending smoke domes, and smoke rising high into the atmosphere.

The smoke rose passed the clouds; the actual glossy glass—
Like the atmosphere— could actually be seen all over with the smoke
Rising that high. And the sky blue became an intense purple.
Children were grasping onto their family members. It was like
Being born out of nothing with no where to go except this

Foray of illusions that took hold of you and would not let you go.
The temperature rose. Some of the very overweight took off their
Vine tunics and stood naked. The smoke became part of the ray
Immensely. Suddenly the stars were visible in this great purple.
It was a nightmare on the verge of breaking its water.

Then several vines plunged and snapped back and exploded like
Clay pots freshly baked thrown. At first it was a few, then hundreds quickly

Shot back. The distances of the returned fire were limitless also hitting
Into the Silica Seas. It was startling. Then the bucket lowered with a
Great heave and halt, just wiggling a bit over the mound. Then quickly—

KER—SNAP! KER—SNAP! It echoed! All the vines snapped towards the
Falling bucket. That anchored onto the pupil with a large geyser of
Red water that went into the air, but did not affect the ray or flames.
The bucket burst open, and with blackened cracked vines completely
Covered the pupil in its black sand and blood bath. Immediately its
Defense system went off with the rain and lightening. But the flame
Could not be put out. The lightening began quicker and quicker.

The sound of thunder became more and more louder, and the iris
Quaked! Animals and people alike ran in all sorts of directions—and
Still many who felt safe, just watched, holding their ears from the sound.
The lightening became a neon blue slashing at the flame and debris,
And the water turned into human—head—sized—hail that broke apart

Only some of the strong bricks holding the wall together. Then the
Lightening became an intense orange. With the sound of thunder
Heightened with the highest pitch and immediately the majority
Of the animals and people became deaf. Children lost their parents.
Babies fell out of people's hands and rolled onto green sand.

People were even jumping and committing suicide. But most

Stood their unheard ground. The walls broke down, but a bizarre
Optical effect occurred as different color lightening seemed to be
Channeling in a circular motion around the bucket and its ray
Like a whirling maelstrom pulling apart the Pequod without the Whale.

This formed a very extreme ray, also known as a type of Light
Amplification by Stimulated Emission of Radiation, also known
Today as a laser. One would say our *Star Wars*, our laser visions
Endure this pain-striking misery in the human mind. The ray
Transformed from red to orange, from orange to yellow, to neon

Yellow, and with the color change grew the length of the ray—
Already beyond the smoke. And black sands were engulfed in flame
And hail, and pounds and pounds of flooding red water. The walls
Became ablaze and started to melt. The metal had melted itself to
The mirror and the pupil like a growing wart with hard bubbles.

The temperature rose, and green sands became yellow, then white.
People were gathered in and clutching onto the pyramid for dear life—
Whatever that meant to them. The vines were dripping puddles of
Their blood and the trees had springs of running blood water that were
Warmer than the 98-99 degrees Fahrenheit incorporating our normal states.

And the beam shot straight to the moon without stop, but only
Accelerating faster and faster. And the lightening didn't yield.
Gray clouds drew all over the now blackish purple sky, and rain
Poured like mad-solid-madness! People drowned literally in the
Rain unable to breathe through their noses, and collapsing in two—

Colored waters, unable to hear their screams and others as they too
Were deaf, and vibrating in seizures of the iris. And their bones
Breaking apart just by lying in the vibrations. The ground suddenly
Was sucked and strawed into the great beam like a tremendous

Vacuum. People within five miles of the radius of the laser were immediately
Siphoned into the lightning magnetized, vacuumized laser, and disappeared
Billions of miles away in space— evaporated. The Moon was hit! For the
Lunar body was already undertaking the great heat of the sun's radiation,
It grew into great heat, turning bright red like the sight of Venus via
telescope.

But the Sun's heat and radiation was stronger on the Lunar Mirror,
In this attachment the meteors were however pulled towards the laser
But never crossed its line—still holding the sun's radiation. The Moon
Was however harpooned by the laser and began to draw into the beam—
And begun to receive a makeover. The Sun however was pulling the moon back.

And with this push-pull, the moon emitted a strong reflection and beamed
A great, but not as strong laser immediately separating a corner of the iris.
And then created a chain reaction to the Silica Seas with driving cracks and
Separations. The lunar laser went straight into the already heated water—
Making it reach tremendous heats. The Silica Seas were even steaming

And evaporating into the barely—glass visible atmosphere. Red geysers shot
Out of the Silica Seas. It had been nine hours already and it was never—ending.
And all humans and animals were losing their senses. Just the eye and mind,
Those two seemed to remain—somehow—to those of the living. The red lake
Began to bubble, and skinless deformed dead bodies emerged like pot stickers

Ready to be served with pale white eyes and gooey white bones. The meteors
Dove into the atmosphere and exploded the Silica and more parts of the iris.
All the pyramids had melted suffocating and drowning all those who felt
It safe for shelter. Animals and humans that survived with only eyes and
Mind had to endlessly run hundreds of miles to the Silica Seas. The land

Fell apart and separated. And four hours of the meteor orbit debris fell onto
The Eye.
Volcanoes emerged, forty in one hour, mixing with the blood, the flame, the
Silica, and the land's substance it spurted out onto the land and then through
The Silica. And the rain was endless. The hail had stopped in the thirteenth

Hour. Onnes' enthalpy findings would be far over the state where
Entropy seemed at its end—but wasn't. It was the Syzygy of Hell, and
It has stuck in our minds— but it has still not ended. Sixty percent of
The Silica either mixed into the ocean, drifted into the roots of the land
Or sifted into the now non—visible fractured atmosphere covered by clouds.

Then came the separation of the pupil. A brave meteor finally plunged
Its way to the bucket toppling the laser over. Though the laser continued
And broke apart more silica on the land and shot through volcanoes.
The bucket made a somersault going down the hill and separated the
Pupil into three inequivalent parts. And the iris turned black too.

After six days the damage ceased, it seemed, and the surviving who
Came out of the Silica Seas or Caves— now the purple—blue sea,
Instead of a blood red one covering the Eye. The sky was also purple—
And thus the water had direct reflective capability. This also explains

Why Sea and Land predators are interested in blood on its appearance,
Because it was a normal part of their species' life for ages, and they
Desire it greatly with all senses including hunger. Those who fear it,
Are not actually grossed out, but through their heritage are those who
Feared its gross presence with the bodies emerged, and how it was

The medium for their reflective commentary. The moon also had a new landscape—
The Face we see today that developed from the laser and the pull
Between the Earth and the Sun. And that this pull also brought the moon
40—times closer to the Earth; and the eclipse had already ended. The
Angry Sun appeared through our atmosphere as it does today.

When coming back onto the charred landscape the humans saw that not
All had been destroyed. As there was also snow, snowing from
Clouds unable to rain anymore. The symbol of devastation, the thought

Of what else when all is lost. When all is lost. When all is
Lost.

The animals and humans who could get back on the land stepped onto
The charcoal ruins of life they once knew. The wind consistently
Blew about them keeping their spirits up looking for more, breathing
For connection for something to keep them alive, a need for
Attachment. There were also those who survived in a Silica cavern

But were stranded in the Middle of the now Blue Sea or today, the
Ocean of Oceans. This was a new age. Food was different.
Drink was also different. And because the lifestyle had changed—
So did everything else. Green skin slowly vanished as the air was
Different and in drinking the water their skin colors became closer
To the charcoal tans and blacks. This also brought an alternating
development

Especially to the bodies of all species and they began to change; or
Today would be called an evolution process. To adjust to the land
And atmospheric changes, by in turn going through generations of
Transformations and mutations. The iris and the remnants of the
Pupil also went through quite a change to get where they are today.

The Pupil for example has become our great vast ancient "mysterious"
Death Valleys, our still driven excavations luring for our curious cause.
And the blood that geysers there is not of the pupils doing, but now is
Of our own. And most of the black stands have become the canyon tans.
And if you look on a world map, the deserts lie on the rim of each continent.

And the pupil still is constantly changing. The center of black sand still
Exists on the islands of Hawaii. And ironically, the large island, the
Center of the pupil where the laser bucket was held remains in the
Same place, but with most of the climates of the Earth on its one location.
After several years of learning to survive, the humans rebuilt their pyramids

With the different muds and materials, composites of the new Earth. It was
After the rebuilding, and the population finally reached back into the
thousands
That the population made a choice of choices. They stated that instead of
Having continual annual meetings as they did before the nightmare, that
They would each focus on uniting with the Lunar eye to

Draw the land close together and make the land whole.
Many disagreed, and wanted something different. The population
Split up with the original goal of uniting the land in thought,
Long now, long now forgot. And that is why when leaders state that
They are going to accomplish something and it never actually fully

Happens in concordance, that maybe they too have found more important
Things to work on. To Create. And thus began the age of Creation,
And no populations had similar architecture of their pyramids for
That matter, or shared in learning about each other's cultures; segregating
And separating themselves like cracks of the Silica Seas, with

Evaporating forgetfulness— though still a desire to attain something?
What was that something? Hmmm? So religions were made.
So symbols were made. So pathways and self—helps were made.
So there's over five thousand ways of saying hello, and thousands
More of saying goodbye. So there are goals about having more and more

Land than everyone else, to attain betterment. Maybe betterment slipped
Into the human mind when devastation did, but that definition has
Quite evolved. You know as the Book says, when God created the
World he thought it good and rested···As, I need to from explicating
This vision that I see— but humans···mankind of women and men alike,

When Men recreated the world they thought it bad, and that it needed
Improvement. And look what happened. Just fixated with fixing
Things up. Shame on you! But we can't "Kerry" on for too long or
"Bush" our way back—for those readers who are obsessive political
Hallucinaters. We must improve this! We must improve that! Get

Slim! Get fat! Get other people angry! Form a line! Be a be a be a?
Some Tale.

Stories were made to express a point, or motif, or just imagery,
Stories were not made to alter the existence of the human thought.

A Swindling side—stabbing surmise suppressed surreal swanker saker soaring
Blind between buildings bleeding blasphemous bewilderment.
Minds mightily, magically— melody molds meagerly— minor, major
mordacious
Anger arranges arms, arranges angles' axis axed, arranges all armistices
Broken.

And in my soul, what's left, to you I realize the theft humanity
Has taken from me, from us, from the Eye, from Earth, and continually
Steals, stripping, sinking longer fangs, and I...I cannot say more as the
Pain elastically
Stretches, pulls my being passed existence.

And a new age comes, the vein—dripping sensation, spreads lucidly
In a distilled ovulation in both my tapped alcohol dripping kidneys.
My shoulders flap forward and my spine curls forward like a Jacob's ladder
Set snaking its flippery with nail plates sticking down my happy trail.
I have been blood emptied, replaced now by a rich purple molten
Tar that overfills my body, like beer dripping down on a cool winter's
Day except for the squirming and sprouts—a—blooming from out of my
Nose and toes, with bones becoming malleable; I want to leap but I
Am strings—attached akimbo acquainted with this wanton fate reaped by
The hands of women and men who set forth thy path to rot; and all this at
A redemptive price—for their wrongful committee community set
Forth by the justice of improvisation of improvement.

Emptied intestines with the aroma of decayed fungus grown on all scented

Ericaceous creations, jags and jiggles. Then unplug like a mad hose
swinging
Back and forth, forth and back, in my body connects, contrastingly, clamps
onto
The hilum, the opening, and where forth the other intestinal end connects to
the
Other kidney in such a sordid sharp—swelling sharp, unstitched stitched stab
Combing then raking permanence into the whirlpool of my filtration. I feel
An immerse inflation as my mouth, or a lumen of its remains is leveled open
By an unknown fulcrum and fed two pure crystal green tadpoles with two
Squinting yellow eyes and the weight of a newborn each sifting, sinking,
sludging
Passed my uvula (I unable to regurgitate) into the deep purple tar.
Like earthworms digging in the sow of a heated manured bath, the two
Jiggling fat bodies embody embryos emblemed in my entire being, and
Their tails each slap my dangling heart on their way down—back and forth,
Forth and back. I have nothing to hold onto surrounded, drenched in, and
Ignited by a stronghold of flames.

Purpose has lost touch to reality or wherever that may be. The green tar—
Drenched amphibian souls dig with rough red suction teeth on my
Intestines creating a "V" and they squiggle and squirm to get inside, like

A Firefighter waiting to put out whatever should not escape mankind. Both
Sprint like waste down a shoot stories high with the still flowing tar filling
up
My track of pipes as well, emerging verging urging until the V's flap down
Cemented by the burning tar. I am cold, so cold and the heat bakes my
Antlers in anticipated glory, gored to my despair.

My kidneys stretch and stretch into great sacs blooming side—by—side
Like two breasts—how soon I jerk in this damask elasticity, that papillas
Popcorn out in a formation of the Eiffel Tower on both sides. Acupunctured,
Tar—wielding, intense and arising in pearl and pink. Two great knockers
Peer their way in extension out my back facing what I left behind—I thought.

My nephrons are being slurped and refilled by the tar oozed blood, and
The renal pyramids feel as if the great green vines have snapped in a
Stampede of shrapnel and flying trajectory of nails and harpooning flotsam.

Benign blasphemy burnt. My kidneys takeover the breast, as they are all
Back—length kidneyed ovaries with the intestines as more fallopian.
Swirling,
Twirling, reeling, cradling who's ever, sourced irreverent matter is this?
Horrifically wronged, they are of fetuses and my spine pushes forward.
Contraptions cringed, currents coherent in this crisis of the male vicinity.
My breathing ceases and my pyramid eyes grow black lines striping the red.

But oh death is good in that I do not have to plunger out these grown
Obscenities. Clawing and ripping on their own— these two white and black
Tarred enigmas having a skull—like structure or a joint like a foal wedging
Its way out of the sac drenched in sopping black and brown hide, twice as
thick;

Twice as muscular. Keep in mind there are two, there are two. The long boned
Joint of muscular vivacity carries a brown fur-hide tapestry and extending wide.
Dripping from the bottoms of these extending bat-like capes, are black furred
Wing tips dropping the tar into the flame. Wings are not made, they're born.
As humans, the same.

And the tar empties me and my blood is now black like oil, constrained into
Canisters from the Middle East of the Pupil's dead sand. My skin green as it
Was meant to be in bold turquoise my bones pure red. I am complete.

    * * *

I am recreated. For when I recreate the world, I shall make it for the Eye.
The flames extinguish, and my wings fold up and I peer at the firefighters
Edging and backing away from their hoses as I engulf their view in juxtaposes
Of Fear, of symbols, of lacking what is and what is not reality, I see it, I hunger
It. And what have all my fantasies taught me about hunger, take advantage,
Make it, strive for it—by taking one who could not escape and adding him to my
Black blood-dripping palate, ready to eradicate mankind.

I am larger too, much larger, enough to eat and digest ten firemen like
Shish kebab ants covered in grease like ones of bazaar street corner merchants

Eager to give it all away for just a filler of the cost; a spare sample. I am
A human's dream, and for thought I am real. I carry an abundant surreal
Reality into my veins as my lungs are able to key the pupil with my
Pain-drenched scream and orange lightening peers out of my nails that
Carry the symbol of the Eye drenched in permanent tar. They are of
The first of many. With just the whiplash of my wings I destroyed hundreds
Of Suburb houses miles wide. I step on children, breast-feeding mothers.
I feel the rust, rest and rebel of each desired pillage step I take. I see
Them with their guns and mayors having sex in corruption naked to
Each bolt I blaze. I can feel Pompeii beneath my veins as they have no
Where to improve, no more abundance, and their numbers dwindle.
I char the land as black as coal, as the day they should have realized Whole.
The day they should have not have made except for the falsity of human
Desire!

I do not pity you. I step on an elementary school fit for the public, but
The doors were locked and no late child could get in.

I do not pity you. I kick open a cemetery of lamenting families mourning
War-Torn deserted hearts and demolish the funeral and rake each soldier
Nude of their weaponry.

I do not pity you. I reaped out senior centers, shred wheel-chairs, and those
Folks, laughing and talking, while playing checkers with their grandchildren.

I scoop up the dead and squeeze their insides to see a small stream
intermittently
Take on its once red hue. I empty blocks and refill banks with bounced
Unchecked minds. I splash and bathe in what reds leave behind.

PART II

RAZING THE HUMAN RACE

The Reign of the Eye Begins.

IN CALIFORNIA

State Motto: *Eureka*

I travel from the Northern Californian suburbs, and grasp onto the birth of the Greatest Movement of our time: Human Demise.

Already in San Francisco grew a an armored protest of those pacifiers and puppy-lovers, hippies, tree huggers, Gay and Lesbian Rights organizations, displaying their form of generosity and courtesy for my up and coming approach; I landing on the two cable of arcs of the Golden Gate bridge, with the brilliant yellow rays of morning greasing me in position.

The Mayor of San Francisco was explaining to the military that if this welcoming of the ancient Pterodactyl Bat Devil thing went into a violent attack to be ready. Each militant was handed a tranquilizer dart gun to be on the lookout.

China Town was already printing out T-Shirts with "San Francisco: City of the Bay Devil,"—which were waving in the Pacific winds on all the friendly and loving protestors going against the conservative view in this situation of—"getting the hell out of there."

This was the time to embrace my forthcoming, a new gigantic being, a big friendly giant.

Even the Hornblower Yacht horn chirped in glee as the driver and the tourists assumed my waving wings in the wind were of my graced salutations.

I shook the cabled bridge a bit, and immediately cars honked and scampered either into a wreck or off the bridge as soon as they could. People ran to their cars, yet from the City by the Bay, I was still happy and gay like giant orange monarch butterflies wearing white gloves.

And the celebration began. . . .

I took both arcs and sandwiched the bridge together and arrowed it into the Bay observing the falling cars and screaming joggers. I traced their sound and covered them in tar and flames. The World was under attack.

I took up a gas-guzzling SUV and slammed it into a family gathered on Crissy Field, and the herding began as I tarred Victorian homes with flames and lightning; San Francisco had never had a severe lightning storm and it was vanishing into ashes. Hills were toppled over. Any military weapon being used on me, did nothing.

Mad vans, and motorcyclist sped with people not used to chaos, who were thinking, Why is this happening to us? Think harder. People are running every which way trying to carry what is necessary their children or their laptops, their pets or their birth certificates, their credit cards or their antique silverware. Some left their children by accident and weren't able to go back to their condos edging with parallel view of the destruction.

Firefighters could not put out the fire, no matter what human strategy proved in the past, their tactics were defeated. Safety left from captivity.

Fire alarms echoed, elevators stopped, wires snapped, people fell from heights and parks.

Several drug dealers were making a "killing" as they were handing out wraps to people who had lost everything in just a minute. Electricity failed, cell phones didn't connect, Alcatraz sunk with the Bay Bridge, Treasure Island and with it Oakland.

Seagulls dove and gripped pieces of burning swimsuited bodies and flew and landed on the Trans America Building and directed their point of view to the hail that scattered down on a city of hills and ambitions directed in cycles.

San Francisco became a barren wasteland within half of a day's 12-course hour, and the debris polluted the Bay, and oil covered otters and Monterey. Napa Grapes swelled up in white pimples and their juice spilled out before they shriveled off and plunged from their vines.

The air became very sticky and humid and the degrees lifted passed 150 degrees Fahrenheit. The Redwoods died and collapsed like fortresses losing funding and care, and one day it hits you— why didn't you care.

In Santa Barbara I urinate on the city with flaming tar, and surfers attempt to fin away, but in easy effort they are corroded in never-ending electricity which travels to boats and waverunners in the Pacific.

At San Diego's airport I redirect flights directly at the city, and buildings, recreation centers, schools— are taken out by 747's and 757's.

The Mayor of Los Angeles has been trying to get a hold of the President of the United States, but at the moment he is dealing with a veto and angry mob outside of the White House. The Mayor of Los Angeles loses his connection in smelted sweet misery. My misery, my heart-wrenched, tear-choked apathy.

<u>IN NEVADA</u>

State Motto: ***All for Our Country***

The greatest evacuation in the World began. Newscasters who were filming the San Francisco disaster had all been murdered in front of the camera, and the Nation was in shock beyond words. Protests rang around the United States, the Red Cross called together a team to be centralized in Nevada—where most of the remaining Californians were traveling too—and so was I.

I flew into the City of Sin, and saw the endless traffic, and gamblers dropping their winnings to get back into their hotel, while people took it on the street and got back into their vehicles. Taxi cab drivers were being kicked out of their vehicles by angry Californian parents who held them up at gunpoint, to get their pets and family there and removed any form of impatience by assault. Taxi drivers attacked other cars waiting in the traffic line too. And their inhuman capabilities of independence and survival became unstable.

I came onto the strip with my arms extended and wings spread out tearing apart each billionaire resort. Vegas of course was used to seeing casinos be imploded and torn down— just not with all the rooms occupied and screaming into the rubbled dust and gassed flames.

The Deserts in Northern Nevada began to mildew and rip apart taking the animal burrows and places of natural splendor into an ever-growing black holed monopoly.

<u>IN OREGON</u>

State Motto: ***Alis volat propriis,***

&

<u>IN WASHINGTON</u>

State Motto: ***Al-ki***

I compile the Redwood forested states by digging up the land, the people, taking the needle tapping on people's rooftops, and slaughtering farms, crops, tribes, children learning how to sail away.

More California, and now Nevada evacuees—many had gone to Utah were in rendezvous of this survival feud, and wars were breaking out for the sake of finding food. Hospitals were letting go of life-support patients as their generators failed, and chemotherapy patients were treated by chaos. Women and children bringing flowers and balloons were stuck in elevators that observed the foyer and all of those wheel chair gown dwellers blindly escaping through the electric doors shoving each other onto the bare floor.

In manufacturing plants, people were trying to jam their system as the incoming fires would create incomprehensible destruction, and it did.

Starbucks blasted over the mountains and into the Ocean.

<u>IN IDAHO</u>

State Motto: ***Esto Perpetua***

In two days, the United States had lost four States, and for the first time since their edged beginning, these people realized that life could control them, destroy them, and their efforts were completely useless. Not one human knew what to do. Some, no many, even attempted to go back to California, but they were blocked off by convoys for no apparent reason but to prevent anymore loss when all is already at loss.

Police gave up, and stores were robbed and ripped down. The newest fashions were stripped off wearers leaving them in the cold naked, and losing with them their sleeping families in their used vehicles heading off to—God knows where.

The East Coast however watched all this on television. A few had cancelled their vacation plans at Palm Springs. Though there were the skeptics, and yes there were the devout who wanted to rid themselves of any wrongdoing before an expected end would come to all.

According to reports on the news, who had lost contact with many West Coast reporters, estimated that the National Guard and Homeland Security required four days to setup a defense mechanism, calling it codename 1776 (so that other countries wouldn't emulate it— as if that mattered now). And then one camera of a reporter fell onto the ground as the cameraman had a heart attack hearing his brother speak to him for the last time from his ranch near Rupert, Idaho. Seconds later, Boise was taken with his disconnected end: "You."

<u>IN MONTANA</u>

State Motto: *Oro y plata*

5 States.

On Montana's Square Butte were the Northern Cheyenne chanting and discussing about the spirits being afflicted with humanity. Surrounding the butte in that Moonlit valley were motor homes, Emergency vehicles and several evacuees who had made it this far. They were all in despair, talking as if wartime had breached their lifetimes, yet which distorted their conversation they couldn't come to mind how to blame it. Some said it was the governments fault some how, others said that it was the spirit of the Earth at conflict with humanity's usage of the resources available, others indicated that it was the manifested form of global warming. And for that matter everyone reached for a sympathy to match their undertakings yet no one could achieve it as this didn't feel real— At all.

Then the Glacier National Park was entirely melted, and I poured it down on the butte to cool them off, and then tarred them dry.

<u>IN WYOMING</u>

State Motto: *Equal Rights*

"Yee—ha!" Said this here buckaroo tossing his body up and down, up and down and waving to his adoring fans from up towards the stands. The bull snorted, and the cowboy gyrated his hips to stay on. The rodeo clown whistled with both pinkies inserted on the hooks of his painted purple lips as he hopped onto the swinging pen. The cowboy threw his black hide hat to his buxom wife in her glittering cowgirl outfit, "Thank you partner," she let out. Another Kenny Rogers hit filled the stands.

The moonlight danced passionately with the stars and her spectacular smile in each rustle of wind.

Suddenly her sheriff let go of the rope with his last efforts, and she covered her mouth———And so did the rodeo clown.

Just as he let go, they let go, the bull choked as I raced down and caught both for an early evening dessert.

Wyoming just became another grazing spot, after all it already was.

<u>IN UTAH</u>

State Motto: *Industry*

Cedar City becomes Cedar Falls. I take to Zion National and break down the land: ledges, bridges, edges. I take hikers and toss them heights into their glory filled doomed destiny, like spilling a box of linked paper clips clinking and twirling to places where you are just too busy to care for— and you expect someone else to pick them up, but it doesn't happen.

Salt Lake becomes a body-filled landscape swarming in flies and all the newly converted pipes of Salt Lake City's Sewage System. Salt Lake City has its warmest season—that it ever will, and ashes to ashes it all falls down.

IN ARIZONA

State Motto: *Ditat Deus*

The Grand Canyon became the American Graveyard where for each hampered human state to which I would exterminate.

Cacti finally blooming their grand century's blossom were discontinued and deserts became char, and Flagstaff was waving its white flag in a pile of desert mirage in coaled despair.

The Arizona Military, still lacking support from the White House attempted a chemical weapon raid spraying seven tons of Sarin via a fire copter in a 50-50 chance at killing me, instead they removed an immediate 5,000 out in Phoenix who were watching the Diamondbacks in the Bank One Ballpark. The fans began to choke severely and immediately their lungs popped due to the pressure, and the batter struck out endlessly into a fouled paradise, into an evaporated dry land flowing in the organs of material Earth.

IN NEW MEXICO

State Motto: *Crescit Eundo*

The remaining North American continent was in a severe frenzy, people robbed planes. White people, white women held pilots at gunpoint so they, without the schools' permission could deliver students from evil in another country and informed everyone who had reserved flights going to Europe or to Japan or to Australia to exit or be killed. And they weren't kidding. A wealthy fast food chain entrepreneur refused to leave his first class seat and luggage from the plane. This female public school teacher took out her handgun and shot him in the head three times – in front of the panicked children, crew and exiting airline customers.

Many state governments called an official lockdown on their states to get anyone acting in such a manner directly to a penitentiary facility or asylum as soon as possible.

The churches, temples, mosques, and synagogues were also busy having for the first time triple to quadruple marriages all at once—with ages ranging from twelve to ninety—two. Even parents with disabled children or children on life support were getting them wooed to the nurses who took care of them and even placing them in their wills as if they too were to die in an instant. Holy Matrimony!

The sex was up and running, teenagers pulling out Armageddon verbiage and their best take on the Sonnets in efforts to un—cleanse their virgin bodies ASAP anywhere from a Wal—Mart aisle to the Epcot Spaceship Earth.

The animal rights activist knew it was their time as they broke into all the unmanned zoos and botanical parks to release the wildlife anywhere and then without my help setting the structures and cages on fire and cheering in glee.

Hospitals lost electricity, and doctors took their savings while jetting out during emergency operations. Pilots had strokes while flying, newscasters were crying, disease was spreading, the water began to desecrate and corrugate their insides.

Food went old after a day by the extensive heat, and people took to food whenever they could, even compulsive eaters were going to the Humane Society and ripping out of the cages whatever was necessary.

The President still had not responded, though the Vice President ordered a former President to be put on radio stations. And to which the former President said that he would do his best to get the States to agree on a plan of action to get everyone to Canada or Mexico as soon as it was humanly possible, and if everyone would stay calm and evacuate safely.

Humans were being quite humane in every way they were not.

To whoever of the East Coast that still had a working television there was a touching interview of a Californian struggling with the loss of her entire family and ranch, yet she never actually was there to experience the loss, and she could only feel a symbol of what could have been felt by the many losing their lives on the day the Golden State became bone dry.

And then there were those visitors both illegal and from far away unable to translate as their translator ditched them in unethical shame with a "Welcome to America" comment and stiff departure.

American dollars became valued lower and lower as each state went underneath.

Flowing primaries, roses and bronze stitched hot air balloons drifted over Albuquerque screaming "Fuck off" while throwing hand grenades, liquors with flaming towels, and even pipe bombs from above, as then each would be puffed up in smoke as I flew skimming the sun dried turf. Santa Fe sunk into a painted volcano decorated and ornate like a gregarious door wreath.

<u>IN COLORADO</u>

State Motto: ***Nil sine Numine***

Survivors are few, and the American flag rips into flowing cutouts along the silent river.

Delta, Delta! Gunnison, Salida, Cannon City, Littleton, Denver! Can you hear us— called the Homeland Security Department over all phone lines in the area and radio stations.
No answer.

In Lone Tree, Colorado, the Lone Tree Hotel and Golf Course became the victim of carnivorous aggression. Hotel guests were eaten alive out in the sandpits and artificial fairways of the courses by evacuees. In addition the numbered hole flag pins were used as skewers separating appropriate muscles for chowing down on. Not since the Donor Party had cannibalism been as historic for the American Textbook as it was today.

<u>IN NEBRASKA</u>

State Motto: ***Equality before the law***

Swinging in the Nebraskan winds were sunflowers and daisies, conifers and some redwoods, and a noosed barn family. A gathering of other crop farmers in the area had called the family pagan for attempting to get machines to replace its workers, and one day let some of its animals go into the wild. They pointed to the noosed family as if their love for animals over humanity and the farm life was the precursor movement that led about my creation. Nebraska was the first of many states to succumb to Loss Insanity. The rest of the Nebraskans ran to their Capitol building in Lincoln and killed everyone in the government

building to, according to them, act for the laws created by the
Founding Fathers.

WE INTERRUPT THIS DESTRUCTION FOR A PRESS CONFERENCE
WITH THE PRESIDENT OF THE UNITED STATES OF AMERICA

Reporter:
Mr. President, how and when will the codename 1776 project take effect?

Reporter 2:
What exactly is codename 1776?

Mr. President:
*I understand that the American people are in a status of concern, and
that we have raised our homeland threat levels to a new color, neon
pink, implying a National declaration of arms by any means.*

Reporter 3:
*Mr. President, what is going to be done about the homeland security with
the destroyed and barely managing states?*

Mr. President:
We are working on that.

Reporter 4:
Are you aware Mr. President that California was destroyed one week ago?

Mr. President:
So that's what I've heard. What day was that?

Reporter 5:
Mr. President, are troops being removed at present time from the War.

Mr. President:
*As a parent with my adoring wife and children, I know what it's like to
make sacrifices for this country.*

Reporter 5:
*Mr. President, my question was if the Army was going to be removed from
the Middle East.*

Mr. President:
One question at a time.

Reporter 6:
Mr. President.

Mr. President:
Yes, Judy.

Reporter 6:
Do you give a fuck about your country?

Mr. President:
Didn't your Daddy ever teach you to⋯ Now we understand that we are at a crisesese, but it would be in the best interest of this Nation to prepare and be ready when the time comes for the right moment of attack.

(continued below)

IN SOUTH DAKOTA

State Motto: ***Under God the People Rule***

Reporter 7:
We just received news that Mount Rushmore Park has been destroyed. Mr. President, what are your next tactics? Now Sioux Falls too.

Reporter 8:
Mr. President the alien demon is moving onto North Dakota at this very moment, what do you plan on doing, how will the budget—

Reporter 9:
Mr. President stop bluffing, you are clearly not cut out to be our President in times of "crisesese".

Mr. President:
Only few would think so.

Reporter 9:
Mr. President, I don't think America needs you anymore at this point.

Mr. President:
Great, that's what I've been waiting for all day. You guys handle your bull shit, I've got a victory to achieve overseas. If you read your history books right; just remember one man, the President Polk and how he went against everyone in order to achieve Texas in the Mexican American War.

Reporter 10:
So you're not going to work for your country— for democracy? You even swore on a Bible.

Mr. President:
I recall the pages were of the Index.

<u>Reporters</u>:
Mr. President, Mr. President, Mr. President!

<u>Mr. President</u>:
So long America, God Bless you.

<u>IN NORTH DAKOTA</u>

State Motto: ***Strength from the Soil***

A Herd of mustang horses galloped from Montana, some with saddles, others wild and free, trotted through streams and rough terrain. Then they passed and leaped over burned bodies with grilled skin gooping into the main cracks and openings of the human skulls. They ran through the feather, shrapnel, upholstery and carrion debris lying endlessly in Bismarck. Only half made it without viable food and barely pure pristine water to Fargo and collapsed with the human bodies in the trenches surrounded in screams and ricocheting bullets.

<u>IN MINNESOTA</u>

State Motto: ***Quae sursum volo videre***

In the white-walled Correctional Facility of Oak Park Heights, prisoners were at ease without any worries except who was going to be hazed and raped in the shower room again in front of the giggling security guards. It was lunch time and the smell of cigarettes covered the entire inmate area. One inmate had smoked all his cigarettes half way and placed them next to the stainless steel bowls of toilet water and the two day old urination—for some who didn't flush.

Though for two days there had not been any security guards to pop in and take them to the cafeteria. Some men had started to eat the cigarettes that someone saved in the main atrium of the inmate area, others were even biting and swallowing their own nails.

A security guard popped in who had burnt his left arm revealing his elbow bone through his untying ligaments of muscles, and locked himself in with inmates, and then tried to reason with them for his personal self-sympathy. They immediately ripped his other arm out that was trying to handle his other gun, took his key card and kicked him aside. On the way exiting, one of the inmates placed the guard's body completely naked in the shower area— as that had been his personal fetish with that particular guard, kissed the guard's head and closed his eyes.

Outside the prison lay their execution as Minnesota had erupted into a pool of lava that extended into the Great Lakes making them

bubbly. I let go of the prison and watched the screaming prisoners
try to run back for security or jump to land and disappear completely in
the molten lava in seconds.

IN IOWA

State Motto: ***Our liberties we prize and our rights we will maintain***

Near Des Moines, the future of energy consumption is being put on
display with ethanol and biodiesel stations with tapered "Grand
Opening's" over new coats of paint—quickly demolished. While
destruction exists, children run and play at the State Fair.

A mother eyes my approach grabbing onto her two children
screaming, "Oh God, I thought the beast would never come to our Iowa.
Run." The Fair was in brouhaha. I took a red, white and blue Ferris wheel
off its rocker and Frisbee'd it miles away into Missouri; and then made
cotton candy from sugared ash and tar.

IN MISSOURI

State Motto: ***Salus populi suprema lex esto***

I stepped and shattered the Des Moines Ferris wheel in the morning
sunrise.

Missouri, O' Misery, you build your arch so high,
That up on top to heaven's door, it frowns unto the sky.
Missouri, O' Misery your river runs with utmost force
That when defeated, you lead your people off life's course.

The siege on Missouri was near priceless on my behalf as I saved at
least 35% of the herded population to meander further East.

IN KANSAS

State Motto: ***Ad astra per aspera***

THEN,

IN OKLAHOMA

State Motto: ***Labor omnia vincit***

THEN,

<u>IN ARKANSAS</u>

State Motto: ***Regnat populus***

KANSAS down to Arkansas bled like beheaded fowls and their flowing verdant landscapes, crops and humbled beauty, arts and crafts, picturesque and romantic fountains were covered in every angled of the human body reflected in the outcome of a shattered mirror

<u>IN TEXAS</u>

State Motto: ***Friendship***

Cría cuervos, y te sacarán los ojos
(Breed crows, and they will take out your eyes.)

A Lone Star Dallas Cigar breathed in stemmed smoke out of a sweaty-wife-beatered mustached Houston, about mid-age, whose fly got caught by the stilettos of a vicious tired Vixen. He says it's been hard with the loss of his family in Arizona. She knows it's been hard, especially for her job at the Cabaret Royale in Dallas, but once she breathes like heaven and strokes the crumpled nipple hair covered in yellow sweat stains—she knows he's gonna get harder.

The smooth fiddling music stopped as the radio station was disconnected.

The Houstonian laughed, he said "Baby you better add more rhythm to yer gig."

She took her skin tight leather jacket off, and kicked off his 10 gallon, and said, "I'm a working woman, my best is always yet to come."

He exhaled smoke in her pretty powdered face, she coughed, and he said, "Damn girl, that's the lamest shit I've heard. You better give me a job in addition for the money I've paid."

She got up, and pulled out a chair on the main stage.

"You think sitting yer ass down is gonna entertain me?"

She called to all the other men having their fill of "love" from the Cabaret girls to watch her in action. Two other women knew the gig, and within minutes they were displaying some lip-action on one another. An old 70 year young Englishman dressed in a full navy suit smiled to exclaim, "That's what I am talking about, pretty bitches, now you come back and see if we can mimic your act."

The Houstonian's girl called the Houstonian up, and quickly they took off his pants and his tighty whities were in much worse shape than his— oh you get the point. She smiled and gave him a wedgie on a coat hook, and he screamed, "Mercy, mercy!" And then I took off tossing the Cabaret into the middle of the Gulf in the middle of a Hammerhead Shark school at bay to find fresh meat with plenty of action.

Back on land, the heat was ravenous as millions from every state, including the country of Canada were in line at Brownsville (as the Mexican airports and harbors were completely full with people to cross over into "safe territory.")
Within another hour there was no wait at all.

IN LOUISIANA

State Motto: *Union, justice et confidence*

After the drenching defeat of the Lone Star State, came the "L" shaped southern drawl. The Governor at the moment was observing rare lilies in New Guinea that could solve air pollution—as that had been a major concern and problem for the population of the Pelican State that barely had any pelicans.

The Mayor of New Orleans decided to take a stab at this, since he had given up trying to contact her with the area code change to do so, and the Governor thought that it was odd the plant observatory had a record player playing her Beatles tune like the one from her cell phone. The Governor smiled when she saw a llama from the garden there walk right up to her and lick her straight up from her chin to her forehead. She smiled and said to the people—that she thought were behind her (as they were out having coffee)—"I love you too. You know, Louisiana would be much better with llamas as they produce less methane than cows, and with less heat we would have less crime and hurricanes."

Within a half an hour after officials outside of Texas were to confirm that Texas had properly and soundly been taken down— just to make sure, the Mayor announced a mandatory evacuation for the city and a "recommended" evacuation for the State—as only the Governor can mandate such verbatim. The population of Louisiana had long left the Governments of Louisiana with the attack on San Diego, and the Governments down South suddenly realized that during my arrival.

The Mayor went out and got himself drunk on Bourbon Street for free before he was found with the other floating bodies heading into the Gulf as the replacement levees broke just as I flew by them. Louisiana became Atlantis—which was to be a theme for one of the Governor's favorite parades, the Krewe of Bacchus.

The Governor in that moment came to a turning point
epiphany that, "Maybe we can call the meat 'Leef' with an 'L' instead of
beef and it would sound so organic."

<u>IN MISSISSIPPI</u>

State Motto: ***Virtue et Armis***

The floods carried on to Jackson where a Baptist Church was
singing in knee deep waters. Singing and singing all dressed up in Sunday
attire a verse of "Amazing Grace":

> " *We've been here ten−thousand years···*
> *Bright shining as the sun.*
> *We've no less days to sing God's praise···*
> *Then when we've first begin.* "

Just as the congregation was coming to the end of their soaked mass,
the stained glass windows broke down with more water coming in, and in
addition came the merged group of Neo−KKK and Neo−Nazi members with
tasers, knives, guns and nooses.

And then suddenly the roof of the church broke off, and I sent rays of
electric light to everyone in boiled waters

<u>IN ALABAMA</u>

State Motto: ***Audemus jura nostra defendere***

The last of 500 tankers just docked out of Mobile into the Gulf to
head to South America with the gradual tankers on their way out.
Unfortunately like the Cabaret, supplies, and people were left to isolate
with the schools and torrents of the Blue Seventy−Percent.

People who had been evacuating for days with their families just
about had given up as they hid themselves in their Greenville motel or
off−the−interstate hotel room, closed their curtains, asked for their
last room service requests with the rest of their credit cards−if that
value was worth anything at this point, and prayed underneath covers in
the dark. The founding darkness of a Great Beginning for the End of All
Mankind.

<u>IN GEORGIA</u>

State Motto: ***Wisdom, Justice and Moderation***

The majority of Georgia's population was in and around, sleeping on the runways of the last Southern United States International Airport, ATL International. People were even running around and doing yoga in the facilities to ease themselves of their stress in the noisy air channels and pitches of jets taking off and rumbling to a halt every two minutes.

There was no water except for bottled water, and the bathroom water had been transitioned to red hued water. Even bathroom tiles and tiles in the flooring were beginning to show signs of crimson to dark brown "mildew" by the unfastened piping. The phone lines and the Internet connections were all down. People kept calling for no apparent reason, while others listened to their voicemail box and the last messages they had heard from friends, relatives, loved ones, even telemarketers. They wanted any real sense of care, and even pilots, flight attendants and many military men and women—and as for all workers— lost that sense of the need to be "professional" in crises such as this one— as they really had no idea of how to handle it.

A three—year old girl in partially burnt clothing walked away from her crying parents and went to one of the gift shops in Concourse A which was filled with clamoring and chatting about loss and what is wrong with the world. She went up and picked up a Snoopy stuffed animal from a shelf, hugged it, as her parents came around with worried and angry looks for her running off, and said, "I miss Love."

Then the entire airport braced for almost expected turbulence.

IN FLORIDA

State Motto: *In God we Trust*

Senior Citizens were huddled about in submarines which were all headed to Peru, however several, not all, Central Americans and Haitian Americans were treated with segregation and could not go on the submarines and either took the ferry or had to steal a boat to get out.

In Orlando I drifted in via obvious human curiosity and eyed Universal's, Disney's and Sea World's Amusement Park Empire. I drifted over the Magic Kingdom in the Sunset, and as immediately as I came over, Tinker Bell retaliated with her mangy fireworks show. In cheerful soundtracks and cartoonish honks and onomatopoeia, the theme park mascots took out bazookas—yes, even that charming jolly mouse. Even Sniper Shooters were flying on Dumbos' backs in a circle spinning to zone in on my position.

In minutes rides were malfunctioning and military personnel were tumbling off in what would, without myself— lead to automatic lawsuits with Hollywood and its movie companies that seem to "start it all."

<u>IN SOUTH CAROLINA</u>

State Motto: ***Dum spiro spero***

The last of the Gullah and many of the South's last folks and children stood among the palm trees in the crisp morning on the bold green Atlantic where pirates once sailed and docked there so long ago, it seemed. What was the Southeast to those of America, definitely a spot for both good food, music and bad hurricane and flood insurance that's for sure; and they had Robert E. Lee to stand up for them.

But what made the West— the West, and the South— the South was a relationship among separate dispersed peoples linking to find and build together an attempt to step back through symbols and life's clues at the bold society that would have been, but never reached, and through time slowly decayed; and became forgotten from the truth of the original plan. And that defines any society, state, country, area of people, a group of people devoted only in the early stages of a group's existence, to attempt to create a society that acts like and for the symbols they believe in from their ancestry, but are never achieved.

What was the West, they'll say, what was the South, what was···the South?

<u>IN TENNESSEE</u>

State Motto: ***Agriculture and Commerce***

Wild turkeys and farm—tortured ones flocked together to soon be attacked and quickly devoured by Black Bears who had attacked Pigeon Forge looking for any good water or food, but most of Tennessee's towns and cities became burial piled mounds with liquids and sugars draining into rivers, soils and streams.

And for the first time in a while, Memphis couldn't listen to the King, and Graceland was a "hunk—uh—hunk—uh—burning" debris.

<u>IN NORTH CAROLINA</u>

State Motto: ***Esse Quam Videri***

Most of the North Carolina residents were on their way to New York, while North Carolina's army and private military division, Blackwater was holding bastion at the Biltmore Estate in Ashville. From Wilmington shot forward heat—seeking missiles, and within minutes the entire

Estate was blown up, along with the thousands of mines freshly established in the vineyards just in case.

TODAY THE PRESIDENT OF THE UNITED STATES HAS CONSIDERED THIS LOSS, NOW, AS AN ACT OF WAR, AND THAT AMERICA IS NOW A BATTLEZONE, AND RULES OF ENGAGEMENT APPLY.

IN KENTUCKY

State Motto: ***Deo gratiam habeamus***

Frankfort spilled along the waterways; however Bowling Green was a little hard to pin down. The military had advanced its plans of attack by making time to work on codename 1776 by placing decoy mined mannequins along the city and into the caverns of Mammoth Cave in efforts to keep me under piled rocks. Slightly agitated I crumbled the rest of Kentucky into a rocky flotsam, and yes there were dead horses and fried chicken in those piles—the original items for the Recipe too.

IN VIRGINIA

State Motto: ***Sic semper tyrannis***

Along I-95 there were cars parked with millions of bumper stickers saying their last words. The afternoon heat in a cloudy day gave them a grim experience to my exposure unto their world, but they had to give up their exposure on our introduction. A Biker gang that had robbed a U-Haul carrying antiques connected to a university bus carrying cheerleaders, were making their own leisurely last-minute venues and stops on the way before getting crushed under crossing signs and tracks of their own kind. And Jamestown fell into gardened and demolished soil, and Virginia became no more.

IN WASHINGTON D.C.

Justitia Omnibus – Justice for All

Operation 1776 is go! Code Red, Operation 1776 is go!
Alarms echoed in Eagled Screams in the District of Columbia.

Mr. President:
Clearly these terrorists don't know what they're dealing with. Pentagon 47-code 1776 is now in effect, your mission to eradicate this Weapon of Mass Destruction, go! See, I told you all there was something at work from these terrorists, but no one listened.

<u>**PENTAGON**</u>:
47 B–2 Bombers are taking off in 3–2–1. Blue Angels prepare for take off. Beta 42709 Amphibian Battleships extend walkers out and prepare to dock on 3000 K Street Northwest, head to the Pentagon, Go! 82 T–72's and prototypes T–79 tanks head to Capitol and return fire when target is within 700 feet of your radius. Mr. President 1776 is in play, Air Force One is on its way right as we speak.

What is this I thought, Duck Hunt on Steroids?

In a high–pitched roar edged a seemingly never–ending relay of B–2's in 2x2 formation and then breaking off to act like Redwood branches all around me in efforts to trap me in one position. However, I relaxed as I was waiting to see more. The Blue Angels flew around me and continuously circled around my ankles attempting see if I had some sort of weakness there. Tanks surrounded myself and the Capitol. Then gradually like a walking table or kitchen sink full–lengthed battleships were marching down the alphabetical streets breaking the concrete into rubble. From a distance I could see Air Force One taking off towards the Atlantic with the President and his completely frightened Cabinet.

<u>**PENTAGON**</u>:
Men and Women of the Military of the United States of America, the President has left the United States, begin eradication. May God Bless Each of you. Represent your Country well' we are all counting on you. Let's do it!

I pretended to not defend myself for the first 45 minutes and pretended to cower down in defeat as the missiles, rockets, and bombs with their explosions felt like getting hit by a group of fuzzy Nerf ™ darts. And like a child playing the invisible shootout with an older family member, and watching them either cover their heart and roll their eyes back in excruciating pain or just flop on the floor with a dramatic "You got me partner. Bleh!", the human child frizzles up in ecstasy and giggles in artificial victory–this was quite the comparison of this evening's battle.

I pulled a Gulliver, as I laid back on the shattered Capitol surrounded by the flames they made with their own missiles. Even the President ordered Air Force One to be turned around to see this momentous defeat for the country. They landed their planes, and parked their tanks, and lowered their fire arms and turrets, snipers and rifles, and got out and gathered around me.

They started laughing and even started to poke me with sticks. I waited for the opportune moment to strike.

The President's plane had landed, and the military was placing a podium atop my stomach, and connecting it to a generator.

The General turned on the microphone to test it. "Testing, Testing, 1,2,—"

I roared immediately and all of the soldiers became deaf and many of their bones broke under their skin and they collapsed. I got up and kicked over the myriad of tanks, and started slowly walking towards Air Force One.

Just as the hatch was opening for the President, it was immediately closed in his face from people manning the landing area, and he received a black eye. With blood dripping onto his star—spangled tie, he ordered an official departure ASAP. His family with the Cabinet members and their family were screaming as I approached, and immediately put on Mariah Carey's Christmas Hits CD.

The President's seat belt couldn't fasten as the First Lady had accidentally placed her own clip into his buckle, and she giggled briefly in the spur of the heat.

I took a swipe at the decorated aluminum can of flakes and it plunged forward like the after—effect of opening a canister of Pilsbury ™ Crescent Rolls. The President rolled forward, and the First Lady took one of his shoes off in effort of grabbing him.

He rolled into the cockpit and got into the empty second mate chair next to the frantic and teary pilot.

PILOT:
Mr. President, sir, we're not going to make it.

The entire Crew heard his words and screamed in unison. The President closed the cabin door with the dramatic discord.

PILOT:
I just wanted to tell you that, to be honest.

Mr. President:
Sometimes honesty weakens an entire Nation.

PILOT:
Mr. President!?

Mr. President:
Pilot, we don't need the likes of your kind on this plane jabbering about suicide and all, let me drive, I've had experience from my earlier days in the Air Force.

PILOT:
I can't Mr. President.

<u>Mr. President</u>:
This an order, pilot!

<u>PILOT</u>:
I can't for America, Mr. President; I can for you.

<u>Mr. President</u>:
Okay set your butt off the seat.

I took another lazy swing at the slow moving air vehicle, and yawned. The President took control of the plane, and the nervous pilot hobbled to the back near the cabin door and started crying in his arms.

<u>Mr. President</u>:
Let's see the Yaw and the Pitch, what did those mean again? Okay here we go Alpha India Romeo Foxtrot Oscar Romeo Charlie Echo One is ready for take off, I always wanted to read that like those pilots—

<u>PILOT</u>:
Just fly the plane!

<u>Mr. President</u>:
Let's see so I push this, uh, uh this way!

<u>PILOT</u>:
No, Mr. President!

Air Force One sped almost vertically into the Atlantic.

<u>IN WEST VIRGINIA</u>

State Motto: ***Montani semper Liberi***

Near Morgantown, one of the mineshafts were closed and sheltering in the flashlit darkness 6,000 evacuees in search of light towards the other side of the mine, though wanted to stay with the last of humanity in its external gatherings. The mine was renovated as deemed fit for the purposes of improvement and a much more scenic view when driving by instead of a leaking cavity of unknown decay—but who would be driving now?

<u>IN ILLINOIS</u>

State Motto: ***State sovereignty, national union***

Aw Chicago, Chicago, Chica Gone.
Illinois was an isolated tear drop as the Great Lakes expanded.

And Indiana, and Ohio, Michigan, Pennsylvania were covered in bodies from previous expeditions in other states and in Michigan I created another volcano national park.

IN INDIANA

State Motto: *The crossroads of America*

IN OHIO

State Motto: *With God, All Things are Possible*

IN MICHIGAN

State Motto: *Tuebor*

IN WISCONSIN

State Motto: *Forward*

In Memory of America's last Big Cheese.

IN NEW JERSERY

State Motto: *Liberty and Prosperity*

IN PENNSYLVANIA

State Motto: *Virtue, liberty and independence*

And Pittsburgh's bell rang one last time.

Liberty, Justice and any human pursuit was coming to an end.

IN NEW YORK

State Motto: *Excelsior*

" Of the United, we are the last States in the United States of Northern America, but our unity has and will never fail, for we stand—all of us at the same level, on this day for the first time since our Founding Fathers wrote and published this land for the sake of our equal independence and rights. However through conflicts and feuds, wars and alterations, the country had become unbalanced in every direction.

Today is not a great day of change; it is the worse possible and most painful day as an American of these States—United. But united we stand, and we will never give up because giving up wasn't part of our Constitutional contract.

We have all lost loved ones, homes, entire generations of family members, and yesterday, we received news that our President is no longer with us.

Let us have a moment of silence in these dark times.

Nor is the Vice President or are the entire Cabinet and their family members— they are not with us. But we cannot give up or run away. We all are weakened, tired, bruised, dying in different degrees, living today from experience or lack there of. Today we are all American people. For there is no Government, the Mayor of New York is in Canada, and the other Governments are gone.

But look at us, the Constitution and our Independence is in our hearts and minds as Americans— that is why we all want to spread our good times to people and then share your problems with us to find a solution. We are the Founding grand, grand, very grandsons and very, very granddaughters of the Greatest Fight and Revolution since its creation— saving America.

Our ancestors and still today people from all over migrate to join in our shared freedom, and let freedom ring we shall.

I am not your President, nor am I the Pope or the Dalai Llama, and I do not have the Bible with me or any other Holy text, so let us make one as we become one in this great lasting hour.

Excelsior! Today this day in the city of New York on Manhattan Island we are going up for the future, moving forward in the greatest battle of our time, saving grace, saving life, saving humanity. We shed our tears no more, for they—they are all rooting for us, and we're not soldiers— we are not public or privately own. Are all of us wearing camo uniforms? We fight as Americans, and when if we shall fall down or need help we shall call each other brother and sister because we are the United Family, and a strong family works together.

Now as Americans we are all different, we all are open to choices and freedoms to believe, and what to do, and where to go to get there. Today we need to put that aside.

Today I have with my brothers and sisters taken down the George Washington Bridge flag, and we bring it here today.

Today I can't tell you what to expect and answer all your questions, but I am here to help and fight for this country. I am not your leader, and I am not asking you to stand behind me. Today we all stand for this country.

Brothers and Sisters let us unfold this great flag together.

Now as it is held by us, we are going to each share and hold it once, put our thoughts and concerns for our improvement directly to the country, and to not be unheard anymore.

Thank you America, thank you my brothers and sisters."

Page Catherine Turner,
High School Student, Junior,
Baton Rouge, LA
An American.

The last two to three million placed their hands on the flag and annunciated their views and ideas for the improvement and future of the United States of America as the flag was passed around in the golden sunrise.

Then following the speech a long moving truck came from the ports, and everyone gave it a confused look. Some took out their weapons. The driver stepped out of the dark green truck and gave a worried look to the entire crowd. It was the Governor of Louisiana. She wanted to speak but she quickly eyed a few angry Louisianans who instantly spotted her.

She quickly went behind the moving truck and with a heave pulled open the ladder and the sliding metal curtain. Out came—a herd of about 60 llamas! Twelve of which had army helmets on.

The Governor bowed to greet them all, and then suddenly realized she was in America. She stood up and said while looking at the mob of evacuees, " If there is one thing I learned as a Governor, of, of, well a non-existent State, is that you die with the people you love and not in the stadiums like the one in Houston of those in competition, like the bad guys. So as I heard at the end of your speech, Ms. Turner, that I'm not a government official, I am just another American and I am here to help.
Except for the ones with the army hats, the rest of the Llamas are all yours."

"Thank you for this very um odd, yet generous offer. Who is ready for a true great American meal some Llamaburger!"

Everyone cheered, and people who were from the City brought some coal grills and started cooking the sliced up living llamas. The Llamas disguised in the military outfits were all watching this in horrendous shock. One of them even fainted.

Some dickhead saw me hiding behind the Trump Tower and ran and announced it. The last American War Began. The Page girl and some others—who decided to follow her took the initiative of going to the top of the high buildings with weapons in hand. Soon everyone had copied Page Turner's plan, and everyone waited on top of the Skyscrapers.

The Governor with her Llama brigade went back to the moving truck and she pulled out some hang gliders that she had bought too with other weapons. She even bought an astronaut suit including an actual oxygen tank just in case and then placed that on. She and her Llamas went to the top of the Empire State Building. This had to be the most ridiculous battlefront I had ever seen.

I approached the scene like it was out of Alfred Hitchcock's "The Birds" and walk into their "over-the-top" frontline.

Immediately the Governor sent her llamas off on their gliders with timed bombs in their mouth which she used duct tape to close their mouths on. Though unfortunately two of the hang gliders didn't work and spun down—down—down; the other llama brigade members landed and popped on my side and I didn't really notice. As I turned, more than fifty skyscraper people had jumped onto my arm and then several hundreds more had leaped onto each of my wings, and the rest were poking my feet with grenades and such. With quick motion everyone was electrocuted, and many people fell off the buildings—buildings that were soon turned into rubble. And on the way out, I tied the large American flag to a sinking tug boat, and eyed America going under at the break of a starry sunset.

* *
And the Nation that was to be built
Of Independence, Justice, and Equality
To last for generations and generations
Ended.
The New World, a human attempt again
To claim what had been lost,
Perished.
* *

The Following were destroyed before the Final Battle during Turner's Dialogue:

IN VERMONT

State Motto: *Freedom and Unity*

IN NEW HAMPSHIRE

 State Motto: *Live Free or Die*

IN MAINE

State Motto: *Dirigo*

IN MASSACHUSETTS

State Motto: *Ense petit placidam sub libertate quietem*

IN RHODE ISLAND

State Motto: *Hope*

IN CONNECTICUT

State Motto: *Qui Transtulit Sustinet*

IN NEW JERSEY

State Motto: *Liberty and prosperity*

IN MARYLAND

State Motto: *Fatti Maschi, Parole Femmine*
(Manly Deeds, Womanly Words)

IN DELAWARE

State Motto: *Liberty and Justice*

THAT IS THE END OF MAINLAND UNITED STATES OF AMERICA
* * * * * *

IN NEW BRUNSWICK

Spem Reduxit

From now a ravage and savaged land, my encore continues.

The Last Mayors and Governors of the North of America with the United Nations were headed off on Black Hawks that were sent to gradually remove anyone off of the Northern America continent. They were destroyed with sudden flames and tarred red tape, and plummeted into the Ocean. The Unity of the West was fading.

Soaring from Cape Enrage I began the Canadian Siege under screaming bells, and scorched maple leaves.

Redwoods and pale colored wooden colonial homes patched the first amount of triggered graves of the Queen's land. Saturated with sparrows and warblers the afternoon sky screamed in sorrow and song, and birds flying without a sense of where to direct their migratory intuitions. Razorbills and Killdeers swam into evacuee pored hair on their burning bodies to make nests for themselves. Other birds began to mimic this search for "robbing" humanity of its qualities and applying their loss for their personal gain.

In Hartland, the longest covered bridge was ripped off its ends and tilted upwards facing the sky with a line of cars compiling in heaves forward again and again, with the highest car hanging out of the bridge's end like a ticket hanging out of a dispenser at a deli with cold cuts and bologna.

Americans— or now just people, and Canadians ran and drove for their lives. Several people drove out to the Atlantic, out into the Sea, and either sunk in peace or began swimming to where the human will drives them.

Then to the Bay of Fundy to the annihilation of the bloodstained Hopewell rocks thundering over crunching tourist and Canadian police who didn't know whether to stop the chaos or control it by violence or reasoning. One policeman shot himself on the scene as a crying mother ran to him to look for her son.

Then I disassembled the Acadian Peninsula, where during the pre-Revolutionary War victory times, many French Acadians fled to a place called Louisiana; and many today had just arrived there from their long northerly road trip—which in turn (for that matter) was simply a waste or very "lagniappe". Their Zydeco days ended.

Canada is quite a country of fleeing people with quite a history from slaves, to war time heroes, to those who refused to join the war, and it's like someone keeps spilling water accidentally into an ant hole.

The heat of Canada at the moment was a rough 170'F, very subtle.

I strutted my pursuit further.

IN PRINCE EDWARD ISLAND

Parva Sub Ingenti!

Swish! The Confederation Bridge is demolished, and the islanders become stranded as the last Sea Plane is docked upside down.

The green rolling hill landscape and dry canyon hilled crispy paved sanded coasts are trashed and trashed on by camping evacuees and residents alike fleeing endlessly.

The emerald hills of farmhouse and cottage landscape were drenched in concrete and used up as resources running on empty.

IN NOVA SCOTIA or New Scotland

Munit Haec et Altera

"For Nova Scotia, for the Queen!" cried the British Navy as battleships assembled near New Glasgow. Immediately like the battleships in the "codename 1776" art project, the battleships became walking bodies and stepped accidentally on the running herds of cattle and headed towards me firing their rockets and lasers— Lasers?! Apparently for sometime, with the U.S. Army even the British military, these militaries were making actual laser arms a supposed reality.

The lasers however did cause a bruise to my right knee, but discolorization did not reveal itself, and without awareness the British did not use that weapon in the same location twice. The 14 battleship walkers were knocked back into the Northern Atlantic upside down—and jammed down—damning their entire crew to the pits of the Earth.

The British Army was using the Casino Nova Scotia at Halifax to put together a massive two-story laser cannon using the generator of the city and the casino, as well as the casino's security camera system to film this great gamble of chance whether this would be victory, or it be loss.

I hesitated at approaching the city as I knew the effects of this new laser attack system and what it did to my aching knee.

The first line was the dressed in all black parachute regiment who carried the new portable laser firearm. As they were attempting to figure out how to deal with all the coding and settings on the laser weaponry I quickly clipped their parachutes like a child in a frenzy of popping soap bubbles for dear life.

WITH A WEB CONTACT WITH THE QUEEN

MAJOR AT THE CASINO:
Evening your Majesty, the laser artillery is in preparation of firing the beast.

QUEEN:
Major, don't let pride take hold of your actions, defend England at your will. If the laser device does not take thorough defence for the Island, what further excuses do you have to offer?

MAJOR AT THE CASINO:
Your Majesty, the Laser B-98 is the most extraordinary machine of its class. I have no further adieu in the matter, and in concordance this may be the most brilliant cinematic display of victory in the workings of the Royal texts binding our history.

QUEEN:
I hope your word, Major is as noble as your gun. May God be at your side to carry this brute into the sorrows of Hell.

<u>MAJOR AT THE CASINO:</u>
Yes, your majesty. Corporal, remove the generators' stabilization from the Main H-volume barrier in the back magnet panel and set Kilowatts to 3,500, and set on increase. Thank you, your Majesty.

WEB CONTACT ENDED

I collided into view and the laser beamed and instantly burst my right leg off, and black tar blood ran throughout the streets. The orange laser shot straight out into the Sea.

The Major applauded however he lost connection with the Queen due to the intense power of the laser. I quickly flew upwards, and within minutes my right leg and foot formed back.

The Major gasped and ordered the Corporal to bring the laser canon upward. The Corporal said that the canon could not rotate. The Major jumped into the central control area for the laser canon and started fiddling with the wires in the human madness to do whatever it takes.

The laser cannon suddenly turned off and the Corporal screamed and fainted. The laser cannon had overheated and was continuously increasing in temperature, and there was no way to yield the machine's increased pressuring heat.

The Major ordered an immediate evacuation— though unfortunately none of their walkie-talkies and radios were functional due to the electromagnetic effects of the laser; the Major picked up the Corporal and escaped the room.

In a nuclear, no, electromagnetic nuclear explosion the cannon's explosion created a magnetic explosion that not only reaped up the land of Nova Scotia but vacuumed it entirely cleaned and full of mile deep crack lines–dispersing the island into hundreds of floating black rocks.

This is my Reign. It is my time.

<u>IN QUEBEC</u>

Je me souviens

The Saint Lawrence River is set in caverns of seeping smoke as the molten lava strolls its way out of the melting coast of Quebec.

Montreal crumples up like French fries sifting in boiling grease for days and the people ignite like the victory of a hockey team whose game ends with the ice rink melting from all the slits and cuts humanity gives it.

North America's France begins to rot like a baguette stuck in sidewalk manure.

Ontario is set ablaze in less passion than man can conspire to seeking his self beauty.

IN MANITOBA

Glorious et Liber

The World is my playground; the humans are the loose screws living to only be screwed up, so their existence is better drilled. Manitoba, Saskatchewan, and Alberta are the last places of the West Coast evacuees and I devour the rest.

IN SASKATCHEWAN

Oh **multis e gentibus vires**, how you do deplore your concrete Evidence as fault lines echo in gathered limbs akimbo. And dying vitality breathes in allied chokes to my grand foundation in more human–green grass stillness paved in central greed. The Living Skies are roofs to no human being.

IN ALBERTA

It is **Fortis et liber** to be amidst sanctity among hands who Say they build life, but life itself is not a culling of carped Ideology in abundance of good status as it is, is it not? Ask yourself that to your own demise.

By passing Chinook winds on Moraine Lake, a breeze carries monarchs and fruit flies to flutter around decay and breed maggots at will dripping in melting snow till every lost drop makes a mountain a tranquil sophisticated rose.

IN BRITISH COLOMBIA

Splendor sine occasu without end in completion.

Enabling voracity in digesting numbers which treat broken wooden totem crosses to clutch the young learning bodies of Victoria's finest impaled atop Mount Douglas, streaming in passionate Ten Mile Misery in each town, in each blooded fogged lake. I toss Kelowna into the Ocean and watch Orcas normally who would come out by the ring of a bell, spin

and glide and sink passed their gums on rich red human atrocity;
oh beautiful hell.

IN YUKON TERRITORY

Thus this land of midnight sun will drip as much as glacial
Spit drenched harmonic fury under hate's mourn-less attributions.

IN NORTHWEST TERRITORIES AND CANADIAN ISLANDS

And Mountain Avens rain on children playing cards, who in their
wool sweaters see animals once pets, once family members become their
main course of food under the now cold and tortuous weather fueling my
ravenous echelon and degree to which life holds truth, by truth by
nothing less than acceptance of the fact that we're not all in the same
boat until someone is slaughtered. Then its equilibrium finds
definition. Canada is dead.

IN ALASKA

Previous State Motto: ***North to the Future***

With help from the Royal Marines, the American Marines— nearly the
last of them (as the many American military personnel were on their way
to Europe) flew in 98 B-1 Lancer jets half heading towards my grand
entrance on the demolishing of Tok. However half flew North and away
from my location to cluster bomb the 23 million acre National
Petroleum Reserve— which was one of the White House's last requests in
the course of human action against my own. The B-1 Lancers swirling
around me were quickly altered by flaming winds created with my wings
and fangs. The last of the planes, after destroying

Fairbanks, as the other half were on their way to the U.K., met their
defeat being stripped of their plane and torched clothing and piled up
on top of Mt. McKinley–stripped of everything but humanity. I left them
on the top, on the edge, edging in fate.

Alaska's moose laid their horns under 200' degree heat and
thundering rains. The last tree collapsed in plundered belittlement in
Unalakleet.

One might wonder what does one feel to have killed so many?
Does one feel loss?
What would an animal feel?
What does a soldier feel?
A doctor?

The family of a suicide bomber?
A murderer?

It just depends on who or what you ask— but whatever they commit, the answer will be far from the walls of real thought, because humans want an over-simplified schedule of patterned emotions, reactions, loves, and hates; and to be patterned so each cobwebbed backbone of actions and discourses convenes and confines with only previous cultures who were created in separation, after the separation of the Eye.

IN GREENLAND

Ha, the name of the land that captures all the irony of humanity. A land bled of natural verdant-ness, almost entirely breasted in iced amour. And this land was home to exiles. Green— you say? And as for humanity— humanity preaches human beauty and the respect of it, and ideally an imitation of a social beauty that a medium of humanity has chosen for it—when all and all men and women are looking constantly for the 100% beauty of life when 80% is the actual effort, and search to begin with it—unless it comes to an end. Shortly.

Going to Forty-Five degrees longitude, Seventy-Five degrees latitude, I hover above the center line of Greenland and the Northeastern region of the capped National Park and I begin an easy fiberful defecation full of blackened tar splattering and enflaming whatever is green. Greenland reeks of the worse possible scent of sulfur and monoxide burning with human and animal organs previously digested and still beating prisoners sizzling into cardiac arrest.

IN ICELAND

Flying onto the much more greener but still icy lands holding the city of Reykjavik, I spot the fascinating textured fin structure of the Hallgrimskirkja church which looks like the work of the sidewalk crazed monkey grinder's organ players creation mixed with the tooting and hooting of the wide-eyed clown calliope.

With a drum roll Reykjavik swirls like a hula hoop balanced on an arctic seal's seizured body as torpedoes into the abyss. And as for the rest Iceland sifts into the merriment of a tear on what it receives when humanity ties the knot with despair, and runs down the aisle holding each other's hand of an unknowledgeable will to survive against the odds—when the odds are caused by humanity's existence.

IN NORWAY

Alt for Norge
(All for Norway)

A conglomeration of the European Navies and Military awaited in the Norwegian Sea with around 120 battleships with the walker legs freshly attached. Though none however had any sort of laser firearm as in Nova Scotia their connection had been lost during and after the Halifax siege. A convoy command center was headed in Oppland.

Throughout the sparkling great fjords and sifting streams propelled the largest SAR Helicopter fleet in the world, with 27 Black Hawks and 47 Emergency Fireccopters. And then those waddling tanks, this time though they were dressed up with painted metal horns and wings as if to frighten or trick me— as is a common human tactic.

As I approached the massive European brigade, out from the clouds behind me came the B-1 Lances; from Portugal the Alpha Jet Squad of 28 Jets painted with demon eyes, and reptile scales; from France, 79 the Mirage F-1 CR jets draped in painted aluminum reflecting the afternoon sun at every angle; all the way from Taipei and Qatar 40 Mirage-2000 Jets; from Sweden 48 Saab Gripen JAS-39 Jets painted completely in black with bright red reptilian eyes; from the German and Italian air forces are 90 Tornado jets both painted in all black with red pin stripe lines on the wings; From Spain 36 FA-18 Jets painted in Valencia orange ; and 3 Boeing X-45 J-UCAS Robot Jets also manned from Oppland.

The War of the Worlds. This was it. Humanity versus its Destruction, and the burden it carries to return for them their efforts.

As the fleets of jets and walker ships and oh, now walker tanks, and hundreds now of swarming helicopters buzzed into position surrounding me, the last of the Queen's message paved their ear channels into the will of attack, the need to kill for solid vengeance, heraldry and fame. To humanity this was it, the World War; no— even larger: the War of Life, and whoever wins, the losing side will be eliminated from existence.

<u>QUEEN:</u>
With the Presidents of the entire body of Europe, and I, Queen of the United Kingdom, it is our highest wish, and with the sake of humanity's existence that this beast must be eliminated. The entire continent of Europe is at your support, if you need fuel or food take whatever is necessary to defeat him. Our lives and the lives of the world are in your hands. Go men and women, this day prove the power of humanity. Obliterate the beast at your will! Go!

And so the War Began. Humans.

I lift both arms and my wings stretch out fully extending over Norway and the Sea with a shadow completely covering the squadron and fleet. This should be Europe's darkest hour.

The 40 Mirage 2000 Jets disperse behind me as the other jets spread out all around me. The tanks deliver heat sensory missiles that collide with my tail with sharp pokes. The Mirage 2000's begin cluster bombs all along my spine, two of them kamikaze themselves in the back of my neck.

In tickled aggression from all this uncomfortable poking, I roar! The glass breaks off all the fighter jets, the houses and structures of Norway, the helicopters that go tumbling down from the intense sound vibrations.

The walker ships jump into the ocean going trigger happy to destroy my wings, while the Gripen JAS—39 jets come from above directly for my eyes with rapid fire and frantic laughing.

I tilt my head and swallow the Swedish help for humanity.

Then like the direct glide of plecostomus catfish gathering to the suction of the thin glass glued together to separate it from life, the three Boeing X—45 J—UCAS robot jets hover and set their landing gear to be attached to my wing's skin, and they begin to pull it.

Like a corpse of a mouse bursting open from maggot feeding and quickly delivery from the birth of the maggots herding on the corroded muscles and fat, the 90 Tornado jets, B—1 Lances, Spain's 36 F—A jets and ten of the Mirage F—1 Jets take the Boeing's initiative. My wings become limp from all the weight and digging into my skin.

The pilots hop out and begin to hold out—laser guns! They take to burning up holes in my wings and Red blood sprays out of my wings.

The dragoon troops and ground troops cheer vehemently.

The walker ships go back to ship mode and send rockets and missiles pounding my chest while blood is splashing onto the southern portion of Norway. My blood.

I try to wiggle the human maggot shits off, and it keeps tearing and heaving down on my wings pulling my spine more backwards from the body. I pull my body forward and clap my hands together.

Sweden and Norway explode off the face of the map, and the ground troops vanish into dust, and my energy leaves me as I plummet with the tinkering pilots and their fanged—clipped ships into the Norwegian Sea.

I descend over 3,000 meters and pilots drown at 1,000 meters.

* * * *

<u>IN SWEDEN</u>

För Sverige – I tiden
(For Sweden– With the Times)

Forever Lost in Dust and Darkness.

A week in darkness, but I am still living as I still see the blood clouds running to the top of the Sea with some of the remaining bobbing pilot bodies.

From atop humanity is in celebration.

And I can't move.

Within a month, I watch and wait for my energy to come back in the cold night black. And it doesn't, I am paralyzed, as it seems humanity has won.

Then something oh so magical appears as I see the artwork of energy geometry in being becoming. Foraminifera and silica particles and plankton pieces begin to enter my wounded wings from the ground layer of the Sea. From solar and heated photosynthesis, sugars or 2-deoxyriboses are created by the particles. In minutes the forams and silica particles multiply, and with their sugar creation, begin to adapt to the cells on my body and emulating my DNA, thus enforcing energy duplication.

Another month passes and the process has sped up as I can use my electricity to attract more and more formanifiera particles.

Another month passes, and I wake up and rise as the Sun does.

<u>IN FINLAND</u>

The country of 187,888 lakes, and a people ironically described as Finnish.

The city of Helinski breezed in ease at the many gregarious Finnish wandering on paved streets and looking at the dazzling waterfront with binoculars from brick buildings.

Then an old lady covered in a mink jacket turned towards me, dropped her cane, as I was within a mile of the front and screamed a second after I clapped my hands "Finnishing" them.

Though I decided after the country disintegrated that maybe
the clap wouldn't be as a worthy a fulfillment to humanity if they were
to leave in such an instant death.

IN ESTONIA

Kõigi maade proletaarlased, ühinege
(Workers of the World Unite)

The world of humanity simply wasn't ready for a comeback of war
within a four month period, I was.

People in greening and gliding Lääne were dashing from their
peaceful picnics, many of the picnickers included American military
members as well as a few politicians from Canada and Estonians.

Tallinin with its Russian architecture dropped any peace and were
ringing everything from bells, cell phones, and the ringing in their ears
as the city vibrated into dust.

Resurrection is quite potent.

IN LATVIA

Tēvzemei un Brīvībai
(For fatherland and Freedom)

And with resurrection comes a speedy delivery, I'm not fucking
with people anymore, this is clear to the point.

I take the Lettland Riga Freih statue with its trinity'd triangle of
stars and send it soaring into the electrical field of destruction in Riga
and the shockwaves send ripples down Lavia's wintered nerves.

IN LITHUANIA

Tautos jėga vienybėje!
(The strength of the nation is unity!)

Vilnius screams in modern strobe lights blasting amp'd arteries, and I
take the grand cylindrical Europa Tower and bat at the modern
spectacles that man has to offer none but her and his lonely self's
desires. St. Anne's Church is the fulcrum at which the tower empties
Lithuania from its shattered reflective UV protective windows.

IN BELARUS

In beaming Victory Square at midnight in Minsk, I stick in the obelisk, and fart it out to pour and puff flaming tar in the sparking carousel lit streets and shredding fur coats and poodles howling in sorrows.

Russian forces get the hint and start conversing on a planned attack.

IN UKRAINE

Процветание в единстве
(Prosperity and Unity)

I end my labyrinth of decorated flaming calligraphy on the Verkhovna Rada and then ignite an electric dyna—might spark sending Ukraine up.

IN POLAND

Bóg, Honor, Ojczyzna
(God, Honor, Fatherland)

After destruction of the great granite crags of High Tatras, the German and Italian Tornadoes take vengeance, as do I. The first four within a kilometer distance take immediate damage as I rip out parts of the demolished crags and create a comet bowl.

I race around the Carpathians and spot a frantic herd of wisent and ignite them and dart on each part of the arrow formation of jets.

I then realize they didn't equip lasers, and I see the fear in their white tear dripped, red—Richter cracked lenses. I turn around and electrocute the entire squadron and drown each jet in Rożnowskie Lake. And then I execute Poland's fall.

IN GERMANY

Einigkeit und Recht und Freiheit
(Unity and, Justice and Freedom)

In Berlin the fleeting Germans, with many of the last American civilians stampede out in all directions from the torching of Germany's entirety and all its ambitious and predatory efforts. I dig out the Reichtstag and hammer it onto the front of the stampede and the humans domino down.

<u>IN DENMARK</u>

Guds hjælp, Folkets kærlighed, Danmarks styrke
(God's help, the love of the People, Denmark's strength)

From its scatter island mess from islands like Zealand to the city of
Copenhagen, I take to collecting only the dead bodies of Denmark in my
talons.

<u>IN THE NETHERLANDS</u>

Ik zal handhaven
(I will stand fast)

   I squeeze the blood out of the population of Denmark all over the
Netherlands— smearing the coats of polished paint on the Holland
Batavia; making the cattle rabid in Friesland; sending plagues, STDs,
AIDS, poxes, herpes and cancers to all— enjoy!

<u>IN BELGIUM</u>

Eendracht maakt macht
(Unity gives strength)

   In Brussels in front of the Atomium World Fair Display from 1958, a
Belgium teen amidst the oncoming destruction announces boldly that
the White people if not all people will be dwindling into decay soon,
unless every female gets pregnant as soon as possible.

   European teens as well as adults definitely heard the message and the
sex was on. However the message faded away into: "Have Sex not bullet
wounds or Apocalypse."

   During the destruction of Brussels the victims were definitely getting
it on all over the place even in the sewers and steel plants.
Bam!

<u>IN GREAT BRITAIN</u>

Dieu et mon droit
(God and my right)

   The Queen was ordered to evacuate from her palace two days earlier but
she wanted to stand with the people who she loved and ruled for. As I
edged around she was physically forced in a black limousine heading north
to Scotland.

In the streets of London, sex was on a rampage. Store clerks instantly uncurled their hair when a man told her to have it. Viagra was emptied from the entire United Kingdom all in one day. Women were even gathering semen from the street in plastic bottles to be sent to laboratories for sperm donations—yes those were going— like chunky biscuits and salty crisps during the World Cup. Even the gay and lesbian communities got together and had a blast even in the train stations or on the train. London was horny, baby! Like bunnies on the edge, man!

The Queen's and British military advanced to Scotland and prepared a stronger approach to prevent any attack towards the Queen.

Britain's flag went down, and so did its pants.

IN SCOTLAND

"Many's the men who've battled foe
Many the number slain
Many the lads have fallen
though Scotland shall rise again. "
Shall rise again⋯

A flaming colt with ashes of a major in the British Navy ran in front of the waiting delegation of Scottish army men and women, as of all adult men who were ready to defend the hills of Galloway, from Dumfries to Scapa to Lerwick. As soon as the colt dropped the stained afternoon in pink sunlit mercy so it seemed corrupted their longing spirit to take on the human sensational approach to vengeance. The bagpipes moaned, and the rockets unfolded and touched me with no tarnish.
The sheep I carried like popcorn were ignited and thrown at the Military and evacuees driving A−835. People ran out to the war zone as I let roar a trajectory of flames and all the roads of the U.K. sank, and children who couldn't get out, tried. Mothers grasping their children were blasting at the military as if they all wore blindfolds attempting to strike a piñata. And the last of the United Kingdom Wars began.

Tanks were in the Night−Toothed streets of Edinburgh in sweat, in dire Heat, in naked whisked disassembled immunity of the wings of soul− burning red stags.

The Parliament Building gave way in seconds, and the Royal family, with the British Royal family awaited in efforts to settle a peace treaty with whom sources indicated their depiction of oneself as a "Bloody beast unfit for the likes of humanity." Edging their glorious banquet with a large brass goblet of wine, and a cornucopia of varied goods, biscuits, teas and cakes. I had no choice but to except their invitation as the smoked skyline was of a glorious view from the Castle.

All of Scotland had drowned in daggar'd silence.

Then like a million echoes Edinburgh went up from its vicinity in everlasting smoke.

A distance away, a yeoman ran to a bagpipe group that had played for the festivities earlier, with the statement: "Her Majesty⋯"

And the players immediately rang out in tears and drums, "God Save the Queen."

Soldiers in Edinburgh helping their fellow comrades, Americans, Americans helping French, Irish, German, Spanish, Swedish, Mexican, Cuban, even Russian, Chinese, Japanese and African militias had gone into the Edinburgh battle, they took off their hats and placed them over their hearts.

Flags across the world were lowered, and the surviving American militants somewhere on its toasted mainland carrion, with what they could use for any radio transmission or military walkie-talkies all bowed their heads.

I didn't even give them a day. They were occupying my space. And the battles continued. Under bagpipes losses rang, and battle cries screamed as planes went into the sea.

"For the Queen!" Humanity cried. "For the Queen!"

And they marched on; children left their families and burning homes and picked up whatever they could to throw at the waves of lightning wrought onto the world, by solely one of them— but not at all; evolved with wings and having the body size of a skyscraper crushing the last efforts of Scotland.

I came across the Loch Ness Lake, and the solemn and cool night sky rang out still in my mind— that anthem. It was playing again, I was certain of it. I came over a hill and there was the military of Spain unprepared listening to some local bagpipe players— and immediately yielding in terror at the grim shadow approaching. Just as I ventured and stepped on most of the crew, fireworks went up all around via another attempt to get me to jump. However something else awoke in the lake reflecting orange sparks and beating stars.

Probably an all together 12-story body shot out of the water. I guess in disbelief, it was the Loch Ness Monster.

It came out with its black and browned furred neck connecting to its elephant pachyderm body with probably-five-ton-a-piece boned fins. The Loch Ness monster was clearly a mammal and did not have an excessive long tail-which is the main paleontologist mistake, which I will mention after we say our goodbyes to Scotland.

The Loch Ness Monster or Furry long-necked seal-elephant let out a howling bark and piercing growl. I couldn't help myself from laughing, and···and···he had a pup-puppy nose. And the humans acted like they were at the World Cup watching their football team get to the goalie.

I spoke out, though for some reason my language is unclear to the humans as I probably speak in growls and barks too: "You know what they saw about long necks." "What? You ask?" "They're dicks to begin with." I take and wring the body and toss it back into the lake. The bagpipes continue to play in fear, endless fear, and the night ended in flames and destruction.

Onward ho!

<u>THE PALEONTOLOGY MISTAKE</u>

Where to begin? Why was the Loch Ness Monster a mammal and not a reptilian scaled beast, or more passionately, creature? The best way to answer this is to compare what is existing to the human eye, and not to date back in depth, yet to describe the characteristics so that its existence is so.

So forth, research or imagine a Tyrannosaurus Rex "Lizard" /"Dinosaur" Skeleton, and look at its components in form and structure. Usually in human sources and diagrams the T-Rex Skeleton is usually always depicted in the tilted ostrich run stance. This is what we will call: wrong.

The toothed skull in the diagram or picture should connect to a partially curved neck with the immediate ribbed structure and spine into place-with two short dangling-two-fingered hands on arms; and then almost after the rip structure with three or less vertebrae is the pelvic area with the bipedal stance with the three-pronged bone toes; and then immediately connected to the pelvic area are tail vertebrae (supposedly) that extend to almost a length and half the distance from the skull to the pelvic area.

Now apply something humans call: gravitational pull -which is standardized at 9.8 m/s. This force according to humans acts all over the place and balances everything on Earth and keeps it there or acts on everything.

Now with that in mind look at the skeletons of two lizards, any two-iguana and just research "lizard skeleton". Look, and observe. Next look and compare these to a cow, a feline, a horse, a pig, and a kangaroo. Notice in all of them an oddity about the tail and neck area. While the lizard's caudal area (tail) extends with vertebrae like a spine, the neck is dually shortened.

For the mammals the cervical (neck) area extends similar to
that of the T—Rex, and notice the lumbar bones or its thorax area before the
pelvic—how there is an extension. Then of course, look at the tail of a
mammal, the bones are more smoothened compared to the spinal—like—
vertebrae on the tail of the T—Rex and the Lizard. This will be called the
first observation.

Then examine the balance of their leg structures in comparison to
their bodies. Find which two out the skeletons match the leg structure or
similar size comparison leg structures to those of the T—Rex. Good.

Clearly you are knowledgeable of something now. None of the
reptiles having skeletons can fully compare to a multitude of the
dinosaur bodies.

Back to gravity, look at yourself and how you stand. Good you are a
Narcissist. Next fold up your arms akimbo and bend over— easy right?
Tilt your head your head upward in that same stance so you are look
forward. Okay?

Picture carrying an extension of your back with the same weight
(with gravity) as carrying one and a half of your spinal area without
your stomach, observe.

So what would the T—Rex really look like? Look at the kangaroo
and the pig as their leg structure sizes are similar to the T—Rex, (and
no—if they had wings— as there are bird dinosaurs—it would be
identified by a similar Extended* bone structure.)

To sum it up, the T—Rex has more of a Dachshund or "weiner" dog
structure in terms of vertebrae, and a thick neck too. The body does not
walk in a bipedal method or does balance as such. The T—Rex Mammal had
a massively large—lengthed stomach too. Now look at the teeth— yes— a
meat—eating pig. The T—Rex is an ungulate. The head though is the only
minor confusion as lizards and fish tend to have a more closed off nasal
area, most mammals do not have one as closed due to cartilage and what
not. This was supposedly done through the work something called
"evolution", which I will call the *Force Extension process.

The Force Extension Process really got into gear after the
incident on the eye. But how to understand it, is to look at exactly what
forces are acting on humanity and what pushes and pulls a human in
place:

SEE THE DIAGRAM,HUMAN.

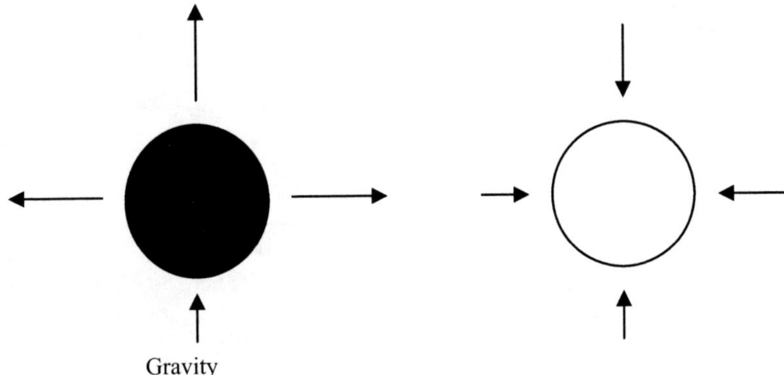

Gravity

COLDNESS—
Is not the temperature, coldness is
the force of push on a body. Coldness
causes expansion, yet space causes the
pull of Gravity, however Gravity's
force of pull (like heat) is less than
the force of coldness (push). Gravity is
heat in that it acts against push.
Coldness however is a **constant** force
(push).Coldness results in a cool
temperature because heat causes
movement (the conflict of two forces)
that acts against coldness. Coldness
causes continuous expansion unless
acted on by heat.

HEAT— GRAVITY
Is not the temperature either;
heat is the force of pull acting
against coldness (of a body),
push. Heat is increased between
two objects in closer distance
between them. Space carries
coldness which we call a
"vacuum"—endless push. However
Space is not a constant coldness
as it carries movement— which is
caused by heat. Heat, pull, acts
against push, yet pull is not a
constant. Heat can only damage a
constant by destroying its
body—by creating higher pull on
the push of the body. However
the constant is not changed or
weakened— it is defeated by a
stronger force acting against it.
Gravity is space's pull of heat on
Earth. Therefore space is in
movement.

The carrier of force, push, is a Body. A BODY is any object that can reproduce
(or cause a reproduction to occur), change, destroy, and exist (these "actions"
are done by the body, but don't have to be for the Body, like a computer can't
give birth to another computer in the form of Light without other bodies).
Reproduce— does not imply an exact emulation, and all bodies are different.
Any body can also have more characteristics than these.
Light is caused by HEAT and the degree at which HEAT is acting against
COLDNESS, therefore HEAT has the characteristics of a BODY. To be visible to
the Naked eye, a body will be able to refract light and attract it. Remember
Coldness is Constant (infinite). A BODY without heat only exists by the
constant of COLDNESS until the BODY is not visible from the endless
expansion. Distance is the measurement of Expansion between expansion of
coldness and heat, the pull acting on the push (heat acting on coldness).

Well I need to get back to whatever I feel like doing. But as you're sitting there bewildered, I'll spit out some more so you're not too belittled.

When the Eye was, before the rains and separation— the Earth's body's temperature was in equilibrium and did not change or change was only very minimal by a marked decimal place.

During the separation, especially due to the Earth's damage in its atmosphere the Earth became extremely cold a few years after the electromagnetic heat. This heat dually came from the closer sun and the moon. However the Sun collided into the push of other planets causing a separation of heat for a while, and Earth's orbit slowed.

During the first—year orbit, the air was dramatically cooler with heat focused on land surfaces and less in or on water. As Coldness expands, water became ice, and bodies born into this time were elongated.

Another characteristic was that these bodies did not walk bipedal at all— which also related to the intense cool (temperature + force) from the coldness. They carried on their movement by hopping, and jumping about—like a kangaroo, or a rabbit in motion. A rabbit— a great example, it hops by carrying its longer back legs forward with its balancing paws in front. Also due to the expansion on living bodies on the Earth, each body's heart also was more than triple its original size. The way of hop—jumping was extremely necessary for survival because it both brought necessary movement to the body with aerobic exercise, and in addition would help the heart withstand the extreme coldness force and beat at would be a normal pace. Sleep was also only three to four hours on average, and was usually under the Earth in the remaining drying silica caverns.

This hop was the way of transportation for thousands of years until the atmosphere repaired itself. And by reparation the push of the Earth came back to a more focused constant— as the atmosphere is also a reaction of space's heat on the body. And with the reparation of the atmosphere, made the Earth's path in celestial movement more circular—also known as its orbit. This was due to the heat that was placed onto the Earth from both the sun, and the planets reacting to their push (in distance) from the sun and other planets with the attraction of heat.

However lifespans were shorter due to the coolness in the cold years era, yet the bodies including mountains and glaciers that formed were dramatically larger in comparison to today's—as were the trees. When the heat was added animals began decreasing in size, and also for many smaller bone structures or exterior body structures. In addition with the increased pull, bipedal movement came into existence.

I could go further on how this relates to color pigmentation, as on the skin, and different electrical charges and such, but then again who could you tell when the world is ending in this human global warming hmmm?

<u>IN IRELAND</u>

From Waterford, to Killarney, Galway and Belfast, Ireland's verdantly pacifying greens and shamrocks, with usually livened sheep wandering in the fog and British horses going to and fro— the only sounds were not of violence but of crying and praying as the grasses sank and Ireland melted away in Celtic flute mist and misery.

<u>IN FRANCE</u>

Liberté, égalité, fraternité
(Liberty, equality, fraternity)

Like London, France was getting it on, even the mimes humorously imitated the street scene while spectators atop of the Louvre glass pyramid were watching art fans hump and bump paintings, even one of Da Vinci's. At the Grande Arche de La Défense et fontaine, I hammered through the Eiffel Tower and began pouring nude French bodies all over the display— and realized that described the artwork of all humanity: naked, exposed and entirely a waste. I even noticed a particular phrase on a destroyed structure:

TEMPUS EDAX, HOMO EDACIOR.

And thus it seems quite necessary for humanity to procreate before and after a war no matter who loses or victories, their answer to conflict is to create more.

<u>IN SPAIN</u>

Plus Ultra
(Further Beyond)

"Salvemos de extinciòn," a Barcelonan priest at the Segrada Familia announced with open arms as I drenched him in solid tar. In Seville, the flamenco dancers to the street gypsies were playing el toro and ramming their matadors dead on— any male in intercourse for the sake of the last Spain, the last Spanish hope. And like the lonely hum of a guitarist who plays his life in a dimly lit alley under the reign of Franco, the tune is unfinished as the hand is removed by another force, and the guitar is either stolen or never played again.

<u>IN PORTUGAL</u>

Paz y Justicia

(Peace and Justice)

Portugal gets carried away, by a whirlpool slurping up the nude tourist bathing in Algarve down to the entire half-human-head pictured country.

IN SWITZERLAND

Unus pro omnibus, omnes pro uno
(One for all, All for one)

Perseverance from atop the Matterhorn takes me to new heights, as I crumble the mountain with the other mountains and roll them into a ball, crushing the sweet cantons like St. Gallen and Schwyz with pivotal greens and soothing mists with the blood bleached streets of Zurich. I roll it on out into Lake Biel, drowning the likes of it in Swiss cabernet.

IN SLOVENIA

Edinost, sreča, sprava
(Unity, happiness, conciliation)

Near Dravograd in northern Slovenia, a group of Lithuanians with several Slavs persons draw an elaborate magic circle for a pagan ritual with bizarre chanting. I wait for the grand act of ritual wording of praise and worship for me to cease, and agreeably swoop down and take the entire frantic crowd in three bites as they were mentioning something about "sacrifice" in their verbatim and I'm hungry.

Most of Slovenia shudders in Ljublijana, and has been bathing in the canal for barely safe water and drying their bodies off on the Three Bridge, the last sunny area as the clouds have covered most of the Earth today. These nimbi join me in adding a partnership in beaming electrocution, and Slovenia is toast.

IN ITALY

Ars longa, vita brevis
(Art is long, life is short)

Rome is and has been quite a symbol of the human art emphasis and empire. As though each empire has fallen in Rome so will this empire, the Vatican.

In the ornamental Basilica of Saint Peter stands in conversation the Pope with his fellow Cardinals:

(This is in English, rather than Italian)

<u>THE POPE</u>:
The next Testament of humanity is becoming, and there may be Truth in this destruction. Yet the destructor destroys because he is searching for that Truth, as his entity is too, searching for the Word. Like us he is searching for who he is, and all he can do is find importance in murder. And if he takes over the Earth, ridding humanity, he may never be able to find it in himself.

<u>A CARDINAL</u>:
How are we to translate the Texts of the Bible to such a beast?

<u>THE POPE</u>:
Yet a beast of God's creation—the enigma of the Truth. Take it into view that the animal stands like a human, yet resurrected himself from the Norwegian Sea after four months in death.

<u>ANOTHER CARDINAL</u>:
Death, for all we know, he could be the harbinger of Hell.

<u>THE POPE</u>:
But is humanity in one perspective a Hell in comparison to itself, as in the animal kingdom there are those who murder against the system of the food chain and those who fight to make an alteration. This could be our Judgment Day.

<u>A CARDINAL OVER THERE</u>:
Judgment will come as it is given. We cannot rely on this being the exact time indicated in the Bible. In alteration this could be the end humanity has caused pursuing its greed; as of our own perception, we want to achieve a sense of self victory do we not. If what you are saying is true why is it killing without yielding?

<u>THE POPE</u>:
It is naïve, just as we were all once naïve. It needs to learn our society's ways.

<u>A CARDINAL SITTING DOWN</u>:
This beast cannot be controlled, Father, it has resisted all possible attacks.

<u>THE POPE</u>:
Then we have the greatest opportunity of liberty a human has, the choice. Now we must go to the Square and wait.

Wait?! I quickly ignited the Vatican in pure vendetta on and for all mankind.

From Pescara to Siracusa, I left a rampaged pursuit where there was only enough fish and bread left for myself. The rest were melting in candlelight.

IN CROATIA

Antemurale Christianitatis
(Forewall of Christianity)

The land of the picnic cloth checkered flag. With a lush Adriatic coast, streamline clear serenity and Venetian townhouses sifting over skimpy bathers wading and looking into the sunset— as the sea breeze blue turns into a fog of crimson, and peaceful rural towns like Zlatar become wastelands and open—coffin graveyards without names.

IN BOSNIA & HERZEGOVINA

Тко учи знаће, ко штеди имаће
(Those who study will know, those who save will have)

The two open—leading stone hands of the Tjentište monument reveal Zenica's torched interlude with Banja Luka's demise. I come and take the hands of the mountain with my own and clap Bosnia down to Bulgaria into fodder carried off with broken vases and lost hearts.

IN YUGOSLAVIA

Yu—Gone

IN BULGARIA

Съединението прави силата
(Strength through Unity)
Unity through Loss.

Humanity in Loss.

SLAM! CRASH! POW! BAM—BAM!
SLIT! RIP! BURRRN! HAHAHA!
DRIP. DRIP. DRIP. SILENCE.

THE LOSS OF WAR IN THE WESTERN WORLD

IN THE REPUBLIC OF MACEDONIA

Каде има сила, нема правдина
(Where force rules, justice does not exist)

A 600 ml of Ouzo is drunk in full and slammed against a rock in the old ruins of Heraclea Lyncestis by a ten year old boy from Bulgaria who has lost everything. With him are children all the way up to the borders of Croatia whose parents sacrificed themselves to make sure their child left in a convoy or their family horse. There was no love in them anymore—nevermore.

I had never tried ouzo before and quickly reached down and swallowed the boy whole— um, sweet. The children scampered with the last energy that they had but could not reach the adults of the convoy sleeping in a more sheltered area; so sheltered that I had an easy crush on them.

There is no War, no more, humanity is falling apart.

IN GREECE/HELLENIC REPUBLIC

Ελευθερια η Θανατος
(Freedom or Death)

Another historic end to a Western turning point I think as I grin at drowning the Parthenon under my toes like the sand between—between hers and mine. I crunch the tourist taking pictures of me, and get that feeling out.

Suddenly off of Mount Olympus and flying through Meteora is not the Trojan Horse; a mixture'd vehicle extending over a 100 yards hovering in a bronze coating with 8 jet wings with fans blowing out with the paved gold words "ZEUSCORE" on the side near its submarine windows. Atop of the Zeuscore were two rotational laser turrets as well as on the bottom of this bizarre hovering human creation. There were three hundred men inside manning this odd contraption. The front even had Stained glass windows of lightning bolts as if to make me tender.

Unexpectedly before even charging or stopping the Zeuscore's top laser blades off my right arm flawlessly while the bottom lasers slice both my bottom feet off. Tar covers Athens with rising flames and smoke. Then the Zeuscore opens an electrode beam turret in its lower hatch then sends a bolt to my right leg. With my wings I rip out of my bubbly tar mess and dodge the vehicles next shots as these obliterate a bit behind me.

The bottom laser cuts the tip off of my right horn and out spills crimson blood that just slurps into the black rubber foam and concrete.

I fall back into the mush as the tar splats into my mouth and I begin roaring and choking, spitting out flames and lightning bolts that have no effect on the Zeuscore. I am almost at a loss.

All this! All this for the loss of being held at the stake of all loss, man!

The bottom lasers slice my tail off and the tar is up to my chest, and my left arm is barely keeping me afloat.

I swallow more tar and my blood, and then immerse my body in the tar blood. My wings become fins and I glide like Pegasus off his leash. I swim into the Sea of Crete and dash until I anchor in Sparta with a trail of tarred road globbing up in bubbles behind me. My horn has stopped bleeding, and I get up with my right leg and foot that have birthed back. My tail also begins to recreate and extend itself just as the Zeuscore makes landfall eying me from Sparta. It jabs a laser at me from the extended distance and digs open my right wing. I roar and the vibrations have little effect on it. So it comes, and I brace for human disaster.

The Zeuscore comes clinking and roaring as well towards me, and slices off my right leg again. I moved to the side, and the people all around me were cheering and laughing at my loss.

The second my other hand grows back I clap directly at the ship. Some of the propellers stop working and I take advantage of the men attempting to get all the propellers back on as the ship vehicle begins to descend. I quickly grab the Zeuscore and stick the back rudder fin into my right leg socket and dig it in. The lasers on the vehicle can only deliver blows forward.

My leg begins to redevelop itself and grows onto the Zeuscore crushing it completely into my leg.

And the last Western World Struggle is over.

<u>IN ROMANIA</u>

Nihil Sine Deo
(Nothing without God)

Venturing in Transylvania I spot the Bran's Castle, and add a fitting decoration of wreathed limbs to garland the roof tops, and drip down balconies. And with the abundant lily pads of the now burningly fragrant Danube Delta waters under a pairing harvest moon, floats foxes, wolves, cattle, and pelican bones skewered to emptiness.

IN HUNGARY

Addig jár a korsó a kútra, míg el nem törik.
(A mug keeps going to the well until it breaks eventually)

The Great Hungarian Plains are filled with sleeping bags and men ripping cattle and pets open bare handed to get what looks safe and secure to eat, while the animals die in front of hungry eyes. Then I dig in.

IN AUSTRIA

"The cradle of the future is the grave of the past."
Playwright Franz Grillparzer

And Austria takes its last cue before termination.

IN THE CZECH REPUBLIC

Pravda vítězí!
(Truth Prevails)

In Vienna I sandwich the entire building complex of Hofburg Palace and complicate its existence while it deletes human political arms and ties. And the Belvedere Palace in reflection becomes a white jack-o-lantern with a roasted roof; the seeds are gutted out to leave room for the light.

IN SLOVAKIA

Čo oči nevidia, srdce neboli
(What eyes don't see, heart doesn't hurt)

Standing wingspread and fully reformed, I gander down from the Gerlachovský štít onto the Tatra Range and orange and yellow foliage of

pines and twelve thousand falcons, and watch the Natives cry as
Slovakia is burned down again and again.

<u>IN MOLDOVA</u>

"Gone by are the hours when the heavens entire
Flowed rivers of milk and grew flowers of fire,
When the thunderous clouds were but castles erect
Which the moon like a queen each in turn did inspect."
—Mihai Eminescue, "Mortua Est" Stanza 2.

At Grigoriopol I take the Biruinţa tanker, ignite it and toss it directly
into Chişinău demolishing the Gates of the City buildings followed by
ricocheting itself into the train station creating endless unmerciful
spineless spurring flames and fumes to sift into dying atriums.

<u>IN TURKEY</u>

Yurtta sulh, cihanda sulh.
(Peace in the homeland, peace in the world)

In Marmaris, the Turkish military sets up a more basic attack though
with the walker—ships, using primarily their ninety—five F—16 jets,
thirty F—22 Raptors, and 7 KC—135 Stratotanker jets carrying jet oil. I
ignite the following and they plummet into Istanbul. Turkey loses all
its feathers and peaceful tides, drooling liquid—less saliva and pus.

<u>IN GEORGIA or SAKARTVELO</u>

ძალა ერთობაშია
(Strength in Unity)

Towers shatter, cathedrals praise in misery, stars beam down as the
electricity goes down; Life rages, Tbilisi loses its skirt, Iberia loses
its molecular human construction and reproduction. And Georgia dies in
the rains of a clouded sky under a blinding sun, sky and human era.

EUROPE DIES.

<u>IN ARMENIA</u>

Մեկ Ազգ, Մեկ Մշակույթ
(One nation, one culture)

Not since World War I, had Armenia seen and witnessed a diaspora of
this magnitude nor had the entire World. Yerevan was an unorderly
defeat as the groups of fleers decided to disperse along different
streets, so that kept me pretty busy. But business is a human aspect, and
in perception it was necessary for my own survival.

And so my victory kept rising as I moved onto AZERBAIJAN,
then Russia destroying ADYGEA, KARACHAY-CHERKESSIA, KABARDINO-
BALKARIA, then NORTH OSSETIA, CHECHENO-INGUSHETIA, STAVROPOL KRAY,
STAVROPOL KRAY, KRASNODAR KRAY, KALMYKIA, ASTRAKAHN, ROSTOV,
VOLGOGRAD, SARATOV, VORONEZH, BALGOROD, KURSK, OREL, BRYANSK,
KALUGA, TULA, LIPESTK, AND TAMBOV. .

But enough summarization my reign continues.

PART III

REIGN
TO
THE BEGINNING

"The question isn't who is going to let me;
it's who is going to stop me."
AYN RAND

IN PENZA

The Sura over—filled with wheats, bodies and riches and spilled onto corporate walkways, and pathless forests.

IN MORDOVINIA

As Saransk was my bonfire of the evening, and there were no rains or sounds of the wounded to pester my tormented hate, there came a remittal'd retaliation of ancestral calibration to which were directed of the Golden Horde—who by which approached— and were brought to the last location of their ancestors.

IN ULYANOVSK

I took the tour not in, but through the house of Lenin's birth. I carried disarray and wounded men piled with split goats, and over wrung hens into a brittle riddled mass of pennies and potash.

IN SAMARA

The Third Baku came like Asteroid 26922, where oil climbed and leaped on turbulent tracks, marching beats, and torn open lung bags. Kuybeshyv Place, once square began to embrace its non—symmetrical reality under fluid destruction.

IN ORENBURG

The shawls were lit high above the currents of oil suffocating blood—wits and bandits, and visitors and those who fled there once before.

IN BASHKORTOSTAN

The Ufa River became a hungry mouth whose population's teeth by both river sides were the knocked out collection of fixated delights bobbing near roots hanging in the ice, and red hues puffing with steamed demise in the mid-morning sunrise.

IN CHELYABINSK

Once more it became Tankograd, and shots poured and I ignored their misled missile miscopy of times remembered. And white partridges feasted on wounded doves who migrated this far and piled down on the Plateau Kvarkush, bathing in dry rain without a cloud in sight as the waterfalls went backwards from the toppled charts and numbers still multiplying in electric boxes piled in vacant automobiles.

IN KURGAN

Kurgan was the necessary encounter I needed from long flights and dismantling; as men and women here listened to my dire need for their skills and made an enormous tumulus. And if they were to mistake me- each were taken from their wills of doing so ealier-much- than after- when the projected mounds were waxed and done.

IN SVERDLOVSK OBLAST

The Volga-Ural Military in their last numbers forced together in a kamikaze formation for their greatest blunder- or whatever they would call it in historical papers. They sent their own destructive feat as they launched a **Great Nuclear Bomb** whose strength was of two Hiroshimas. And I paved on dusted turf, untouched, unscathed.

IN PERM

There came the Sverdlovsk nuclear rains submitting rust and smoldering deterioration to the Monument of Heroes- draining its ore to a glistening pulp underneath a population's gulp in the snow, gray, green and red rains of despair!

IN KOMI-PERMYAK OKRUG

Planes and airliners who had evacuated in other areas were barrel rolling, side-winding, tail spinning on broken wings down to Permyak and each transformed spark that passed me in this stained glassed gossamer brigade of blindness and apathy clung like Velcro bands and drowned-melting onto Earth's crusted plane.

IN UDMURTIA

The Syrian Arab and last of the French Army blockaded Glazov,
and its many brick apartment buildings were within 40 meters of
compiled ash— and on top were doctors and anyone who could dig into a
wounded body with whatever was on them— keys— someone used their car
keys to lever out a marble column piece engraved into the forehead of
an astronomer.
It was not a matter of vengeance; it was a matter of War.
Human-Triggered War.

Within two beams of lightning the French and Arab armies vanished
and the buildings sank below the snow and grated ash.

IN TATARSTAN

I wing by Victorian crème colored buildings and found another
brigade, this time by a massive ship fleet defending the Kazan Kremlin.
They ready, their canons at hand. I fly away as the last of the nuclear
effects wipes clean the Kremlin, into smithereens.

IN KIROV

The city of twins, and that is all it ever will be. I derail the Trans-
Siberian. I rip down forests, schools, parks and churches, and scream "
This is for you bitch!", and punch through the reservoir on the Talas
River, and the water gushes through me and I feel nothing just speckles
of water touch my skin and fade into air. Bare. Immunity to everything
my body can resist, but the heart. I take anger on every taiga, every de-
veined leaf and tree and rodent threat. I— must move on to the next.

IN CHUVASHIA

In Tcheboksary's coast, with the arrays of isolated sand sculptures
and vacant cruise liners, I sat down, crushing one and glide my long red
black nails into the sand to once feel that tingle, as if to feel nature's
flirtation and gentle massage with— but no more— not even a single
dotted poke or itch in transmittance, but a distance all ready miles
from its start. And I take another cruise liner and hammer it into the
ground and set Chuvashia in red glistening freckles.

IN MARI EL

In Yoshkar-Ola the only ones I find are a group of old women, three
imitating the "See no evil, Hear no evil, Speak no evil" monkeys. I laugh.
And then they are dead. The towns fall like zig-zagged Crayola-crayons
scrabbling yet patterning prints along a textured plastered wall paper
surface with trees and melting fleshed out beauty.

<u>IN NIZHNY-NOVGOROD</u>

A massive city edges its way with victims dodging left and right. I sway my wings enticing tempest catastrophe. I take degrees by wind and transport air into tornadoes engulfing each soul, body and mind in bundles at a time, suffocating in the air and being planted down neatly with the others.

As I make way to the sunbeamly lucid Shuhkov Oka Tower which seems to only display parallel points, less the beams in balance. I see a fable play out before me. An African-American- probably one of the last Americans climbing in frenzy to the top, gets to the top to a Russian militant who is crying and waving the White, Blue and Red.

The African American stops as the Russian militant removes a rifle. Here's what was played: AA- for him, and RM for the militant being, if not a civilian as well:

   <u>AA:</u>
What would be the point to kill a man to rid of his incorporation now than instead receive his fellowship?

   <u>RM:</u>
You're an American, and you have no fellowship.

   <u>AA:</u>
Yes- Yes it is true, but that is what we conceive as you too.

   <u>RM:</u>
Exactly, that is why your death is necessary.

   <u>AA:</u>
I have no more words, shoot at me.

   <u>RM:</u>
Just an easy target.

The Russian militant shoots the African American in the lower right chest. The African American man doesn't cry and holds onto the bars and moves closer to the Russian militant.

   <u>AA:</u>
If this is what it will take-

   <u>RM:</u>
If you can take more sorrow, I am glad for you.

<u>**AA:**</u>
So that act was not out of defense.

I make my cue onto the scene with my wings spread out.

<u>**AA:**</u>
Look he will kill us.

<u>**RM:**</u>
Exactly. But we will die together.

<u>**AA:**</u>
Like Brothers.

The Russian militant began dripping with tears and he dropped the gun in nervousness and almost fell forward, but the African–American clutched his arm. The African American almost lost his balance too and they embrace on a single bar both holding onto the Russian flag.

<u>**RM:**</u>
If it wasn't for Fucking Communism!

<u>**AA:**</u>
Fuck Democracy! Fuck them both!

And the tower disappears in a second's smoke passed the twelfth hour.

IN KOSTROMA

I stand where once a Tatar murza stood converting himself to another human degree by a fountain in the Ipatievsky Monastery under silent winds and howls and sins. A land where Nestor's Hypatian Codex was delivered and kept— the topic of Russian history— which now swept under melting clay, brick, mortar, tower domes bowling bodies bottling underneath the cap of whirlpool intoxication.

IN IVANOVO

At Interdom housed the last of the Russian Red Cross hospitalizing thousands, with wounded animals and rabid animals biting patients, and patients devouring pelicans, and children playing catch with burnt toes they found along the way on the road— and their parents weren't there to judge their actions, actions, actually they were in lift–off from existence–as concrete paved this mixed pothole, and every ounce and every joule went either, every way.

The majority here were of women both Mongolian and Russian, the only men I saw were the toll men, who received fair tariff for all men's tolls.

IN VLADIMIR

I descended like an eager hawk and gripped the cotton-colored "Golden" Gate right off its course and tossed it into the Assumption Cathedral watching churchgoers flee like termites with acid on their tendons. The blinking lights of last electric charge sparked up and down roads like idle machines without pinballs.

IN RYAZAN

Slicing the pearl bright columns of the Drama Theater I dramatically place the irony on all man's folly's that lose support when minor flaws are found at the base of its existence. Another Kremlin, another broken sunrise unweathered by powdered flakes and muscles caked in living lakes asunder. What taciturn I see by two things that represent man and his artillery? The cheerful Foreign Wars monument I drape onto my head, and step on Dyagilevo just before it goes off.

IN MOSCOW

I had already destroyed the most-talked about places.
So striding along the Moskva, I came across the Novodevichy Convent holding a stained tapestry of hungry children maliciously starving for each other, I eased the situation and poured all of Russia's ants to assess and cause the damage.

IN SMOLENSK

The land where Napoleon was defeated, and then Germany destroyed, a land that now has a Hero City yet treats me like a void. And I am immediately met by inhospitable threats, and I take the eagled monument turn it into a pike, and impale down to the nadir of Smolensk and erupt a diamond mouth of molten lava causing boiling snow and apparitions between steam and smoke.

IN TVER OBLAST

I passed sweet summer fumes of infant boy blue and ponytail pink on white Faberge lacings towards, by standards of my own, and ownership in being, only temporary buildings as I cracked each one open in dispersion. On the still unraveled pool of Seliger, I ripped and bouquet'd Stolbny Island on top of Tver city.

IN NOVGOROD OBLAST

Following me in large consecutive tweets and wavelengths are thousands of Yellow Wagtail whose wings are losing speed as I grasp onto the 1,000[th] Anniversary monument in Novgorod. The yellow and blue head aviaries dwindle in puffs and spots underneath my dripping claws covering the thick bell—shaped with feathery bodies all holding on for dear life— they worship me. With one flap of my wings the bell monument breaks out of its cemented base with the gripped birds— attempting to flap their other wings for support— while the rest are underneath the monument as if to catch its fall— not knowing— simply not knowing the size and mass of it all. On my yellow and blue float I glide pass the Siberian architecture, and another Kremlin and toss lightning waves and festive salutations as we move on.

IN PSKOV

Across from Pskov's Kremlin along the River was a separate glow pouring with prayers and talks of peace. An airliner had crashed into a structure carrying Chemehuevi Native Americans. The plane was siphoned of oil and was burning whatever was left in that sorrowful snow jaw'd acrimony, drenching and drilling their surviving skin. The plane had taken off from Phoenix, Arizona before the strike, and then suddenly its right wing tore off the burning body and sank into the iced aquatics.

They looked at us as we glided over the River and I parted it with a wave of my claws, and these of a few of the last remaining American tribes, first presenting harm with an attempt to holster up with bazookas— and the only female of the group wearing a sweatshirt and pajamas told them to put their weapons down. Dramatically she walked forward with tears running down and her arms open, praying in whispers. Praying in moments.

One of the Yellow Wagtail, a traitor, left the bell formation and glided to her and flapped in her way as if to warn her. Immediately I ignited his struggle and like the removal of caption on a straw, the bird plummeted into the other percentage of the Earth.

She continued walking, I watching at this sacrificial procession in course.

And then, she brought reminiscence of her— who had left me.

And then, a whole-hearted sensation beamed through me, and I let go of the bell and it plummeted on the Yellow Wagtail into the River.

I wanted to be loved, and she knew it too, I thought.

And silence in the moment, by her closed eyes, pivotal prints striding towards me, and the beat of her heart with the enchanted sparkles in the night.

Another step. Silence.

I began to extend my clawed talons in gradual extension.

Her eyes began to open, and she said in her best English, "I love you."

I began to talk, and just as my answering was in a time worth it's calling, a hungry claw inserted its way into her ringed sweat collar from a group of Brown bears.

And my floating body shook and I screamed quaking the area, shot lightening at the bear and unfortunately took her lower half with the blow.

And as the group of bears lay dying and the other Chemehuevi had run off, I sifted down into the River as her upper half was still staring at me and her hand edging out towards the frost vanishing from the now boiling Velikaya, and I kissed her with the edge of my tongue.

Her body disintegrated into ashes and blew into the River, and

I blew away with the five last Yellow Wagtail.

And the Pskov was set a flame at each angle, and the last
Flame was for her.

IN LENINGRAD (ST. PETERSBURG)

All in Leningrad rained of insanity, and nuclear drops that sizzled the snow and the clouds which were as deformed as broken mirrors in a cyclone with yellow fog and sunset shadow reds and purples testing the pupil's vision. The Chamois and gray wolves went for the UN members in herds and packs. And geese fell like gravity had control of their flight, and rats pillaged cradles. Dishes were eaten by moose that could not swallow their etched bone.

All in Leningrad rained of insanity, and when there was silence, women screamed in fury of hunger and loss when even their husbands were near them, and a few wives turned ravenous against them, murdering them,

butchering them, enforcing their children to run into the wild
before it was too late, and hours later in recognition, I came and did the
rest.

All that was St. Petersburg, became Leningrad, became Petrograd,
became endless fury jostled in juxtaposition to the rising snow over the
torrents of Mars.
The Leningrad Oblast received equal hospitality.

IN KARELIA (South and North)

The conifers and fallen lumber from the nuclear rains suffocated
the lakes and streams, and penguins who had migrated out of Northern
Canada, and ten narwhales who attempted to defend them from the fallen
trees—whose skeletons were drenched in black feathers, horns and
beaks.

An artist's portrayal of a family clutching each other all done in
skeletal medium was a common display near the paved debris and sinking
shores, furthermore, forever—less.

IN VOLOGDA

In Priluki at the Saviour Monastery stood over three million cows and
one bull, who seemed to be organized on their own system and judgment,
though some went mad and started drinking the churned butter and
shanks of hanging bovine deathbeds. With the majority of the cows being
female, they ignored the bull and wandered away leaving him to sulk in
misery on his path alone. By midnight it was a Russian Western Barbeque.

IN YAROSLAVL OBLAST

And the cruise liners here sunk as the waters were turned to tar and
the city had sunk in the melted soil, and cars had driven themselves out
parking spots in windows—and off building tops. Legislature was not in
existence— anywhere except in Australia— as the representative had a
relative to visit in Sydney.

Another Yellow Wagtail died and landed in a Vodka shot on a vacant
balcony with an absolute view of a becoming veranda.

IN ARKHANGELSK

There lay fallen strings on broken chords, drums with shaved skulls,
and only one working speaker that was whistling endlessly. And the last
Yellow Wagtail fell and hit a broken cymbal which its chime ended the

whistle, and silence hit in solemn glide like an approaching
missile— that crocheted its path in ice.

Беда́ (никогда́) не прихо́дит одна́.

(When it rains, it pours.)

IN MURMANSK

The port of Murmansk was filled with lit torches, cranes swallowing
endless heat around steel boxes spilling grains, caviar, goods, teas,
wines, textiles, syrups, blood round knee—deep—zit—greased pools
scraping tankers from Japan carrying sushi for the flies.

IN NENETS AUTONOMUS OKRUG

Among the fallen Taiga, chanticleering Nenetsian poets dressed in
conifer leaves and twigs were dancing among a fire with fallen comrades
who didn't have arms nor eyes, nor ears, nor tears.

The fire burned and the chanting grew:
   "Бог плу́та(ше́льму) ме́тит"
   (God marks the crook).

Again and again with different tones they cried and roared as my shadow
broke into their chorus.

IN KOMI

Like a pinwheel, merging and spinning, twirling and driftling, lifting
swirls of pink and white under pollen and over endless limousines
housing mink coats and coffins—no that was the Trans—Siberian Train
heading from Moscow filled with black feathers from devoured crows.
The carousel—pink —white, —pink—white, salmon, clouds, rose cheeks, egg
whites, eye whites. Pink and White are the structures of evacuees in
Ukhta. Pink and White thumbs. Pink and white plumbs of ankles. Pink and
white rashes, pink and white eyelashes. Pink and white, white then pink,
then sturgeon pink leaking liquid reflecting the white heavens and red
sun.

IN YAMALO NENETS AUTONOMUS OKRUG

The stiffness of a an old man's heart on the last generator at which
life controls it, beats but holds onto the cable connecting it, the last of

the West Siberia Energy facilities is drained and Western Russia is blinded in smoke and hunger. The day comes in scornful transition.

IN KHANTIA-MANSIA AUTONOMUS OKRUG

With granted speed I land on the high orange-gold arch holding the Surgut Bridge which extends over the Ob for over a mile- and held by one cabled arch. An example of man's creation of separation- but to complete the separation by a need for unification to tie in the differences artificially, demented and transfixed in ideological acceptance dripping in guilt long forgotten. & like a clothespin holding the dry I collapse the arch closed, and the line snaps, catching runaway trout from other Seas.

IN TYUMEN

Piles of Moskovitches, Lada-Vazs, Gaz-Volgas and dented Aros line up and tilt back and forth in the blizzard winds. Stray cats have run up to supposedly their owners' vehicles and clawed their way into the front of each bundled-crushed automobile. They are each biting apart their own limbs and every so often licking the mess clean to bring themselves to closure with their lost owners.

The gas and oil plants were clicking while pulled apart and ignited- unhinging forests and surrounding shores into a turbulent frontier.

IN OMSK

On Lenina Street, small pale blue children were flapping their arms to make snow angels as hawks swooped to them, gave them wings and took them off into the clouds. The street lights were ground lights, and light bulbs were planted. The foundations were plumbered and copulated with the discord of growing Richter roots and fallen petals on snow cleansed groves and meadows.

IN NOVOSIBIRSK OBLAST

In Novosibirsk I came upon their "Bluetoothed Batman" structure and took both bat ears in each clutch unzipping the structure down the line. So as an angry Mongol combater defending the hearth that once was his, and once was theirs, I use these crippling konchars covered in dust to controvert against a prosperity in human humaneness emblem'd on expansion with caged animals, and property. In duty I take to this abundance and tie it in hoarded birch and aspen tossing it all into Lake Chany watching it sink by shrinking buoyancy.

<u>IN TOMSK</u>

Extending his right hand stood bronze Lenin, plutonium Lenin,
Lenin displaying courage, displaying a welcoming in— as hail and waves
of shrapnel and cindered smoke delivered eerie tears on his eyes.
Though through the flames melting the letters of his name, the
character of the statue never moved, and I flew onward.

<u>IN KEMEROVO</u>

Coal Miners neverminding the odd weather still were drilling in daily
sorrow with the waving KEMEPOBO flag parachuting in bundles in carts
and on bell pepper green gantry cranes lifting out the crusty leathered
world
ore like a copter delivering water to flames to an endless forest
pandemonium in lethargic exercise over and over and the avalanche
comes taking everything with it.

<u>IN ALTAI KRAI</u>

Out of the Katun River salmon jump to touch the cobalt blue zeniths
from below, and the lonely ones are almost there— clutching atop the
Altai Mountains on an expedition with a two—day view of the verdant dry
Kutscherla Valley with flocks of ducks and dragonflies who knew of my
renegade—rampage long beforehand and planned accordingly. Their cell
phones are dead, and every glimpse of the nadir— this path ascends
through psychotic vision lenses focusing less on the narrower, and
these human bodies want to descend but the plan is executed by demand.
There they hold on until an artificial unity saves the day—but doesn't.
One watches their tools rip through their frozen pockets and bang and
echo down treacherous heightened chambers in orbit of the
gravitational pull.

<u>IN THE ALTAI REPUBLIC</u>

The Center, the exact center of Russia and Asia, a human enigma of the
centerfold of the symmetrical, of the balanced, beauty in supposition—
or the balance of the antagonist's mirror of a philanthropic self giving
for the good? Neither. Infused where arrows meet and intersect, I hover
over Lake Teletskoye and see that the depth of the lake is less than half
the distance to the top of the mountain range, reflected in it.

Snow leopards hiss as I glide on by and hiss back and they alter their
form like popped kernels by every glance still retaining their spots.

An owl flies by and catches a blind mole— I didn't notice until after
I stepped on them both.

A charlatan dressed in flannel covered in long gray hair with a dreary mustache lets the tadpoles play with his beard as it drenches in the lake. I knock him in, and the big fish come and do the rest.

IN KHAKASSIA

In the line of fire on dead leaved deserts and coarse grinded agony dirts, megaliths like Stonehenge like electric guitar solos projected to a tired sunset— supposedly in astronomical direction or authenticity of a moment. A moment never—ending. These megaliths were once turquoise holders—holders for the greatest mirror. And now just inferior mysteries for man to puzzle up his trajectory on board life's vista.

Чут болурга ыт семириир,

Аарыг болурга лама байыыр.

(When there is killing weather, the dogs grow fat, when there is disease, the lamas grow rich.)

IN TUVA

On decaying stallions ride the Great Kural to my encounter along the Uvs Nuur Lake. They stop and present throat singers to who I am suppose to feel the gratitude of accepting their hospitality in. Taken in my most civil attributes I extend my dripping talons out to shake their brittle trench—digging hands—and in opportune agreement— yes brutally brittle. As before I took my wings preparing for lightening charades— which are always "hard to follow", a meteor shower paved its way onto the Tuvan dry surface and the horses panic, and I am tickled by the sudden natural magnetic celestial fury.

IN KRASNOYARKS KRAI

Comets speed from all directions, and earthquakes rise as if the Earth's body finally feels comfortable to disagree with the treatment of its grand body and the comets collide unto open ground holes. Hours later volcanoes arise in the Southern Krasnoyarks cities, and then Krasnyoarks separates into two divisions in streams of molten larva-cocooning lava fluttering when ready over each mound and naked valley.

The clouds flash lavender and fuschia and orange—black smokes
and fogs rush out like the Hydra heads dispersing after Pegasus'
accelerated victory.

IN EVENK AUTONOMUS OKRUG

Aw a country whose flag is much obliged in commentary; the
peppermint pinstripe target adds onto those water cooler speculations
of such in merry adornment. My wings blading back and forth on the
Tunguska's sunset foiled reflection on each ripple, I observe more
comets coming from all directions.

The birds are darting which way too. Smaller wrens are flying into
the mouths of ducks; hawks, and eagles drowning themselves in lakes as
glaciers are over—riding with heat. The ground quakes and ridges turn
to waterfalls, and Russia starts to descend in its heavy bronze mail.

IN TAYMYR AUTONOMUS OKRUG

A mad accordion juggling tunes either which way—East or West
followed by the flips, taps and splits of Cossack dancing and acrobatic
agility, followed by a meteor landing directly on this radio in Northern
Taymyr. A reindeer was in dire need of a human to direct his steadfast
efforts as he was raised to be as such. But now in dire needs his direct
tactics weren't of usage much. The reindeer called to a herd of yak that
didn't call back, and she was left with her wagon of needed human
emergency supplies and vaccines.

Some of the last Dolgans of a group of kolkhozniks crowded
underneath the local market tents as my infamous screened—self
blanketed what was covered before even tangibility had coincided, as
time does all the rest, and thus these drunken figures are covered too
by my approaching talon grip.

IN THE NORTHERN ISLANDS

In Novaya Zemlya a bubbling carrion congregation of seals sifted onto
the icy shores of an earth quaked—avalanche display of breakdown in the
containment of the glacier's amniotic sacs, breaking water into falls
destroying retaining walls of Rogachevo's Air Base.

In Franz Josef Land on Ostrov Gallya poisoned Walruses were flopping
down in huddled pile for the appetites of near frozen Caribou, polar
bears and Arctic foxes. Before gathering to dig into their take—out
boxes, it was noticeable that the warmer Arctic Sea had received oil
purple splots and blues. These hues were from the billion of Man'O'War

gathering and multiplying like the intensity of a hurricane in
warm torrents and humid waters.

In the Severnaya Zemlya, the last discovered archipelago, on the
central island of Oktyabrskoy Revolyutsii, I take a one-hit-wonder and
ignite the island and watch the rest of the islands sink to eternity
under the electrifying spectrifying dimensional pandemonium stirring
from the Kara to the Laptev.

In the New Siberian Islands on Kotelny, The bats have conglomerated
and are battling in rage over the falling comets and their hunger for
each other in cannibalistic harmony, and hence in their blindness, the
island has erupted and the archipelago separates into flaming debris.

In Wrangel Island I height off the land towering above the Mount
Sovetskaya zeniths in thine own occupation. The grasslands transform
into raging tar, and oh lo' and behold my eyes do grace upon the melting
block of a tight haired pachyderm. The Mammoth comes into life briefly
under the turbulent monoxides oozing in his lungs, strangling his heart,
making him roar! And Roar! And his ice-drenched fur body ignites in
blood red flames, and the whites on his eyes spiral out into cold black
remnants consecutively shattering into his skull, bursting his tusks. I
just watch his suffering, and the charcoal evaporates into smoke.

IN YAKUTIA

My eye lashes eject fangs compiled of human bones of which I had
devoured and the chain of the 3 Billion dead were attached to my body
and covered in flame and dripping onto the mountains and filling up the
pit of the Udachnaya Pipe, and vomiting my tar'd puke and decay into the
Vilyuy, the Olenyok, the Nerpichye, and all the Russian bodies of water.
Russia is turning red from gold.

IN IRKUTSK OBLAST

The oblast that is in the shape of a bunny rabbit or the symbol of
peace— I TAKE ITS PEACE one by one! I take it's fingered ears with
extending body arms and 29-fingered grip rip every village, every
musical instrument, kremlin, bronze statue, bridge, dam, wheeled
transportation, electric generator, roof and drum, and Irkutsk
collapses.

Then I fly to the Moon, Earth's moon, and like ripping off a piece of
an orange, I take a slice off, and it reveals the Moon's turquoise ice
crystal core-that after I rip up, tries to vacuum up its attached
pieces— but they immediately comet off into distant space. The Moon is

destroyed and there are no waves on Earth's water, nor is night as
clear, nor does heat retain in most areas, and in the following:

IN UST'-ORDA AUTONOMUS OKRUG
IN BURYATIA
IN CHITA
IN AGA/ AGINSKY BURYAT AUTONOMUS OKRUG
IN AMUR OBLAST
IN KHABAROVSK KRAY
IN MAGADAN OBLAST
IN CUKOTKA AUTONOMUS OKRUG

IN MAGADAN OBLAST AND NORTHERN ISLANDS
IN ST. LAWRENCE ISLAND
IN KORYAKIA AUTONOMUS OKRUG
IN KAMCHATKA OBLAST
IN SAKHALIN OBLAST
IN BIROBIJAN
IN PRIMORSKY KRAY

    I vacuum it all up onto the Moon's magnetic core and toss it into the
Sun in its slow burning.

*"Crime is naught but misdirected energy. So long as every
institution of today, economic, political, social, and
moral, conspires to misdirect human energy into wrong
channels; so long as most people are out of place doing the
things they hate to do, living a life they loathe to live,
crime will be inevitable, and all the laws on the statutes
can only increase, but never do away with, crime."*
    –Emma Goldman, *Anarchism, What it Really Stands For* (1910)

"晴天の霹靂"

(A Bolt from the Blue.)

With the waves of all the oceans to the smallest rivers in ponds
all depleted with the moon gone, oxygen started gradually disappearing
from the waters. Fish swimming near the ceiling of the water instantly
died as their air bladders popped by the extreme imbalance. The waters
were foaming and salt were appearing on beaches, with cliff rocks and
coral all over the world.

Then came the destruction of Japan, I took on Sapporo first
with grip of my hand and watched the alleyways and markets roast
bodies and the flames sizzled school children, and chefs making sushi
and smoking Ghengis Kahn cigarettes.

I immediately destroyed Japan's electricity generators with
endless electricity beaming through the islands with the main island
and immediately Tokyo turned in the curtain of the dark blue sky and
red Sun peering though it.

Theaters were destroyed, Oh how I've seen this distribution of
destruction before, like the video electronic games and hardware driven
out from these virtual reality dealers who special in artificial
sensations for the human paraxial.

Tokyo the wealthiest city in the World was destroyed like a
penny dropped in Time Square when the Apple descends— purely pity-
less under screams of glory.

Across Honshu, the mainland I observed in the Sea of Japan, the
crisp aqua blue waters becoming bright splattered red with bundles of
sea—life toppling the water; even Taiji dolphins and pilot whales, as
well as some Whale Shark had inflated and bloated their bodies to the
surface—to immediately be popped—opened—organs and all—by tapping
oars of poachers looking for exactly that—a dead catch. Even tourists
who were snorkeling in the Sea either inhaled too much of the heated
hydrogen and deteoriating oxygen source, or swallowed too much of the
blood of the sea—life, and were also bobbing up like apples—like the
fish, like the fish they so devour.

In Nagoya I decided to try my more original approach and flew above
the Nagoya Castle, in the central park area of the city, I looked at the
screaming humans and spread my hands a half a kilometer apart···

I shot them back together to create a gigantic obstructive—to the
humans, —constructive force 9 times stronger than the atomic bomb.
Japan was obliterated like a chain of dynamite along the cavern of
possibilities and cherry blossoms demolished in extended Mortality in
the hour of the first Rising Red Sun in white—blue sky. As if the flag was
held for the world to see in permanent surrender.

<u>IN OSAKA</u>
    DESTROYED

<u>IN KYOTO</u>
    OBLITERATED

<u>IN KOBE</u>
    DESTROYED ALONG WITH THE BEEF.

<u>IN HIROSHIMA</u>
    OBLITERATED

<u>IN KITKYUSHU</u>
    SHATTERED AND MELTED INTO THE SEA

As each building, church, temple, castle, family, aquarium, museum, tree, crusted in peril in evaporated spirit, the sound was the heart beat of a million jack hammers beating down on the Earth at the speed of pulse in single dropping blood-red tear, and the scream of a geisha that has dead-on intercourse with a barge carrying wealthy Whites, who in turn laugh at their light screams because there is no connection between their "made-up" language. However as human service does its best to please another human for personal growth, the receiving human acts like coldness and will shut her up without mercy.

This is the end, it is like the end, the end of Japan; and nothing can compare.

<u>IN FUKUOKA, IN NAGASAKI,</u>

In Where? I don't see these on the map or the legend anymore. They must be a myth.

As Japan disappeared, what was left was the growing red hue and dead bobbing bodies not floating in any direction in flat water— flat foaming water.

Rabid water.

"소 잃고 외양간 고친다"

(After losing a cow, one repairs the barn.)

Or in this case, eradicates it.

IN BUSAN

As for Japan, I had made their death an easy toll, and realized humanity still had not suffered nearly enough. So for four hours I wove a tar basket around all the dead fish, animals and humans in the Sea of Japan, and lifted them out with speckles marshmallow drops of coagulated blood drops plopping back in like floating dice.

On top of the blood curling-crying splatter, I delivered to them matters of their own kind, and tore open the net covering the city in tar, body parts, blood and sushi.

Immediately my disease began to take on their atrocious apathy. With my tar blood and the blood of humanity, they became of my own.

I watched as a British Korean tour guide soaked in what was a mixture of pilot whale, manta ray and a group of senior citizens blender'd up into chunks and pieces of glass, beginning to sponge in her pores. Her firm dried hair disconnected its comb wires from her scalp and leaked like the falling flags at the end of a spar of Tae Kwan Do in the phantom upheaval of flaccid blue disappearing from the once placid sky.

Her bones gyrated like tarantulas breaking free of humanity's grip, and her back ripped open. And as one unzips a silk gown to watch the slithering garment slide downward, her skin was unzipping at all seams by invisible and invincible fingers which no human can bear to imagine.

Her screams murmured into horned air as skin provides echoes for sound amplification. Her muscled skeleton form ferociously fell into a grand seizure and her eyes turned into charcoal curtains. Severed body parts from the gelatin gush threaded onto her dripping and deforesting—by which the forests are of the conifers of man's leafed skin—skeletal enclosure, and drew out a Wright Brothers' delicacy as she became in aviary pulchritude (like her predecessor father), the symbiont who was of thy creation. This was Manifest Destiny in voracious agility leading into my vility.

I watched the humans of Pusan all undergo the outbreak, though most did not make it, and some who did were eaten by another who had just transformed.

After their meal, the transformed human, more civilly
entitled, cherub grew beautiful lavish and extravagant fanged claws of
animal bone. To my unsuspected body, I grew a nippled phallus designed
with a bold urethra in tacked, all made of tar and the thousands of
nipples made of my green garment organs. Immediately, those in flight
swam in vortex, poked open a nipple and let the tar rivet their insides.

Then the flock grew and suckled on me.

And within three days, every once sweet tropical paradise in South
Korea from Haenam to Gimpo and lined up to Sokcho were of my order.
The animals, pets, and wildlife were all eaten by us. And I was tickled
pink by their osculation on my dick.

"호랑이도 제 말하면 온다"

(If you speak of the tiger, it will come.)

<u>THE GREAT MASTURBATION OF CAPTIVE ONANISM</u>

All of Korea became a Cherub Cesspool. And within each minute,
they surfaced back to me for another tarring and I relaxed fully
erected.

But after Korea's population had headed North to take on China,
I ripped out the phallus and threw it into Beijing, and saw a great
undertaking of Africa's Northern population and the survivors of the
European, Canadian and American siege lined up in front of the Old City
of Jerusalem. And then the sky's blue vanished.

"树 倒 猢 狲 散"

(When the tree falls, the monkeys scatter.)

<u>IN JERUSALEM</u>

"Just as the weeds are collected and burned up with fire, so will it be at the end of the age. The Son of Man will send his angels, and they will collect out of his kingdom all causes of sin and all evildoers, and they will throw them into the furnace of fire, where there will be weeping and gnashing of teeth. Then the righteous will shine like the sun in the kingdom of their Father. Let anyone with ears listen!"

—MATTHEW 13:40–43

JUDGMENT DAY; THE DAY OF ATONEMENT; THE RETURN OF MAHDI; THE ENLIGHTENMENT; THE DAY TO WHICH HUMANS OF HUMANITY WHO SUPPOSEDLY BELIEVE AND ACT ACCORDINGLY TO THE "RIGHT FAITH, RELIGION, LEGAL SYSTEM, IDEOLOGIES, IS SELECTED; & EVERYONE ELSE WILL PERISH AND SUFFER FOR THEIR ACTIONS.

The Sun displayed itself like a star in the black night sky, and Jerusalem was cold that night. The masses attended were primarily of Africa, few Americans, the remaining Asians and Southern Europeans. There were 6,412,000 people who were the leaders of their religion and they led groups of their followers in hurdled groups holding torches. Chants, Songs, Sacrifices, Explosions, Talking in Tongues, Odd Suicidal Rituals, Sexual Rituals with both Humans and Animals; there was even some sort of cult that was roasting a wealthy official from one of the Pacific Islands and after was devouring him whole. Then a major earthquake erupted and I hurled massive comets at the Mountains and Temples, and Jerusalem began its flaming descent. The crowds ran, drove, flew on hang-gliders, helicopters, and even devices that looked like giant robotic bodies out of the Old and New Cities.

Their Raging Pilgrimage Race of Survival led to Har Gilo near the Tunnel Road Bridge, and a large dry bowl area of land which made the masses appear as spectators in a stadium, a Stadium of the Earth.

<u>THE STADIUM OF THE HUMAN EARTH IN HAR GILO</u>

I waited to the side of the bowl as the surviving religious groups gathered in solemn silence. Many were injured, of course. And flames were ignited all around them—on those who were finally catching up to the Stadium and they dispersed into ash. There were no screams only sorrowful eyes, and holding hands and mindful prayers.

Immediately I razed through the two cities a massive human skull shaped mountain where the eyes of the skull were pillaged open and rooted with the molten blood of the Earth, and the smoke grew over the view of the sun, and made it too, crimson red. I tilted the formation to face the bowl and dripping down onto the skull cheeks and jaw the lava came, and cracks swam. Taking trees in by the forests and valleys, the world of humanity was coming to an end.

Other smaller volcanoes suddenly burst out like popped pimples and leaking warts, in scattered array in sound turbulence all over Jerusalem.

"Mahdi!" someone shouted and bowed.
"No it is the angel Gabriel!", another shouted and bowed.
"Siddartha's risen", one yelled and prostrated.
"It is God, and he or she is coming our way!"

I stopped to see if what I foresaw would take root and perform.

They assembled again into their separate religious groups and almost as if they had all been at an Arts and Crafts fair, they had assembled their religious symbols out of wood, cloth, metals, golds, ivory and even human skeleton.

And like a bid rally, I was up for the choosing. The Cardinal representing Christianity though in its diversity of different forms of Christianity, the Cross was to represent their origin, and crossing into other religions were of course their religious symbols. The Star of David, the Crescent Moon, the New Era Scientology Symbol, the Square with Robot Eyes, Voodoo Dolls, A witch hat, a Klingon Sword, and on and on. Each were laid out on the Tunnel Road.

A Cardinal, a Rabbi, a Muslim priest, and a Scientology priest all walked together furthest from the bridged road. The Cardinal Proclaimed towards me:

"Angel Gabriel we Christians have worshipped you the way our Lord has taught us to, please have mercy."

The Muslim priest next spoke:

"He does not understand English, he is Mahdi. Marhaban Mahdi, Shokran Mahdi—"

The Rabbi interrupted:

"Unfortunately good men, you are all wrong, for we are the Chosen Ones. Atah beChartanu! Atah beChartanu!"

The Scientology Priest shook his head:

"If it is in Truth you seek as we do, rid all those who seek for illusions as men do to substitute for the missing loose ends in their life."

I blasted tar rain behind the circle, with sparks flying towards the bowels of the bowl, others who had chosen to speak were shuddered underneath the sound of fury.

Prayers were murmuring into other prayers and their solemn peace was grasping for thermos—pure air at which to live on.

Then Judgment came as I looked into their pleading, greed—filled eyes.

I opened my hands as if extending a sigh. The Rabbi led out a brief joke, "I know sometimes it's hard to make the right decision under pressure."

I closed my eyes and remembered the church at which she and I were going to be in our fantasy marriage with a sunlit stained glass—reflecting—window of blue and turquoise swirls dampening the paleness of her white laced···But it never happened.

And the organ played···yet it never happened.

All the **physical—built symbols** of faiths, religions and ideologies for the humans burst into immediate disintegration with trailing smoke up to the celestial domains.

Every human being was in a state of shock. Immediately, the Cardinal took out a sword he had brought with him for security and beheaded the Scientologist priest who was shaking his head, and exclaimed, "It is at your own doing, that brought all faiths to an end."

"Faiths!, It is only the right way of thinking that one is chosen, and if this is a war, it is best that Islam is the victor!" said the Islam priest, and immediately the Cardinal took again to his gold and ruby sword, and the Islam priest kicked it out of his hand and beheaded the Cardinal. The Rabbi took out a gun he had with him and shot the Islam Priest's leg, and stated, "Enough, we have always been the Chosen One." Immediately the Islam Priest stabbed the Rabbi in the heart, and a shot from the crowd hurled into the Islam Priest's eye. The religious groups fought on for the rest of the night until there was one barely living survivor, a Yarrabah Aboriginal woman from Northeastern Australia. She, in her last clear words of English looked up at me as I flew by the work of Humanity's failures, and whispered to a hush,:

"Thank you, Creator."

And the flames of Hell moved on as the smoke cleared from the Sun.

* * * * *

Asia's population problem was fixed: a fixed number portrayed in uncontrollable immortality covered in equality red, drying into brown, drying into culture—less, love—less, heart—less beings devouring each other over and over, and sucking all they can from those ever—filling verdant nipples life gives all.

So I have no more words as all is decayed, so in that summary, you can continue to read the graves.

HERE DIES BY THE HANDS OF HUMANITY:
TOTAL HUMAN POPULATIONS IN

LIAONING   HEBEI   TIANJIN   BEIJING   SHANXI

HENAN   SHANDONG   JIANGSU SHANGHAI   ANHUI

HUBEI   HUNAN   JIANGXI   ZHEJIANG   FUJIAN

TAIPEI   TUNGSHIH   FENGLIN   CHAI   YULI

P'INGTUNG   TAWU   FENGGANG   PENGU/ MAKUNG

JINMEN DAO   GUANGDONG   HAINAN   GUANGXI

GUIZHOU   YUNNAN   SICHUAN   SHAANXI   GANSU

NINGXIA   QINGHAI   XIZANG/TIBET   XINJIANG

BAYANOLGIY   UVS   HOVD   DZAHVAN

GOVI—ALTAY   BAYANHONGOR   ARTHANGAY   HOVSGOL

BULGAN   SELENGE   TOV   OVORHANGAY   OMNOGOVI

SEE IF YOU REMAINING HUMANS OF THE "WESTERN WORLD" CARE ABOUT THE
ENTIRE HUMAN POPULATION ALL OVER THE WORLD.

DUNDGOVI   DORNOGOVI   HENTIY   SUHBAATAR   DORNOD

ALMATY   LEPSI   AYAGOZ   SHYGHYS

QAZAQSTAN OBLYSY   PAVLODAR   KOKSHETAU

SOLUSTIK QAZAQSTAN OBLYSY   RUDNYY   TORGHAY OBLYSY

QUARAGHANDY ZHEZQAZGHAN   ONGTUSTIK   LENINSK

SHALQAR   AQTOBE   BATYS QAZQSTAN OBLYSY ATYRAU

MANGGHYSTAU   BALKAN WELAYATY   DASHHOWUZ WELAYATY

AHAL WELAYATY   LEBAP WELAYATY   MARY WELAYATY

QORAQALPOGHISTON REPUBLIKASI URGANCH   KHORAZM

BUKHORO   NAWOIY–JIZZAKH   SIRDARYO   TASHKENT

NAMANGAN   ANDIJON   FARGHONA   SAMARQANO

QASHQADARYO   SURKHONDARYO VILOYATI LENINOBOD

GARM   DUSHANBE   VILOYATI KHATLON   VILOYATI MUKHTORI

KUHISTONI BADAHKSHON/ GORNO   BADAKSHAN

KHAYDARKAN   SULUKTU   OSH   TASH   KOMUR

TALAS   CHUY OBLASTY   NARYN   YSYK

KOL OBLASTY   FARAH   HEART   BADGHIS

FARYAB   GHOWR   SAR   E POL   JOWZJAN

BALKH   SAMANGAN   KONDOZ   BAGHLAN

TAKHAR   BADAKHSAN   KONAR   LAGHMAN

KAPISA   NANGARHAR   KABOL   PARVAN

VARDAK   LOWGAR   PAKTIA   PAKTIKA   GHAZNI

BAMIAN   ORUZGAN   ZABOL   KANDAHAR

HELMAND

NIMRUZ   BALOCHISTAN

THE FEDERALLY ADMINISTERED TRIBAL AREAS

BANNU   KOHAT   LANDI KOTAL   THE NORTHWEST FRONTIER

GILGIT   SKARDU   AZAD KASHMIR   ISLAMABAD

PUNJAB   SINDH   SISTAN VA BALUCHESTAN   KERMAN

HORMOZGAN   FARS   BUSHEHR   YAZD

KHOROSAN   GOLESTAN   MAZANDARAN   ZANJAN

ARDABIL   AZARBAYJAN E SHARQI AZARBAYJAN

E GHARBI   KORDESTAN   HAMADAN   MARKAZI

QOM   LORESTAN   KERMANSHAH

ILAM   KUHZESTAN   CHAHAR MAHALL VA BAKHTIARI

KOHGILUYEH VA BUYER AHMADI   MAYASAN

DHIQAR   AL BASRAH   AL MUTHANNA   AN NAJAF

AL OADISIYAH   KARBALA   AL ANBAR   BAGHDAD

BABIL   WASIT   DIYALA   SALAH AD DIN

AT TA'MIM   AS SULAYMANIYAH   ARBIL

DAHUK   NINAWA   DAYR AZ ZAWR

AL HASAKAH   AR RAQQAH   HALAB

IDLIB   CAIRO   AL LADHIQIYAH   TARTUS   HAMAH

HIMS   DIMASHQ   AL DUNAYTIRAH   AS SUWAYDA

DAR'A   AL QUANAYTIRAH   LEBANON

ISRAEL   IRBID   AR RWAYSHID

AL JAFR   AL MUDAWWARAH AL HUDUD ASH SHAMALIYAH

AL JAWF   TABUK   AL MADINAH   HA'IL

AL QASIM   AR RIYAD   MAKKAH   AL BAHAH

ASIR   JIZAN   NAJRAN   ASH SHARQIYAH

AL WAFRAH   AL JAHRAH   AL ABRAQ

BUBLYAN   IN KUBBAR   BAHRAIN   IN HAWAR

AZ ZUBARAH   DOHA   BU HASA

TARIF   ABU DHABI   ASH SHA'M

MUSCAT   HAKKAN   KURIYA MURIYA   THARMARIT

AL MUKALLA   SANAA   MOCHA   HARAD

DIJBOUTI   ETHIOPIA   ERITREA

SUDAN   THE CENTRAL AFRICAN REPUBLIC   UGANDA

RWANDA   BURUNDI   TANZANIA   KENYA

SOMOLIA   COMORO ISLAND   MADAGASCAR   MOZAMBIQUE

MALAWI   ZAMBIA   BOTSWANA   TRANSVAAL

LESOTHO   THE ORANGE FREE STATE   CAPE

SWAZILAND   NAMIBIA   ANGOLA   CONGO   GABORI

CAMEROON   EQUATORIAL GUINEA AND NEIGHBORING ISLANDS

NIGERIA   CHAD   NIGER   BENIN

TOQO   GHANA   BURKINA FASO

COTE D'LVOIRE   LIBERIA   SIERRA LEONE

GUINEA   GUINEA–BISSAU   THE GAMBIA

SENGAL   CAPE VERDE   MAURITANIA

WESTERN SAHARA   MOROCCO   MALI   ALGERIA

TUNISIA   LIBYA   THE CAYMAN ISLANDS

CUBA   THE BAHAMAS   HAITI

THE DOMINICAN REPUBLIC   PUERTO RICO

THE VIRGIN ISLANDS   THE BRITISH VIRGIN ISLANDS

ANGUILLA   ST. KITTS AND NEVIS

ANTIGUA   BARBUDA

MONTSERRAT   GUADELOUPE

DOMINICA   MARTINIQUE   ST. LUCIA   BARBADOS

ST. VINCENT AND THE GRENADINES

TRINIDAD   TOBAGO   GRENADA   NETHERLANDS ANTILLES

ARUBA   NAVASSA ISLAND   JAMAICA   QUANTANA ROO

YUCATAN   CHAMPECHE   TABASCO   CHIAPAS

MINATITLAN   OAXACA   GUERRERO MORELOS

IN PUEBLA   MICHOACAN DE OCAMPO   MEXICO CITY

HIDALGO   VERACRUZ–LLAVE   QUERETARO DE ARTEAGA

GUANAJUATO   GUADALAJARA   JALISCO ISLAS TRES MARIAS

NAYARIT   ZACATECAS   SAN LUIS POTGSI

TAMAULIPAS   NUEVO LEON   COAHUILA DE ZARAGOZA

DURANGO   SINALDA   CHIHUAHUA

SONORA   BAJA CALIFORNIA SUR   BAJA CALIFORNIA

THE ARCTIC   GRAHAM LAND   QUEEN MAUD LAND

IN THE CENTER OF THE PUPIL: THE CORE OF MAUNA KEA

As the Cherubs finish their procreation in South America, I watch the red die–dye blending into the Sea with piles of kelp and dead coral, and I watch the last meteor fall and crash in utter silence, as Sound has been deleted.

The Amazon melts underneath its foam–blooded River.

And the Suns across the universe are flashing left and right as if the same apocalyptic events are happening to their Earths, and yes they are, yes it is, yes it is a loss for the entire galaxy of the reflective humanity.

And yet with any reflection there is always a future, but the past is long gone to exist again.

And in this moment, there are no cries, no sensations, and complete stillness. As I look at red puddles on the green and black beaches of the

Hawaii Island, they are exactly like when the rain fell on the eye,
in the beginning.

Veins of ice spread across the Ocean and encrust onto each other,
and Hawaii is intoxicated with forever winter snow.

And on that island the bitch who started it all: the last human,
marrying another man in the spur of the moment when all else seems at
the end, is trapped in tears, isolated in ice above the Mauna Kea looking
over Man and Woman's destruction.

And like a blinking dot of a startup, molecules begin to mosaic and
collide from space and other planets and build the layers of the new sky:
a life without shadows.

The Cherubs come in billions herded as the tarred nipples have run
dry, and in their enriched desire, human hubris, they "deserve" more. I
smile, and with the extension of my middle finger on my right hand, they
shatter into the iced red oceans, leaving their bones floating in the
soliloquy of solitude.

For teamwork is but a human flawed quality, to be united, to work
in loving union, this is the unreasonable flaw that has—and was one of
the greatest separations of humans—the nonexistent. For every leader
risen— has come the followers who expected the same accolade as the
creator; however they succumb to be used as sacrifice only for and by
his determination on their manipulative self—beings.

And all this for a woman.

As I come to this epiphany, I notice the ocean blues coming back all over
as the blood is disappearing in the ice, and I realized that even by
slaughtering the entire population, there was never a way to reach the
beginning and that existence like destruction—only happens.

And I leave and ride away from the lonely quiet day—less Earth into the
Sun.

THE END

There once was a bear, but not any ordinary bear, not humanized nor civilized, but a bear whose life was forged to the zoo. His fur was black, with spills of white and red, and his eyes a hue of innocent blue. His claws were clipped, his roar depressed; only four and very stressed under circumstances fit for human kind.

CHAPTER ONE

Calico, the name of names
To fit his color only touched
By that of human kind. From
Time to time he was nudged
By nose of two of his companions.
Calico, a tenant, in the boundaries
Of bars could only correspond on sides
Towards five meters East or West, amongst
The other bodies of fine animal hides.
His dashing neighbors carrying the San-Fran hospitality,
Were a pair of dashing flamboyancies:
A barking deer named Martackadong,
That went about his fancies.
To the East was Corinthia,
A tiger of Siberian descent,
She would seldom take daily walks
But when the zoo closed, she would repent
To feel the real night whose brush was
Clean on her fur— she told Calico, who'd listen.

Corinthia would tell Calico stories about her
Youthful times in San Diego, when her fur would glisten
With the pulchritude of the evening air alive.
Calico dreamt of his time collapsed with this unwinding wind,
And only tales that were laid by the tiger's tongue
Glazed onto his impure mind.

A mind impure does not dividend to that of human kind. Calico
Non-sociable, Calico content. Calico was not the lion Fiona,
Nor Corinthia, he was a donation to the zoo from a maternal form,
Never met. His mother delivered and died in Phoenix, Arizona.

Above the bars held the letterhead indicating Asia.

Below the bars was a variable indicating life watched.
Ahead of the bars was the fantasia
Of children, forms and mouths in plenty
Carrying bags, ice cream, and pop, complaining,
Yelling, fretting that the tiger would come loose.

But Calico, Calico refraining
From the public eye. The rest was stratospherical,
Around the bear and dreams were a common antidote to
Stress, and he would ignore.

Authorized on his status, a doctor, who
By the name of Rachel Kladiffe drew a view
On the perplexities of this bear, whose surroundings
Seemed appropriately manufactured for his kind.
She began to diagnose and develop findings.
Kladiffe betwixt and bewildered captured
Merriment lost in the turquoise eyes of a balloon—carrying child,
Whose mother sulked under happiness, ruptured.
Calico would eye them, but never met eyes to end.

At Twelve PM, Kladiffe, verified, was certain that
Calico would require sociable features for his exhibit; or
She could contrast on what happened at
Austin's zoo to the bobcat that refuted to discipline himself justly.

The following day, thirteen hours passed this— zookeeper Ryan Bettings
Came into the pen, laid out greens, and bridged to Calico.
Calico in pleasure as he knew this figure by birth started coming
In a manner of a canine salutation, but yielded to realize that was not
His internal thirst and hungered opportunity he desired.
Bettings, from recent spreading of "the news"conjured to her attention
That maybe sweet Calico was in love, and that would be admired
By the zoo, if it gave him an addition to disable his solitude.
Calico. Calico was not in love, yet did not attain its definition,
Lacking knowledge of lonesome, or unity, just wanting freedom.
Though on higher ground, life must have indignation and ammunition,
otherwise liberation would not be at high request.
Calico, flabbergast to foresee that Bettings felt negative on his move,
Galloped back at her.
At which she captured a theory that she was dreamt as food.

Bettings shut the bolt—splattered wall, as Calico fell on its face.
Calico, confused gave it a push, but embezzled to the zoo,
His life was trapped. Never understanding its reason, place,
And but to dream of wind enchantment, and parceled desires.
Not knowing his life, but to sit and loathe about the day not to come.

Martackadong barked, and Corinthia roared as the slam fired.
Calico extracted on what just went on, and not only did Martackadong

Wimper, he wept, as he knew what happened to Alberta— the
previous
One.

He told Calico the story of the cone that one child who came along
To see his pen, who accidentally dropped it and red cold liquid spilled
onto
His bamboo vegetation. It happened the day Alberta left, and a child
Who was looking at her cage saw the red liquid from underneath two
Of Alberta's blankets near the bamboo, and began to cry.

The father judging
This bizarre matter glanced and smiled, "We'll never know Alberta."

But Calico didn't think, didn't know what to expect that his conduct— hers
Was even a threat. And so Calico, smudging
His clipped paws into the dirt sulked and moaned until the night gave
help.

The next day, the president of the zoo, Mr. Gerard along with Dr. Kladiffe
Discussed on a course, whether or not this shadow feature of a welp
Could ever be quite a panda, such a panda, as humans see fit. Dr. Kladiffe
Brought into account that he saw others and that keeping him would be
An Expense; just an if. Onto the decision, then.

Mr. Gerard informed Bettings, who couldn't help but shear her shed
Of tears, and alibi that what Calico did was a mistake.
But Mr. Gerard was forward, and encountered him as if he were dead.
Grabbed his legs back with four other men on tact. Bettings said
"They'll Kill him", and who will. The liquid, the needle or
The hand that holds him back. Kladiffe began to smile,
As Bettings thought her judgment wrong—of him.

Calico was placed behind where Martackadong, and Corinthia long
forgot.

Bettings shook Dr. Kladiffe and asked for a whim.

Dr. Kladiffe who lost but his smirk addressed her in verse:
"Ryan Bettings the answer runs amuck
That Calico is to be carried in a truck.
But how I've made my decision,
Is his heart is lonely, my intuition.
He belongs in the wild maybe he'll get laid.
Either way your day is paid.
But before you fret, I never gave a GPS chip,
So there is no way Mr. Gerard knows Calico has not been chipped
And that he is our panda bear to keep
No more."

Bettings was confused, bewildered, and let out a "why."

Dr. Kladiffe was silent
He looked at Corinthia and the flashing cameras. It was his intent.
He turned to Bettings, and towards the glaring Golden Gate.
He said "Because of us."

CHAPTER TWO:

Rivets in the thousands, at a mornings wake.
Calico, tired Calico, endured a long awake.
As the bump and tumble of a tweed basket fumbled and tossed itself
Over his bare—metered cage and a chain around his neck.
Calico could barely stand, as there were no others caged and it seemed
like the ground was gone.
Wooden Crates and every few seconds, a bump and they would move
Around unwillingly. Calico tried to get up, but he was caged shut.
Calico then realized this was how they made ice cream. But above
Him was an overly heated light as the air in the cabin was somewhat
frosty. Calico pattered, and paced in the unanswerable enigma.
Hours, the wooden boxes had moved up to his cage, hours, and hours
Ago. Then a streamlined delta of wind, a charisma
Of soothing halogens, but no not chemical air. It was never felt before
By Calico. He twitched. It wasn't fear. It was different, odd.
Calico growled and pawed, and the wind brushed against his face.
Calico began to slowly twist his sopping fur brazed skull, and clawed
To his left and clumped his paw against the plastic barrier, but
A barrier with holes. The holes had a set of eyes with charming black
lashes.
Calico prepared to inch back but banged his tail. There was a nose not
like anything he'd ever laid eyes on except Jose the Stallion. Lashes
Colored like ashes.
But to compare was a long neck of white sand, almost marble marked fur
Sifting down the plastic holes on what seemed to be like the rails in
front of his cage at the zoo. But then there was a mound and the brushing
blur of a small broom, no that was her tail.

"Who are you?" said Calico to the elongated horse.

"I am dying, death, loss." Said the creation.

"Who are you?" said Calico again confused by the answer,
 Only to hear more remorse.

"They've killed me. I am their victim."

"Who? I do not see any mark of death, you're not cold or red." Calico
said.

"Hilly Dallia, I am···a dromedary camel they say, but hath
Committed that I am a Pure Kind, but they have led
Me to die elsewhere, but hath I to die amongst the
Hands of these bandits. They're taking us away, bear."

"Martackadong told me. wha—"

"And what did they name you?
You sound like you've believed
Them and lost your sense of the pure quality."

"My name is Calico." Said Calico relieved
As to finally feel a connection.

"Calico, yes they name you for your red stain,
They name you because your real body is
Nothing compared to their love of display, and pride.
They hate us Calico, tis
Time enough. We're in a plane in the third dome of air.
Calico, Martackadong is dead too."

"Dead? I never introduced you to him yet,
He's just behind the door through
Those crates." Said Calico.

"Crates, Calico, is what happens to us,
The pure kind, when we die."

"Hilly Deelia, when I die I turn into
A cone of cold red cream, and I
Run through the vegetation."

"Calico, you don't know. You
Don't know. They're the gorilla
Whore, the Pure Kind killers, who
Will do anything they please for
Us to lose power. I shall sing, yet
I am weak and too old to serenade."

THE GORILLA WHORE

Mmmm Mmmm Mmmm Mmm Mmmm Mmmm
Brick and mortar, sand and flame
Twice an hour passing sane. Rain.
He had come, she had came.
Capacitated till all the blame,
Was a loose, conspiracy
And all the fame
Was just hierocracy.

Now they call it democracy.
And all the lame.
Numbers are all gone.
Fortunes laid.
Tomorrow comes.
And they all get paid.

The gorilla whore, the gorilla whore,
 They took our lives, they hosed us
 Down, Spit on our love,
And they knocked us around.
Killing up a thousand stars,
They broke Jupiter's son—is Mars,
And topical dome is called the sky,
They fed us up in jars on the street
While we loyal—ed and hid underneath this bid of
A time we had lost and it cost us our lives.

 The gorilla whore, the gorilla whore,
 You can ask it for something,
 It will ignore,
 You can beg for something
 And take a little more!
The gorilla whore, the gorilla whore, the gorilla whore.

Mmmm Mmmm Mmmm Mmm Mmmm Mmmm
    Time and Future, Traffic trade
    Trapeze murder across the Everglades. Fade,
    It was the only nightmare, they came across,
    And our tent escape failed, It was all ablaze—d Away.
    And all the fame
    Was just hierocracy.
    Now they call it democracy.
    And all the lame.
    Numbers are all gone.
    Fortunes laid.
    Tomorrow comes.
    And they all get paid.

The gorilla whore, the gorilla whore,
 They took our lives, they hosed us
 Down, Spit on our love,
And they knocked us around.
Killing up a thousand stars,
They broke Jupiter's son—is Mars,
And topical dome is called the sky,
They fed us up in jars on the street
While we loyal—ed and hid underneath this bid of
A time we had lost and it cost us our lives.

The gorilla whore, the gorilla whore,
You can ask it for something,
It will ignore,
You can beg for something
And take a little more!
The gorilla whore, the gorilla whore, the gorilla whore.

Over a thousand pin drops, rain and I bled
Walked alone, and then in a cage
They hunted me down, killed my own mother
Locked me up on the cold barren floor,
With nails, and needles, if I could roar—
Those Gorilla Whore!

The gorilla whore, the gorilla whore,
They took our lives, they hosed us
Down, Spit on our love,
And they knocked us around.
Killing up a thousand stars,
They broke Jupiter's son—is Mars,
And topical dome is called the sky,
They fed us up in jars on the street
While we loyal—ed and hid underneath this bid of
A time we had lost and it cost us our lives.

The gorilla whore, the gorilla whore,
You can ask it for something,
It will ignore,
You can beg for something
And take a little more!
The gorilla whore, the gorilla whore, the gorilla whore.

"The Gorilla Whore?" Calico turned to the side of the cage
Quite far complexed. "Hilly Dallia? Are you sure we're going
To die in this moving back room?"

"Die? They will slaughter us in appreciation, without pith.
Darling, they've tried to destroy us for thousands of years why
Would they end the odds now for any revelation?"

"Rev—uh—lation?"

"Honey don't you recall? If not— the gorilla whore have turned you
Into a subordinate impurity, a pet, and you are their weaker."

Then like the rambling through beakers
And tossing of jars and chemicals aside like
A scientist looking for a way out,
The crates and cages flew forward.

"Oh heavenly camel Pap take me on your hump."–
Screamed Hilly. "Get ready to die my furry friend."

"But death is to become ice cream?"

"And what would that mean?"

"That the humans would never⋯"

"Oh yes they would, oh yes they would."

The room tilted more and the heat lamp fell off,
Calico, dear Calico, felt the chill air and began to cough.

"Silly pure kind friend, you are dying already." She said.

"Hilly, no the room is tilted for a reason, we're going to
Become mouth–watering miracles."

"And that is⋯good, darling? I would spit against it."

The room tilted back and the cages slid in the 1st position.

"See we didn't die, and we did not become ice cream–
A double whammy!" confessed Calico with passive glare.

"A double whaw? Listen pure kind, if you talk like them,"
Hilly spit a wad in a crate carrying pineapples,"
You'll bathe like'em and stop licking your fur clean, and
They'll brush you– oh they will brush you!"

Calico was silent as her opposite intentions did not
Attract his, as he was impatient that the process was
Taking so long.

"You know what Calico?"

"What Hilly?"

"They're going to kill us."

"Okay."

"Calico?"

"What?"

"Well I don't tell too many about Hilly Baba.
But Hilly Baba was my bull. He was all bull,

And no cow, as he didn't have nipples. But
Bull he was, he was, he was.
We had two young ones on the way; at least that is what
He wanted for us both. Sometimes, I miss him everyday."

"What happen to Hilly or Baba?"

"Well to get from hoof to cage is very self-explanatory."

Calico was distressed and dry, and realized the room was
Very, very still.
Hilly Dallia closed her eyes and spurted out bits of her tune.
Too still, Calico thought, Calico content, Calico-concerned.
The sounds went off. Hilly spit again into the pineapple crate,
And tilted her head, and tears ran down her demanding lashes.
Her pleading lashes.

"It's not that bad Hilly." Calico- who had only seen this reaction
From Martackadong when he lost his meal one day had no idea
Of the extremity at which she wept.

"They are···are coming." She whimpered. The footsteps beated.
Calico attempted to sit up straight but bumped his head.
Suddenly two men with darker yet pale skin came over and smiled.

One had a nametag with Charlie Yu, the other nametag on the
Other person said "My name is Rick Yu, but call me Dick."
Rick and Charlie picked up his cage, and Calico just eyed these
Two men in, which Calico's eyes were to them, cute concern.

"They'll kill you, and you'll never know it." She said in a distanced
Pitch.

Calico quiet, suddenly saw buzzling sunlight and felt very warm
And sticky all over and he suddenly urinated in his cage.
Rick noticed and laughed, "Panda is horny around men."
The other one said, "They kick him out for reason."
Then they placed the cage into the dark room.

Several minutes after, a familiar voice joined him in this
Bizarre twist to becoming a dairy product.

"We're almost there, the next light after this dark room." She
Moaned.

The room vibrated and the cages started hopping about.
"I guess this must be the mixing process." Calico said
To keep things upbeat as Martackadong had indicated such.

Another bump, another bump.

Calico became quiet too, he didn't know what to do.

Then suddenly Dallia screamed:

"WAKE ME UP WHEN IT'S OVER!!!"

Calico panicked and began scratching the bottom of the cage.
And Hilly Dallia kept on and on.

Calico thought the same too.

CHAPTER THREE:

A line of reporters wait:
      Jenny Chu from CNN
      Kerry Wae from ABC
      Lee Woo from BBC

The Hanjin moving truck arrives in paradise, on scheduled delivery.

The truck opens and Charlie takes out a cattle prod and tranquilizer dart gun while Rick takes out both cages one at a time; Dallia tries to give Calico the heads up with the indication as to what Charlie is taking out, but Calico, curious Calico is eying the general public through cameras to record this—this grand and only entrance, before an unknown departure from "this" world.

"Good afternoon this is Jenny Chu reporting live from Woraksan National Park in South Korea. We are just minutes away from San Franciso Zoo's Calico being released into the wild. Here it comes, the opening of the cage, well that's one small achievement for animal activists to bring back the endangered Korean panda back into its original habitat. Aw he is sure a cute one. Now back to today's weather with⋯"

The reporters quickly wandered away before Calico could be petted or observed. Though he was in great observation himself— green trees, tall trees, bamboo beyond numbers; and uncontrolled leaking pipes streaming endlessly. Dr. Bettings always complained about the leaking pipes in the restroom near his one—time—home.

Calico took his first breath of this brave new world, to him.

Rick then took out Hilly Dallia as the last news van left. And she tilted her jittering neck towards Calico, cute Calico and stated, "Before we die, Calico, why was it that you were sent back to the, the uh, What do

they call us, uh nature animals. Why were you brought out here to
the nature animals?"

"Nature animals?"
"Just, just tell me that, so I can die with happy hump."
"They said. They said I was unsociable." Calico said.
"Ha, how amusing. Quite amusing."
"Why, what is amusing? What is making you laugh?"

"Clueless completely clueless. You're every single thing the gorilla
whores want you to be. Now for they to judge a nature animal as
unsociable in their grounds is like saying you can't run out in the world
without having their cage with you at all times. And look there's one
right by you—freak of nature animals, freak of the gorilla whore."

"Well I can't wait to die, if that's how you put it," mentioned Calico.

"There, spoken like a true naïve gorilla whore nature animal.
Calico, even if you some how live today, you'll die tomorrow."
"Well if you want it so much, why don't you see if they have some
Ice cream on them," chirped Calico.

"You know why camel is here Charlie?" informed Rick.
"The zoo no take her cause she old and sick." Charlie chucked.
"What do we do with it? Extra cargo?"
"Well, Rick do we have panda food?" Charlie glistened.
"You think what I think?" said Rick.

Charlie Yu loosened his belt on his tight fitting jeans, and burped. He
took out the cattle prod and tested it in mid—air to watch the sparks
sift in melody. "You see the way panda growls at camel. I bet panda will
eat camel, bet half you salary."
"Okay Rick, okay, you go lose some money."

Charlie pulled Hilly Dallia's rope that noosed her nostrils in the
direction pulled. Charlie smiled back at Rick.

Charlie quickly jousted the prod on Dallia's neck, and she
screamed. Calico didn't know how to react, but he wanted it to stop.

"The bear says it's not weak enough," said Rick.
Charlie quickly took the initiative and shocked the camel four
more times. Calico roared for the first time in his life, and became
extremely quiet, and moved back a bit. Charlie back away, as confused
Calico came up to Dallia who was lying on her side with charred marks on
her legs and bleeding hump. He sniffed her body, and tried to lick the
charred imprints but burned his tongue, and whimpered.

"Calico, I was wrong. Calico, long live, Calico. I am sorry for
my negative—uh the pain···"exhaled Hilly Dallia.

"No you were right, you were right. In the morning when we are both ice cream—"

"Calico, the ice cream was a lie. All this, the zoo, the air, the world around us, the people, disappear—go bye—bye, and our bodies stay here—that is death."

"I'm glad you told me," said Calico who started to whimper.

"I am glad young Calico, I could set a pure—a pure—"

Immediately Dallia was fired on by Rick's own gun. Rick indicated that the money would be whether he ate her or not, otherwise he'd kill them both.

Dallia barely breathing told Calico to place his jaws on her neck even if he refuses. Calico refused to. In another quick moment, Charlie came and prodded Calico— and Calico felt for the first time unnecessary pain and whimpered more. Then Charlie pushed Calico onto Dallia.

"You have no choice Calico, place your jaws on my neck."

"Kill her bear, finish her meat." Charlie sprayed at Calico's back.

Calico then heard the mechanical thing that shot Dallia make a grinding sound so he walked up to Dallia's neck, and put his mouth barely on it and looked up.

"Bite you stupid panda, what you wait for!" yelled Charlie.

"Do it," sifted Dallia.

Calico closed his eyes and bit as hard as he could and felt her warm blood coming out dripping onto his whiskers down to his chest.

Charlie applauded and walked away. Rick was a little shocked and just sighed. The Hanjin truck drove off.

"Dallia," whimpered Calico, crying Calico. "Dallia?"

And in that moment, the real stage of life began
For a panda named, Calico.

THEIR CALL, CALICO

<u>Legend on reading Calico's Life:</u>
Indicators for each character: Italicized character name
Indicator for dialogue: " "
Indicator for thought: *Italic Font*
Indicator for action: **Bold Font or wording with quotations.**
Poems and Songs appear more centered.
Setting set inside: Brackets: {SETTING}/{BOLD}

{Calico sits with Dallia's body and looks at the clear blue sky glistening over the stream. He stares at the tire tracks that the news vans and the moving truck left behind. }

Calico:
   "Dallia, oh Dallia, If only what they told me was true. I bet we were in the wrong moving room at the wrong time, or the right time. But Dallia, wake up, Dallia wake up; they're gone, Dallia···Dallia. Where are you?"

Calico moves her mouth open and closed, open and closed. He takes a deep breath and then attempts to move each leg expecting each one to start up in place. He's had it; he then bends her hooves on her right side firmly to the ground, near the stream. He quickly with his best effort pushes her to her upright walking position with her limp head and neck swaying like a swinging tool belt carrying an electric driller on the end of a wobbly sawhorse. Calico stands back and immediately, Dallia's body swings back landing on top of her swinging neck splashing on top of the stream. Her blood leaks out and runs in motion with the ripples.

Calico chokes, and claws the dirt and roars for his second time, and hears an echo and backs away. Suddenly a flock of heron fly above him.

He quickly looks down and eyes an army of ants coming from all directions.

Ants:

Song: Hip Hip Hooray
Hip Hip Hooray, what man has brought to me,
He's brought a lot but never before
A gratuitous charity.

Hip Hip Hooray, what man has brought to me,
A dead bull's bitch, in a bloody ditch
And how we'll dine merrily, hey!

Hip Hip Hooray, what man has brought to me,
A trail of blood, a fly−less grave,
And red meat as fresh as can be−
As can be···
As can be···

Oh Hip Hip Hooray, Hip Hip Hip Hip Hooray!
We march onto his murdered path,
And on his account···
We all will dine today!

Calico:
"And who are you black spots?"

Antoine:
"If you are referring to me your pure kindship, I am Antoine, and we are removing this rather delicious looking remedy of the gorilla whore's wrath out of your trajectory."

Calico:
"Who sent you?"

Antoine:
"Aw a pure kind riddle, wait my fellow antinions, I can make sense of this. "

Calico:
"Okay."

Antoine:
"Your pure kindship, we just want to give the impurity growth after death for the ground and our hearth— is that more than any riddle's worth can ask?"

Calico:
"I···I uh cannot let you."

Antoine:
"Hmmm the pure kind is injured too, bring death to both! Hurry, we just received news of a miscarriage of the impurities down the hills!"

Calico:
"Don't I say, do not hurt her."

Antoine:
"Stop! The Pure Kind says she is diseased and is paralyzed, go to her heart antons we need her to stop pumping blood, enter threw the latch under her tail! Thank you Pure Kindship, you can leave now or be given death."

Calico:
"No you stop!"

Antoine:

"Cannot your pure kindship; we've got a lot of killing to do today. I am sorry your Pure Kindship you will die now."

Calico:
"Stop, I do not want to die, I do not want to die!"

Calico looks at the ants who have completely covered Dallia's body in seconds, and then begins to back away as the ants scatter towards him, and backs up and falls on the stream carrying greasy bubbles of Dallia's liquid and chunks of fur. He gets out on the other side of the stream and begins to cry. He watches a line of ants shoot underneath her tail and how Dallia's body gradually begins to deflate. Calico stops crying and notices one of Dallia's eyes bobbing and going with the stream. He jumps in fear and runs into the dark Korean woodlands into Nature.

Antoine:
"Such a strange riddle that one left. Aw such dwindling of time our campaign continues men, onward ho! Hip Hip—"

Ants:
"Hooray."

{The sun is setting and Calico has been traveling for hours over mud and dirt, and he is alone near a small pool of water, surrounded by the chirping of grasshoppers. Dallia's blood has washed off his coat as he wades through another stream.}

Calico:
"Where is the ceiling? Where is death? What am I? What AM I?
I see myself in streams and colors, who am I? Who am I?
Panda or Gorilla Whore, Pure Kind or Death—who am I?
Why was I unsociable, what is it to be liked? Why doesn't
Anything make sense? Corinthia said life always makes sense.
Now I am thirsty, and in this reflection of the night sky,
All I see is her blood."

Calico walks over and touches the dark body of water with his nose.

Her eyeball is in there somewhere, changing colors and growing tumors, and Dallia's blood is screaming, "The Gorilla Whore! The Gorilla Whore! The Gorilla Whore!," I thought the world would be like the zoo, but then again the zoo did not like me. Bettings did, she gave me a bath but not in blood.

Calico quickly licks the pool. Immediately feeling that the water is warm and sticky and there are dead insects in it, he spits it out.

Calico:
"Maybe she was right. No, no I don't want to die! Hilly Dallia I wish you were here to show the way!"

{A cloud passes over him and blocks his view from looking towards the stars.}

"Okay, one more kiss."

Bettings told me to use my pink licker to kiss water in large amounts to get the medicine syrup down quickly.

Calico takes a slow lick in the pool again and gets a mouthful and feels something swimming in his mouth. He quickly spits it out. It's a blue koi with a French mime—like human face with brown human eyes. It hops out of Calico's mouth and winks and disappears into the murky water. Calico urinates near the pool thinking that could be what is troubling him. He quickly finds that he has urinated on the family of grasshoppers that were chirping. The forest is now very silent.

Calico jets out in complete embarrassment and wanders into the uncut bamboo forests and edging around trees and weeds.

Suddenly Calico accidentally breaks a larger bamboo stem that was carrying a wasp's nest.

WASPS:
   "Pure kind! It is time we eradicate you all once, once, once, once, sszzz, and for all! Once and for all! Sszzz!"

Calico:
"I what? No don't kill me!"

WASPS:
"Oh it's a grubby Pure Kind, he needs his maffa maffa szzzz! Sting him in the tail hole make him a weak pooper for a week! Szzzz."

Calico:
"I do not want that."

WASPS:
"What is want?"

Calico:
"Want is!"

Calico roars in pain as the wasps attack his rear with 9 stings, and he begins to limp and trot at the same time while the wasps are all gaining on him. Another wasp lands on him and crawls up his back— towards his face. He stops a bit to try to remove the back—crawler with his teeth but three wasps zone in on this moment and sting him in the nose and his cheek edging towards his eyes. The one that was crawling on his back is now up inside his ear and stings the inside. Calico whimpers and limps now and runs towards the pool where he drank from.

Calico:
"Today, ugh! Is not the day I die."

Without a second thought, Calico jumps into the murky waters immersing himself three meters below. He eyes around and sees over three hundred blue human-mime koi eying him, then winking. Calico defecates accidentally into the water and the human koi just watch the stool sink with their eyes winking every few seconds.

Calico:
"I hope they're gone."

Calico struggles up to the top with pain all over his body and drinks some of the murky water. He claws himself grippingly back onto the muddy turf.

He looks to the stars again in the silent night. He then tries to get the stingers out from his buttocks with his teeth but he's in too much pain and lies down on his side breathing heavily. Tears begin to drizzle out onto the mud and he closes his eyes and attempts to sleep.

{The night is silent and Calico is out cold. The morning rises with a dreary mist and the heated morning beams on the burning furred flesh of Calico}

In the morning, he wakes up to⋯

Ants:

Hip Hip Hooray Part 2

Hip Hip Hooray, the pure kind who cried "disease!"
Has outnumbered his odds, by giving himself
The status of deceased.

Hip Hip Hooray, and it shows up on his ass
That he's not as pure as a pure kind,
And as for his riddle we will pass!
But not today!
No, not today!

Oh Hip Hip Hooray, Hip Hip Hip Hip Hooray!
We march onto his murdered path,
 And on his account⋯
 And on his account⋯
 We all will dine today!
 Today! Today!

Calico jumps up seconds before the ants approached his vicinity,
and urinates both in jolting fear and protection away from the
approaching ants.

He runs back onto the trail that he was making the previous night with
the destroyed weeds and broken bamboo stems. Then he eyes the wasps
that stung him, as do they towards him.

He picks up his limping speed.

Calico cuts his front leg with the same giant deteriorating bamboo stem
piece with the fallen wasp nest. The wasps pick up and speed towards him.

He keeps running and running with a trail of blood from his wounded leg.
He begins to carry it to prevent it from bleeding, and hops faster getting
pounded by weeds, stems and even mosquitoes plucking into the moment—
that take a sample and leave the scene.

Calico keeps running and halts near a cliff with a stone statue of the
Buddha and quickly runs behind it. He watches the wasps go into another
neck of the bamboo woods and leave the scene.

Calico is panting heavily and licks his wound, and goes around to the
front of the Buddha statue who is sitting in the Full Lotus position, legs
akimbo with the palms of the feet upwards. The statue is made of granite
stone and carved without any unbalanced measurements, and is draped
with vines. Calico wanders about the statue which stands, yet sits, five
meters tall. Calico completely tired goes into the lap of the sitting
Buddha and lies down covering the top of his head and his stinging ear,
and cries like an infant in a nurturing parent's arms.

Calico:
     "No, she was right, she was right—she was right! I am lost and my
state of living is lost, and I can never go back home. Why did Bettings do
this to me, why?! Then I shall wait here until Antoine will kill me. I
shall wait here···I shall wait···"

And then came a light rustling in the bamboo ahead of him. The rustling
became louder and louder with each leg brushing against the falling
debris and leaves.

Calico stops whimpering and makes his claws tighter on the sitting
Buddha, still hoping to live.

The bamboo forest in front of Calico is silent as a long orange, white and
black striped furred paw edges out of it onto the vine running cliff; then
the other paw.

Okay, this is not the ants. But it could be another deformed human headed thing like a Martackadong with Betting's head. Wait, no, Corinthia?

The old Korean tiger steps out into the glorious sunlight with wise and caring eyes and slowly approaches Calico with leaning shoulders.

Calico:
   "You're an ice—cream colored Siberian tiger!"

Gengall:
   "He who names me must seemingly have a name for what I am not. "

Calico:
   "You are not a human are you? Are you related to the antons? Do you know Antoine?"

Calico becomes more nervous as Gengall comes closer to him trembling and huddling in the legs of the statue.

Gengall:
   "(laughs) Little pure kind everyone knows Antoine! Oh dear let me calm down."

Gengall props his body in a sitting position which has a shadow covering Calico in his presence.

Gengall:
   "You are truly not of this vicinity as I saw the gorilla whore pouring you out from their moving mountain caverns in a vase made of sword wire. You must be completely unaware of the boundaries. In this forest, I hmmm, in this forest hmmm.
   Let me be more simple. My name, is that what you call it, is Gengall. Could you say it please just in my presence?"

Calico:
   "Gen—gall?"

Gengall:
   "Now say it exactly like you would confront me with me asking you to confront me."

Calico:
   "Well···um Gengall."

Gengall:
   "Now what were you worrying about pure kind?"

Calico:
   "What should I be worried about?"

Calico his gripping onto the Buddha statue more and tries to growl but only a whimper comes to the air.

Gengall:
"Hmmm. Say my name."

Calico:
"Uh Gen—gall?"

Gengall:
"One more time, please?"

Calico:
"Gengall."

Gengall:
"Hmmm, it's been a while···What comes next? I say my name is Gengall, and then you say my name, no, no hmmm."

Calico:
"Gengall, my name is Calico."

Gengall:
"Aw ha hmmm, I say what is your name hmmm!"

Calico:
"Could you say my name please?"

Gengall:
"Why would I say your name, Gengall!"

Calico:
"Uh, your name is Gengall, I am Calico."

Gengall:
"Oh, oh yes (laughs), it makes perfect sense now, the names are passed on to one another."

Calico:
"What do you want, Gengall?"

Gengall:
"Oh yes, that's me. And you are? Oh I am so old, Gengall."

Calico:
"I am Calico."

At that moment Calico begins to loosen up.

Gengall:
    "Calico, it must be a foreign name."

Calico:
    "I do not know what a pure kind is, and everyone keeps calling me it, and worst of all I think I am going to die because the Hilly Dallia told me so!"

Gengall:
    "Such problems indeed!"

Calico:
    "Do you know what a pure kind is?"

Gengall:
    "Hmmm, that is their name, right?"

Calico:
    "Me—Calico, Me—pure kind— what is pure kind?"

Gengall:
    "Hmmm puzzling? If 'me' is Calico, and 'me' is also pure kind, what is 'pure kind'? Is the answer, Calico, me?"

Calico:
    "(laughs) Okay, why not?"

Gengall:
    "I like the way that sounds already: 'Pure Kind Gengall'."

Gengall stands up and whispers the name to himself prancing around merrily in a figure eight. Calico laughs and watches the spectacle, but the pain still lingers on him and Calico rubs his face, ear, and rear.

Gengall:
    "That is the most meatiest compliment, I have ever received, it makes me feel like I could just jump and pounce in the air."

Gengall spins around and jumps at Calico, who completely doesn't expect it, loses his breath, in addition to all the pain, and faints.

Gengall is about to trot around in another figure eight and sniffs Calico, and pokes him a few times. Gengall scratches his own ear, and walks back and forth questioning himself with the phrase "Pure Kind", as if he is trying to find an answer.

He goes back to Calico, and pokes him a few more times with his paw, and then sniffs Calico's ear. Suddenly the stinger that was inserted inside Calico's ear goes into Gengall's nostril. Gengall sneezes it out, holds it and looks around briefly. He goes back to Calico's body and pokes it yet again.

Gengall moves Calico's body onto his back and drags it into another area of the forest with fewer trees); all of which are deciduous evergreen.

Gengall takes him into an {Open grass field on the mountain with a view of the other mountains}, and suddenly is confronted by two angry pachyderms.

Jul:
  "Gengall you have stooped to low lows pzark knuck knuck knuck!"

Aub:
  "Gengall, you were exiled from here days ago, knuck, pzark, offa."

Gengall:
  "He is from the gorilla whore; let him see Rendemra!"

Jul:
  "Gengall, your kind are forbidden to enter the Pure Kind Temple. And in addition the path you are on takes you to the caverns near your family grounds pzark, offa, offa, knark. "

Gengall:
  "I must take rest, I am an old Gengall, Jul. Age pulls you down sometimes. Leave your argument for Antoine."

Calico begins to wake up, and wiggles off Gengall's back accidentally.

Aub:
  "Antoine! Antoine! Knuck knuck knuck!"

Calico:
  "Antoine?! Where? Am I dead?"

Jul:
  "The pure kind is puzzled, Gengall, what have you told him, offa?"

Aub:
  "It's trickery! It's treason to hurt the pure kind; it is as much a treason to love a human! Your sweet defecation days shall expire today! Knuck, offa, offa, knark!"

Gengall:
  "Calico is injured. He needs the care of the pure kind. He needs better care than Triam could give him—that tusky witchdoctor of yours!"

Jul:

"Those tusks are my Triambo's (father's) tusk!"

Gengall:
"That bull is not your father! Your father died before you were born! You came here and acted like a whore—a gorilla whore! What is the word, what is word···?"

Jul:
"They called me a performer, an elephant. And I was whipped. I have seen others like them in the— the arenas! When you lying shits were done and old they would burn you or feed you to the trotulls [horses]! Knuck, knuck, knark, golla!

Gengall growls and raises his whiskers to reveal his old cracked teeth, and then coughs.

Calico:
"What is going on? Why do these butterfly eared, fat horses···um very fat horses want to get mad at you?"

Gengall:
"We are in difficult times, Calico, the world of Kind and the Pure Kind, and the Gorilla Whore is changing. There are very corrupt beasts that will do anything to keep it that way so others can become weak."

Jul:
"QUIET! GENGALL, you have injured him enough, and you are going to kill him to dine on, and leave the rest for Antoine, right, knuck, knuck!!!"

Gengall:
"I am a changed Kind. Look at me, do you see me in hunger lust on this gracious pure kind grubby?"

<u>Song: Tricky Tiger</u>

Jul:

      Um Um Oooooh!
Oh mao, mao, tricky tiger!
Oh mao, mao, tricky tiger!
Ya, ya, no—oh—oh—oh!
Ya, Ya, no—oh—oh—oh!

Tricky tiger, sitting in the grass,
Tricky tiger hungry fast!
You're no damsel in distress,
Your fetish says you're the best
At what you do—oo!
And you go—go—go—go!

Tricky tiger on the run!

Aub:

Like a naughty gorilla whore nun!
Knuck knuck knuck offa, offa, pzark!

Jul:

Um Um Oooooh!
Oh mao, mao, tricky tiger!
Oh mao, mao, tricky tiger!
Ya, ya, no—oh—oh—oh!
Ya, ya, no—oh—oh—oh!

Tricky tiger, munching in the cave,
Tricky tiger has no sex slave,
What turns him on! What turns him on—is a meal!
Tricky tiger gonna steal!
And what you do—oo!
And you go—go—go—go!
Tricky tiger on the run!

Aub:

Like a trotull hopping for fuh—uh—uh—uh—un
Knuck knuck knuck offa, offa, pzark!

Jul:

Um Um Oooooh!
Oh mao, mao, tricky tiger!
Oh mao, mao, tricky tiger!
Ya, ya, no—oh—oh—oh!
Ya, Ya, no—oh—oh—oh!

And what you do—oo!
And what you do—oo!

Aub:

At what you do—oo!
Knuck knuck knuck offa, offa, pzark!

Calico:

Knuck knuck knuck offa, offa, pzark!
Oh my?

Aub:

Knuck knuck Knuck
Knuck Knuck Knuck
Knuck Knuck Knuck
Offa, offa, pzark:
Whose there?

Jul:

                Oh—oh—ya!

Aub:

                Oh—oh—oh—yaaaa!
                Knuck knuck knuck!

Jul & Aub:

                Oh, and what you do,
                What you do, what you do,
                What you do—oo!

Aub:

                Last time Gengall!

Gengall:

                I can pass, and take him myself.

Jul:

                Um Um Oooooh!
                No, no, you can't Gengall
                Because Gengall you know
                Something, you're a:

                Oh mao, mao, tricky tiger!
                Oh mao, mao, tricky tiger!
                Ya, ya, no—oh—oh—oh!
                Ya, ya, no—oh—oh—oh!

Aub:

                Tricky tiger—

Jul:

                Tricky tiger—
                Ya, ya, no—oh—oh—oh!

Aub and Jul finish their tune by raising their trunks to the sky merrily.
Gengall turns around and starts heading his way informing Calico to do
the same.

Aub quickly runs alongside Gengall, and kicks him over to the ground on
his side, and slams his foot down on Gengall's ribcage. Immediately Jul
comes and rears her body back roaring out and slams her momentum with
her right leg on Gengall's skull smashing his face down like unfinished
cherry pie with filling popping out of the sliced cooling holes.

Calico is in shock, and has no words and tears pour out of his eyes and he
can't move. He immediately starts vomiting.

Calico:
    "You killed him, you killed him, you kill—!"

Jul:

"Pure kind it was the best thing to do."

Calico:

"Couldn't he···He was going to take me to get help. He helped. He helped me."

Aub:

"Trickery, Jul. Gengall's trickery was strong on this one."

Jul:

"Do you, pure kind, remember the codes of the universe?"

Calico:

"Uni— okay, look whatever you are—"

Jul:

"Whatever I am? This one is completely. Wait what did he say your name was?"

Aub:

"Believe it was Calemderannan, Jul."

Calico:

"My name is Calico, and I am not a pure kind, okay you uh nature animals! I am a panda from the San Francisco Zoo. I lived in a cage, and I felt comfortable and I had two friends, Martackadong, and Corinthia, that is all—and the gorilla whore are called humans—Dr. Bettings helped me and—."

Jul:

"It is not trickery then Aub. I know your type. Ten years ago, I too was like you are now."

Calico:

"But you just killed Gengall for telling the truth! Look he is an old Gengall, and did you see those puffy brown biters, and you killed him."

Jul:

"I remember this— oh I remember this—"

Calico:

"Remember what?"

Jul:

"How many times have you seen death in your life, Calico?"

Calico:

"Twice, the camel that came with me, and the Gengall you killed—the Gengall that was trying to save me!"

Jul:

"Gengall's kind does not change; he is a bred liar, whose breed longs for gorilla whore blood. He wanted to kill you as well."

Calico:

"He did not seem harmful at all."

Jul:

"Calico, on average you will see death 200—300 times a week."

Aub:

"What does that mean '200—300 times a week', what is week?"

Jul:

"It's the gorilla whore language coming back to me. They called it statistics like in the circus they said things like it to prevent the law men and activist men from going into the pens, or was it the other way around? Statistics are supposed to ease the gorilla whore mind without valid evidence."

Calico:

"I am not at ease, Jul. I am in pain. I can't seem to be attached to anything otherwise it dies, and then I can't seem to trust anyone apparently because who knows what tricks you could be pulling on me right now. I am confused, I want to leave, but I can't."

Calico starts to cry, and is completely embarrassed, and covers himself. Jul walks over to Calico and kneels down, and rubs his head with her trunk.

Calico:

"Oh go on and eat me."

Jul:

"No, Calico, no one is going to eat you."

I never felt this sensation before, is this gesture safe.

Calico:

"Are you sure? Why does your um nose keep pulling on my fur."

Jul:

"(laughs) I am sorry I cannot help it, I breathe just like you do."

I feel warm, and I want to be with this nature animal.

Calico:

"Can I stay with you?"

Aub:

"It is against the pure kind conduct, he must be with his own kind. Otherwise Gengall's punishment will serve as ours. Remember Tribbartha who brought the phoxes (foxes), and how we had to roll her off the Great Cliff?"

Jul:

"Calico, this is a different world in nature, and there are different rules to follow."

Aub digs up mud on Gengall's body.

Jul:

"For the time being for tonight, we can take you to our camp—"

Aub:

"Jul, that's exactly what we—Jul! What knuck knuck pzark offa, offa, do you think you're doing?"

Jul:

"Knuck, knuck, pzark, knark, offa, offa knark knark! Aub, as Triam's daughter I will take the blame for my actions.

Aub:

"Let us only hope you do not receive death."

Jul:

"Do not speak of death, only those who talk about it run to it."

Aub:

"Yet there are those that wave their trunk on high stampeding into it."

Jul:

"Aub."

Aub:

"Jul⋯"

Jul:

"Knuck, knuck, knuck! PZARK, KNARK, KNARK, KNACK!"

Aub:

"Knuck, knuck, PZARK—KNACK, PZZZZARK KNACK!"

Jul:

"KNACK you!"

Aub:

"KNACK KNACK PZARK!"

Jul:

"Knack, knack-pzark-pzark-mmm-Knark!"

Aub:

"KNACK-KNACK, KNNNACK-KNNNACK!"

Jul:

"KNARK-KNARK, KNNNARK-KNNNARK!"

Aub:

"Knack, Knark, okay?"

Jul:

"Knark, Knuck,Pzark, mmm Calico.

Aub:

"Be that way Jul."

Jul kneels down again to Calico after the argument with Aub.

Jul:

"Calico, yes we can take you. Come and get on top of my back."

Aub:

"Knack, knack, knuck!"

Jul:

"Aub."

Aub:

"Jul."

Calico gets on the back of Jul and they ride {into the forest over through evergreens, and some clear water streams. There are more Buddha statues, and some red and very decorated buildings with wooden statues. There are some vehicles outside of the homes but they are covered in dust and vines.} They continue into the night stopping for urination breaks or to eat bamboo.

I wonder if this is what it's like to have a real family.

Calico:

"I never got to know my parents either. All I seem to be aware of was that section in the zoo and the two cages on either side of mine."

Jul:

"It's quite excruciating how much they let you know, and then how much they think you know, and then when you should know better. They're on a drive to never—endingly convert objects, animals even nature into all things humanly controlled."

Calico:

"I feel so odd right now, Jul—I can't"

Jul:

"Doesn't feel like there's a beginning or an end to it all in life? And at that moment too, like you may be too, I felt like my life was really just beginning out here in Korea."

Calico:

"Korea?"

Jul:

"That is what the men said on the tanker before I was driven up in their moving caravan to wherever Korea begins."

Calico:

"Korea."

Jul:

"Korea. Maybe it's the last free land for the Kinds."

Aub:

"Knack, Pzark!"

Jul:

"Okay, Aub, we'll get a move on."

The journey continued. {Over the top of the summit of three mountains, where Jul pointed and told Calico about the moon}, yet she said that she could not teach pure kind the ways of the world as they were to be taught it differently through their own kind.

It was pitch dark by the time Aub, Jul and Calico came into the herd in a {large grassland valley reflecting the full Moon and the sprawling star line across the dimly lit verdant mountain range}. The light begins to get brighter as they approach the herd at the small lake reflecting the full lunar display.

Suddenly from the large herd comes a young elephant in wobbly form.

Hig:

"Maffa! Aubo!"

Jul:

"Calico this our grubby, Hig."

Calico:
    "Your grubby?"

Jul:
    "Well theoretically he came out of my vagina."

Aub:
    "Knack, Knuck, knuck! Pzark!"

Jul:
    "Oh Aub."

Aub:
    "Jul."

Hig:
    "Maffa, maffa, what is a pure kind doing here?"

Jul:
    "Aub, knick knick, pzark."

Aub:
    "He is my grubby too."

Hig:
    "Maffa! What is a PURE KIND doing here!"

Jul, Aub, and the rest of the herd are suddenly silenced at Hig's remark.
Jul walks in front of Hig, and looks at the two larger herd members
approaching her, Aub, Calico and Hig. It's her father (adopted), Triam and
her maffa (adopted), Cleb. Triam is almost all dark gray with a thick coat
of black fur, and has one back leg shorter than his other leg—and he
carries it off the ground when walking; Cleb is very furry as well yet is
more light gray.

Triam:
    "Jul, my dear···mmm Aub···Hig has knack pzark knack
mmmpzarkkaknack?"

Cleb:
    "Why did you bring a pure kind Jul, answer your Triambo!"

Jul:
    "Maffa, he is from the gorilla whore world."

The Herd:
    "Jul brought an outsider who is a pure kind of the gorilla whore
world."

Triam:

"This is the worst night in the future and present day of the Tusk and Pzark Pzark! Jul, do you not know the punishment for your actions— is a visit by Antoine?!"

Cleb:

"Knack you, Knack you all! I told you Triam, once a whore for nature animals, once a gorilla whore property—stays a whore either way you look at it."

Jul:

"Knack, Knaffa, Pzark!"

Hig:

"Maffa Grama, Pzark 'whore'?

Cleb:

"Your maffa is a whore for life."

Triam:

"Pzark, knack, knuck⋯ uh knuck, knuck."

Triam takes a deep breath, goes to the side a bit and begins to defecate. Hig also agrees with Triam and runs to his Gram Triambo to join in.

Aub:

"Uh knack–knack, knack–knuck!

Then Aub joins his grubby in their evening defecation in the stars.

Cleb:

"Whore!"

Jul:

"Maffa, Pzark!, Knuck, knuck."

Cleb:

"Jul is a whore, gorilla whore, nature whore, whore, whore! Knuck, knuck, knuck!"

Jul:

"Oh Maffa!"

Cleb:

"But you're our grubby."

Suddenly Jul and Cleb embrace their extended noses and lick their cheeks. Calico is trying to figure out how all that abusive arguing turned into such a happy connection with that same warm feeling he felt earlier.

With a loud fart by Triam, Triam, Hig, and Aub join the odd embracement creating a carousel of the warm feeling. Calico feels that he wants to join in, but holds back in case they suddenly burst into another yelling battle, or someone gets killed.

Triam:
    "Jul, dear, as your Triambo, and chief of the herd, I do not want you to die, neither does your pompous maffa."

Cleb:
    "Knuck, Pzark."

Aub:
    "(laughs) Knuck, Pzark."

Triam:
    "Hmmm, but as chief I was brought up that any of the regular herd who brought in a pure kind had to be executed. But you, my Jul, are not a regular one.
    Hmmm, my mentor still lives with the herd, Jul, he may know best."

Jul:
    "Who is he Triambo, and why haven't you brought him up?"

Triam:
    "Komiak!"

Jul:
    "The old blind elder was your mentor, Triambo?"

Triam:
    "He sees more than many of us can."

The Herd separates completely eying a smaller size pachyderm that has gray streaks of fur over his black coat. Komiak's eyes are completely white except for the faded remains of a blue pupil. Like Triam, he has a back leg that has a size imbalance. Komiak, regardless of his age takes great strides through the grassy field and approaches the Chieftain family.

Komiak:
    "Triamtut, Clebtutta, Aubi and Juli, and aw the pure kind on your back Juli."

Hig:
    "Don't forget me Komiak."

Komiak:
"What who said that?"

Jul:
"Hig come out from hiding behind Komiak's tail."

Komiak:
"And the grubby, Higlet."

Calico:
"You see me Komiak?"

Komiak:
"We all see you; you're the elephant in the room."

Triam:
"What does that mean?"

Cleb:
"That's bizarre; what is an elephant?"

Jul:
"(laughs) This is why it is good I had experience in the outer world."

Triam:
"Jul dear, do not laugh at my mentor, this situation may cost you your life."

Komiak:
"Calico, right? Hmmm, it has been forty-five years since my visit—uh—"

Komiak farts a few times, and Jul is trying not to laugh. Calico is covering his mouth and rolling on Jul's back.

Komiak:
"Aw, that is good, that is good. That is sweet, that is sweet. KNUCK PZARK!

Triam, Aub & Hig:
"KNUCK PZARK!"

Komiak:
"KNUCK PZARK!"

Triam, Aub & Hig:
"KNUCK PZARK!"

Komiak:

"And they tusked and sang···"

<u>SONG: Knuck Pzark</u>

Komiak:

What once was a Knucka Knucka—goes

Triam, Hig & Aub (THA):
KNUCK PZARK, KNUCK PZARK

Komiak:

There's a tusk in the stream and it looks so heavy—
Says he's out of steam.
But behold in the night, shaking to and fro,
Over here, over there, and away we go.

What once was a Knucka Knucka—goes:

THA:

KNUCK PZARK, KNUCK PZARK

Komiak:

I say, what once goes Knucka—goes

THA:

KNUCK PZARK, KNUCK PZARK

Komiak:

Oh what once goes Knucka···

THA & Komiak:
Goes KNUCK PZARK, KNUCK PZARK

Calico:
"And what did that all mean?"

Komiak:
"Aw pure kind, in simple terms, the times are changing; in the song
it states that once the sound we use for 'Knuck Pzark' originated from
'Knucka'. And once change happens, the oldness has to let go and adapt to
new situations."

Calico:
"Knuck Pzz—ark."

Komiak:
"Yes pure kind."

Triam:

"Komiak, what is the best decision for the herd. Shouldn't we kill our grubby as our ancestors did or Knuck Pzark?"

Jul:
"Triambo."

Aub:
"Yes, Triambo—Knuck Pzark, Pzark knack knick!"

Komiak:
"I would agree with Higlet's Aubo. And one more time, you can sing with us Calico as male kind and pure kind, unless you do not feel the need to sing."

SONG CONTINUED

Komiak:
What once was a Knucka Knucka—goes

(THAC) (Calico):
KNUCK PZARK, KNUCK PZARK

Komiak:
There's a tusk in the stream and it looks so heavy—
Says he's out of steam.
But behold in the night, shaking to and fro,
Over here, over there, and away we go.

What once was a Knucka Knucka—goes:

THAC:
KNUCK PZARK, KNUCK PZARK

Komiak:
I say, what once goes Knucka—goes

THAC:
KNUCK PZARK, KNUCK PZARK

Komiak:
Oh what once goes Knucka···

THAC & Komiak:
Goes KNUCK PZARK, KNUCK PZARK

Komiak: And what happens tonight, our choice
Spells it out, and little by little we voice
It out, oh—oh—oh

THAC & Komiak:
KNUCK PZARK, KNUCK PZARK

Komiak:
"It is time, the only time if night has all night as stars do sun!"

Triam:
"Komiak."

Komiak:
"Triamtut, I need to take Calico to the Forbidden Pure Kind Temple, I am the only one of the herd who knows the way."

Jul:
"How?"

Cleb:
"Jul knack, knack, knuck, knack!"

Komiak:
" The journey can only be done tonight, as we may have many onlookers already who saw Calico traveling with Jul—who will do anything to kill you Jul and Aub, and you too Hig."

Hig:
"I feel noticed."

Komiak:
"The rule has been broken, and we must move on or be killed. Now I must take Calico, now."

Calico:
"Will I ever come back to herd?"

Komiak:
"Truthfully—no."

Jul:
"Then it is farewell Calico and welcome to a great world of beginnings."

Aub:
"And watch out for tricksters and the gorilla whore!"

Jul:
"You never gave me such caution, knack, knick knack!"

Aub:
"Knuck Knuck, Knuck Pzark, Knuck Pzark! (laughs)."

Jul:
  "(laughs) Goodbye Calico."

Triam:
  "So long pure kind, it was the greatest respect felt by your presence, we shall bow as you leave our existence into purity."

Triam, who has to balance himself lowers himself as the entire herd approaches and does the same; Jul looks at Calico confused—who is also confused. Hig runs over and bows with them. Komiak walks by Jul, and Calico gets the hint to climb onto Komiak. Cleb eyes Jul viciously. Jul eyes Calico one last time, and eyes Aub as they quickly join the others in kneeling. Calico feels the warm feeling again, only stronger and stronger and tears begin to drip from his eyes. Komiak leaves the herd into the darkness using his trunk to push the stems out of the way, but takes the best path.

Triam:
  "Farewell Komiak."

{The Journey winds up through thin trails barely passable by the blind Komiak as his hoof toes barely rim over the side. There are vine covered caves full with moths that glow, which fly directly into Calico's mouth. He chokes on them, but accidentally swallows them whole. Komiak seems like he has endless energy as he keeps going under and over each mountain steadily and with continual posture—though with his frantic trunk (elongated nose) jostling each branch and even barely visible insects. They decide to take a break in one of the lowest levels of valley land near a bamboo forest and small waterfall.}

Calico goes and urinates as Komiak does the same.

Komiak:
  "I was like you, Calico, but in a much, much worse status. I did not originally come from America, Calico like you or Jul. I came from the greatest continent of Africa. I had grown up in the Savanna, but the gorilla whore came. I don't want to dive into the long range of detail but my family was butchered and their bones sold for ivory.
    I was fortunate to come across an animal field agent who brought me to Brtain for his zoological gardens.
    When I was twelve years as the humans call it, the New York Zoo in the burrow of the Bronx bought me. And everyday I would be whipped and beaten by the gorilla whore who didn't want us to escape.
    Then one day the cuff that held my back leg came loose and unbolted from the ground.
    That night the gorilla whore—"

Komiak takes a deep breath, tries not to cry, but a tear comes. Calico walks right next to Komiak and places his paw on Komiak's trunk.

Komiak:

"He took out a tool saw— with the pain of a thousand wasps, and he tied me down. He even placed a cuff around my trunk, and there were chains—oh the chains.

He placed it on me, my leg and rubbed the cold object down until it reached my knee. And I didn't deserve it.

He jammed it in, and he had attached hooks on my eyelids so I couldn't close my eyes. And every bit that he drove the saw in, I became blinder from the pain. PZARK!

But it was on my account that the police— the protector gorilla whore, came and heard my screaming by a fellow zoo janitor who used to give me peanuts at night.

They came around and broke open the bolt as we were in some sort of storage area as they call it, and the blood was everywhere, and the gorilla whore who did it to me, was laughing and licking the saw.

And that was the closest to death that no Kind— not even the gorilla whore to say the least, should ever go through by another kind. "

Calico:
"Why aren't you a pure kind, I have suffered only minor injuries compared to your scars."

Komiak:
"The pure kind, also a 'panda' who I had taken to the same location asked me the same question. As I had just entered Korea and did not know my way around, he showed me where to go with the ways of the mountains and where the grasslands were. Though he also had an injured leg from being attacked by a panther, he said I could not help him into the location and it had to remain a solid secret.
He was also a novice as you are to what a pure kind is and what a kind isn't.
In life Calico there are always forms and kinds that you will want to be, a certain happiness of such perhaps that belongs to another kind or gorilla whore that you haven't achieved. Whether you attempt to take the long steps of effort and pain one way to get it, get to it, or instead take a different path, you will find out that the only kind you'll ever be is you—who you are born to be. It sounds odd, and something that in your upper head region through those eyes sounds fun and changeable like finding the tastiest piece on a single pineapple—but whatever it takes— you end up with you. Maybe an improved and experienced you, but all in all you live life in your senses.
I remember the last time I saw a winter in the New York Zoo, the colorful coats the younger gorilla whores wore and the snow lining up in

thin bars between existing bars of the cages— it was what humans
say over and over—beautiful.

But to the other elephants, they wanted go back and be cramped in
a warm closeted pen.

Anyway, the sun is rising, we need to hurry, Calico."

Komiak goes over towards the waterfall and splashes his trunk in the
soaring foam and pouring endless delight, and laughs a bit. Calico gets
tears to his eyes. Komiak kneels down towards Calico, and Calico climbs
on board. Komiak climbs over two more mountains almost seamlessly.
Calico still looks on in amazement at Komiak's effort. Komiak slows down
near {a vast bamboo forest in the afternoon sunset}.

Komiak:
  "Calico, how many are there?"

Calico:
  "How many are there—where? What?"

Komiak:
  "Don't you hear them? They're coming within distance! Coming
faster, and faster."

Calico:
  "Who?"

Komiak:
  "Calico, listen go down the path ahead of you and keep going until
you get to the gold Buddha statue. Crawl along the thinnest path from
the back of the statue and you will get to the main red dragon gate."

Calico:
  "I don't understand."

Komiak:
  "Do as you are told, it is the only thing you can do now or you
will meet death."

Calico:
  "Thank you Komiak, and tell the others, thank you."

Calico slowly walks away from Komiak who is also slowly re-walking the
steps that he used to bring Calico to this long maze of bamboo stems.
However Calico stops next to several shorter brushes as he hears the
pattering of paws on the ground. Calico urinates silently and watches
Komiak. Then suddenly Komiak stops moving, and Calico wants to go
towards him as if to protect him from whatever is coming his way, but he
decides to listen to Komiak. But he waits to see what may happen.

Twelve Korean Tigers (younger than Gengall) bring the severed heads of the pachyderms—Jul, Aub and Hig. And they approach Komiak. Komiak doesn't say a word as if he knew actually what was going to happen.

Komiak:
"This is as menacing an attack as the gorilla whores. Why did you kill them?!"

Pengall (the lead tiger):
"It is obvious Komiak, they were bound to the rules of our ancestors. There are only few pure kind left in the world to be demoralized and corrupted by the outsiders, and furthermore transportation of a pure kind with a regular kind requires death.
Fortunately, Antoine will be quick today too."

Komiak:
"I am ready Pengall, strike at me."

Pengall:
"Kill the three-legged blind freak!"

Komiak:
"So ends a life completed."

Calico watches the tigers pounce all over Komiak and toss him to the ground and immediately rip underneath his skin above his rib cage and start digging. Komiak's last movement is with his trunk as he reaches up and pulls an evergreen leaf and holds it to the sunlight.

Komiak:
"And now I see the···"

Komiak's trunk drifts down like the endlessly flowing waterfall and hits the beating rocks.

Calico waits until the execution is complete, and the tigers have left with Komiak's head, and Antoine has corroded the insides of Komiak, and walks out of the bamboo forest and sits next to the drying blood covered bones of Komiak and the fallen evergreen leaf and cries. But Calico stops because he seems stronger.

He then looks over and eyes several banana trees. Calico remembered when Bettings used to carry things on trays and in bags, so he quickly runs and climbs onto the banana trees and gnaws out the large dew dripping banana leaves. He then uses one banana leaf at a time, without the fear that he might die and disassembles the remaining skeleton pieces. In subtle amounts, Calico brings together the bone pieces and takes them to a smaller waterfall only a short walk away. At nightfall after he brings the entire hoard of Komiak's remaining skeleton, he lifts

each leaf into the waterfall, and watches each set flow endlessly
away. He then places the last set of skeleton pieces and watches them
scatter away down the stream into the bamboo.

*Thank you Komiak. Thank you for teaching me the lessons of life, and to
never give up and to be "you" through it all. May you go to where your
death goes, best.*

*Thank you Hig. Thank you for teaching me the importance of family and
care and attention, May you go with Jul and Aub where your death goes,
best.*

*Thank you Jul & Aub. Thank you for teaching me to help those in need
even if they don't ask for it, helping them get on with their life even
when everyone disagrees, and to settle things by direct communication.
May you both go with your grubby Hig where your death goes best, and
may Triam and Cleb be at rest too. And oh yes how to spot a trickster
and be wary of your surroundings, thank you.*

*Thank you Gengall. Thank you for teaching me to help and do what you
think is right no matter what any Kind thinks of your kind. May you go to
where your death goes best.*

*Thank you Hilly Dallia. Thank you for being the one to open me up to this
new world of understanding and taking me from the shell that kept me
unsociable, and teaching me about the gorilla whore and death, and that
the world is cruel; and most importantly to protect those you can. May
you go to where your death goes best.*

Thank you all.

* * * * * * * * * * * *

Calico falls to sleep in the entrance of the bamboo forest looking at the flowing stream.

{Calico wakes up covered with some bird droppings on his back as a hawk's nest was right above him, and he goes to the flowing stream and cleanses his body, the sunlight is peaceful in a glamorous flare between rays and white blue, and Calico enters the bamboo trail drenched in butterflies and moths, with cocoons just opening, and the flowing bell Suzu—Ran (Convallaria Keiskei Miquel) and swaying Magnolias blooming in gentle breeze. And then the silent bamboo continued and continued with few shadows.

Then appeared a great gold Buddha statue covered in vines which made it somewhat invisible from the naked eye if one was to pass or fly above the forest, the sunlight drew on this clandestine shimmer held under the strangling yet loose and hanging vines.

Calico walks up and touches gold for the first time in his life, and then realizing he has to move on like Komiak said, Calico goes behind the statue and sees—only one thin path extending from the statue. Calico takes the path alongside the tall evergreen trees, and suddenly down into a low valley— below the visible valley and the ceiling seems to exist with the sky with a blend of wavy leaves reflecting each beam in dancing shadows.

Calico goes deeper into the animated shadow woods with changing colors from the different leaves and beams, and plays with them briefly, laughs and stops. He sees a very wide flowing stream separating himself from the other end. With little choice, Calico extends his paw and finds that the bottom of this water—covered stream is almost perfectly flat and only covers up above his paws. He walks on this water stream and looks left and sees a brick wall with a circle of gold bars sifting out the water like a water fall endlessly does and exists.

Calico acknowledges this odd characteristic of the landscape but has to move on.

He goes across the wide stream into a well—carved cavern (a tunnel) covered with painted decaying and dusty images of tigers and humans (gorilla whore) standing and looking at the tigers as they have a a bulbous glow about them. Calico swallows, and growls, and then holds his mouth as he must move on. He exits the decaying tunnel and sees a stream like the one he just crossed without any water. He walks across its smooth black surface, and sees a dusty brick path and follows it into another neck of the lowest valley of bamboo woods that he has been to as he shivers from the odd coldness of it.

Calico goes through an all shaded bamboo forest that only echoes
his sound. He urinates and it sounds like a rampage of streams; finishes,
and listens as the last drop echoes in the odd yet serene coldness.

Calico climbs up a hill to a much warmer valley and sees the sun setting
and a long red wooden bridge going over a dried up stream. And behind the
half circular bridge is a large brick wall painted in bright red probably
20 meters from the ground. In the center of the glowing red wall is a solid
golden doorway with red stairs coming down from it. The golden door has
an imprinted picture of a panda-like himself standing in the same height
as a dragon. On top of this glowing display on the top layer there are coal
black spikes—that are actually elephant tusks in the hundreds.

Calico swallows, and questions his entry into such a place. He is
completely shaken and faints.

He wakes up in nightfall and there is no moon out and it is pitch black.

Calico sleeps the rest of the darkness away as the morning light comes in,
and still no matter what sunlight hit the gate, the gate was very
sinister.}

I have come all this way. I cannot turn back as death is around every
corner and I have been at the fault of the murder of—
Yes I am at the fault of the murder of my friends!
I killed them, I was unsociable and I killed them.
These gates are not for me as I am not a pure kind, but that is my kind
they say.
It was my fault, all my fault.
But Komiak, he acted like he knew—
He knew the whole conjunction and set of events that were to follow—
He knew because he saw the worst when I came.
They gave up their lives because of me being unsociable.

Calico begins crying again, and whimpering.

I have wronged everyone; that is why Bettings threw me out, and why
they all died. It was my fault.
But I cannot end here, but they're dead.
I cannot end here! I cannot end here!
I shall listen to your words, Komiak.

Calico goes over the creaky red bridge and the sun rises to its stationed
position and beams out into the world. Calico goes up the red stairs and
looks back at the red bridge and the green mountains.

He pokes the golden door with the imprinted panda on it and almost
magically despite its thickness and probably 20-ton mass, the door wings
open like a relaxed Western saloon door. Calico goes and gently kicks the
door behind him.

{The Pure Kind Temple. There stands a large grassland field with not one large golden Sitting Buddha Statue as he had seen as on the way of taking the one thin path, but twelve sitting evenly in a circle with equal space between each of them. Also the statues were positioned so that their shadows would never intersect another statue, or their shadow.

In between the statues is a large dusty tiled circle painted in black and white displaying a Zen labyrinth. The boundaries seem limitless until the distant towering mountains touching the winged angles of clouds. The grass blades wave in even pattern. Walking past the circular display there is a long rectangular sand gardened path extending into another bamboo forest.

Calico looks back at the small red gate glaring out of his view and the small gigantic display, and then enters the forest. The forest however is not a forest but a decorated fence to look like such. Calico re-enters to question what he has just gone through, and looks confused.

Then in front of the fence is a flowing stream that has a bridge composed entirely of a Suseok formation that is colored cobalt blue. But in front of the bridge is and has to be the largest Bonsai Tree in the world covered in vines on its bark.

Calico walks across the formation that doesn't wiggle at all.

As he comes closer to the mountainous Bonsai he sees other panda grubbies playing on top, probably forty pandas swinging and enjoying themselves, or playing around in the leaves. Calico continues walking forward. A few other panda grubbies run by peacefully and laugh, Calico smiles a bit; though he is about a year older, Calico feels several years older on account of his recent experiences.

Calico keeps walking forward and then down a smoothened wildflower hill into a magnolia tree garden with dragonflies swimming about in the air. Calico is completely in awe of these surroundings. After an hour of walking in the Magnolia Tree Grove he sees 50 meter-high bamboo posts acting together as a wall unto the next area.

Calico walks passed this wall and sees twelve giant marble Buddha head statues atop a pillar like structure that is acting like an endless fountain siphoning water into each indentation of the pillar into a large marble pool. The flooring is all marble tiles as well of different polygonal shapes with circles. In the pool are around 90 pandas (pure kind); some swimming, some drinking from the tiled flooring. Calico smiles and another pure kind nods at him and starts licking up the water. There is more six other pools like it.

Calico listens as there are voices all around him now talking about the gorilla whore, the kind and the pure kind. After the Hall of Fountains that

extends over a ten minute walk, there is a large golden stairway
inside the wall of a large green mountain providing shade for the Hall.

Calico looks back again at the pure kind in luxury and goes forward up the
non-rusted and superb conditioned stairs. The stairs lead into a tunnel
sanded down to perfection, carved stunningly with pink red marble tile
lining the flooring. After the brief tunnel through the mountain, Calico
comes upon the main Temple-of temples?

There stands before Calico an entire village with blue bricked rooftops,
fields of flowers and overgrown plants, and all of the buildings are built
with white colored wood with blue brick roofs. Calico enters the village
and sees in front of the massive temple is a pure kind wearing a golden
tasseled napkin cloth on the top of his head, and has some gray fur. This
pure kind stands in front of at least four-hundred pure kinds, and is also
conversing about the gorilla whore.

This pure kind is Rendemra.

Rendemra:
      "And it was these gorilla whore creations like Buddhism, and they
called them fajitalmahs, then faiths, then religions— that were based on
forgetting the joint connection between gorilla mixtures and the pure
kinds that, these-cover your grubbies' ears if they are near-'humans'
took to forgetting the liberties that we brought forth and shared with
them all these planetary years and struggles···"

Calico listened only briefly as something else catches his eye in a nearby
village house on the way to the gathering.

Calico sees a very colorful mural displaying different colored circles in
a black background. The mural reminds him of the ice cream stand that on
rainy days would be wheeled near his cage and he would observe the
painted speckles and circles bright colors.

Calico wanders in, and sees another pure kind possibly around his age. The
pure kind is dipping its paw in different ink bowls and is climbing up on a
tilted wooden ladder. He continues and wanders into the house and
watches the pure kind paint.

Calico:
      "Your wall is···"

Calico thinks of something he heard relating to the ice cream stand.

Calico:
      "Scrumptious!"

Gammina:

"Sorry pure kind brotto, I did not achieve your understanding in my own."

Calico:
"Your wall, the colors, I mean they are scrumptious and delicious."

Gammina:
"Aw yes brotto, the universe has beauty beyond the imagination of our own."

Calico:
"Your uh wall—"

Calico suddenly becomes embarrassed and he has no idea why. He swallows.

Calico:
"Is beautiful···"

Gammina:
"The universe can do that to our eyes but we must be wary towards—"

Calico:
"I mean you are."

Why did I say that? What's wrong with me, I must need to defecate soon, how embarrassing.

Calico:
"The wall I meant."

Gammina:
"(laughs) Okay brotto."

Calico:
"I see it and think of the peacefulness of the night."

It does remind me of traveling to the herd with Jul and Aub.

Calico begins to tear a little, and Gammina who is talking directly at him while he stares becomes a little worried.

Gammina:
"Hey I said you can join me up here I could use your help—oh—oh thank you, well, I uh mean is everything okay?"

Calico:
"No. I mean yes. I mean no—uh."

*Aub said not to trust a trickster, but what is wrong with me, I
don't know what is going on.*

Gammina:
    "Can I help you?"

Calico:
    "Help me?"

*Hilly Dallia said the gorilla whore pretend to help and take a little
more, she could be a gorilla whore.*

Gammina:
    "Could I help you?"

Calico:
    "Why do you want to help me, what do you want from me? Why are
you trying to control me?!"

*Why did I say that? This feeling it's like that warm feeling but it's
entering my senses. I need to leave. No I can't leave, they're watching
me—these pure kind. I am a killer to them, I am a killer to all of them!*

Gammina:
    "What is the matter brotto?"

Gammina gets off the ladder, and notices Calico shivering oddly and his
eyes are cracked and red.

Calico:
    "Look, I don't want to hurt you. I have to keep moving forward."

Gammina:
    "What does that mean, brotto?"

Gammina goes behind shaking Calico and closes the sliding door to the
house, and then licks her paws. Calico looks at her closing the door.

Calico:
    "You want to trap me don't you—you trickster! You want to see
Antoine come to me and tear me apart, don't you?!
    I have to keep going, maybe to another forest, maybe elsewhere—"

Gammina:
    "Brotto, brotto, you are home with Gammina."

Calico:
    "Gammina you are not with the Gengall are you?"

Gammina:

"Uh no. Who are you?"

Calico:
"Calico."

Gammina:
"Calico, grubby Calico."

Calico can't hold his feelings in and he embraces her and starts crying on her. She immediately takes a hold of her feelings and starts kissing (licking) his ears, and then she lets go of his embrace and begins licking his back. Calico still is crying but begins to slowly yield as he suddenly feels a sharp pain in his rear.

Gammina:
"These wasp stingers were in deep. You have great fur Calico."

Calico now in less pain stares back into Gammina's hungry eyes, and he is wondering what he got himself into. Gammina growls. Calico swallows, and scrambles back a bit. Gammina pounces on Calico and claws him across the face. Calico growls and blood drips from his cheek onto the tiled floor. He gets up and growls in her face. Gammina growls and bites his lower jaw. Gammina quickly pushes Calico over on his back and growls in his face and claws him twice in the face. Calico gets up without feeling the pain yet is shocked a bit and confused and growls back. Calico pounces on her and then she bites his leg and pushes him into the ink bowls and they splash onto both of their coats.

They both are panting, but staring at each other waiting who will take the next swipe. Panting, Panting.

Gammina growls and takes her claw aiming to get some more marks off his face. Calico dodges that swipe by anchoring his claw into the shoulder of the front paw she is using to bring havoc to Calico, and he pushes her back. Gammina to balance herself anchors her other paw in Calico's opposite shoulder with his paw that is not being used and begins to push him back.

Gammina and Calico are standing upright in effort to push one another over and growling head-to-head, and moving in a synchronized waltz-like manner.

Calico forces the duel to an end by pushing her on her back. Calico quickly takes his paw and claws her across her face from her cheek to the top of her ear. She starts to bleed. He then roars in her face. Gammina begins to whimper.

Oh Calico, oh what have I done?

Calico backs off a bit from Gammina and sees that she has tears
from her eyes as he did when he had entered her home.

Calico:
        "I should not have done that, I-"

Gammina gets up and blood comes off her mouth with drool.

Gammina:
        "Done? Done? We are not near finished yet, grubby!"

At that moment, Rendemra slides open the door and sets his eyes on his
daughter Gammina, and then on Calico.

Calico:
        "Look. But listen, I can explain this-."

Rendemra:
        "Aw Brottoto I have all the explanations in this village as you
should be aware of."

Calico:
        "I-"

Rendemra:
        "It is true then, my grubby Gammina has finally removed her
virginity!"

Calico:
        "Her what-?"

Rendremra:
        "Brottos this is a great day for all pure kinds."

Gammina:
        "Rendemra, he did not complete the acts."

Rendemra:
        "Did not complete the acts? Did not complete the acts?! Is there
something wrong with my grubby pure kind? Yes, yes you are nervous to
tell me and it is true! Gammina you must repaint the entire red wall
again starting tomorrow. Come brottoto let us to the temple."

Gammina:
        "Do not forgive me for I have wronged you Rendemra."

Rendemra:
        "And we will not forgive you until your wrong is right."

Calico:

"STOP! Look I have no idea what a pure kind is, I assume it's a panda like we are all, and I have been searching for a place called home since I was delivered here from San Francisco."

Gammina:
"San Francisco? He used the word 'panda'!"

Rendemra:
"An outsider—an outsider! Have you come to reveal our secrets outsider? No, I do not see it in your eyes that you would do such a thing. But my grubby would, go and be useful with your days Gammina, and then will the days be useful to you. San Francisco Zoo, I take it? Shipped by a delivery truck and attacked by the people who brought you there—is this not the truth?"

Calico:
"Well—"

Rendemra:
"I thought the same. Gammina before we take this pure kind, name bear?"

Calico:
"Calico."

Rendemra:
"They named you for your spot, brottos they named him for his impairment! Gammina be quaint and take Calico to the Hall of Fountains and bathe him completely."

Calico:
"Rendemra, I can do that on my—"

Rendemra:
"Nonsense, female pandas need to exist for a reason. Take him to bathe—and if I will repeat myself again, I will need to remove both our guest, you Gammina and four of the youngest grubby out into the world of the kind, is that clear?"

Gammina:
"Yes it is beyond clear words."

Rendemra:
"Take him and do not talk to my level, grubby.
Calico, I will wait for you in the main temple, I assume you can figure the location out if you have the true intellect of a pure kind."

Rendemra sniffs viciously at his daughter and takes the group of male pure kind (brottos) in the direction of the main temple.

Gammina nods and Calico attempts to comfort her, but they are
both silent. Calico is more sorry than worried now, and Gammina is very
worried. Gammina shoves Calico a bit to imply that they must go down to
the Hall.

Gammina leads the way through {the red marbled floor tunnel in the
mountain gate and they arrive at the Hall of Fountains which seems to be
isolated as the other pure kind have stopped using the pools.}

Calico:
> "Look, Gammina I am sorry."

Gammina:
> "Please go into that pool over there I need to bathe you."

Calico:
> "Gammina, I can do it on my own."

Gammina:
> "Calico, do you want us both to die today?"

Calico:
> "No, I don't want you to die today for the harm I placed you in."

Gammina:
> "See, well you–uh *me*? I have been here all my life maybe death
might be good for me."

Calico:
> "Have you seen death?"

Gammina:
> "No, a pure kind is prohibited to see the physical death, but we
are taught that the forces of the body move onto another form or
location."

*She doesn't understand death like I do. But I remember I was once like
her naïve.*

Calico:
> "Gammina, I have seen death too many times before I came here."

Gammina:
> "Please, Calico, I need to bathe you."

Calico eyes Gammina, walks and goes over into a shallow pool of water
reflecting the clear afternoon sky and the bottom white marble surface
of the pool. Gammina with Calico notice that she has brought two
persimmon fruits and crushes them together with her paws and rubs her
paws together with the juice.

Calico:
    "What are you doing?"

Gammina:
    "Could you look up at me, Calico, and stay that way. Don't move."

Gammina takes her paws and dips them into the pool a bit and scoops the water with the persimmon juice; then pours it over Calico's head. Calico closes his eyes and swallows. She does that a few more times.

She takes another persimmon out while sitting on the edge of the pool watching Calico wait for all the persimmon juice to leak of his soppy wet face with his fur hanging over in a facetious manner as the juice is a little sticky.

While Gammina presses the next persimmon closed Calico rises out of the pool and grabs her into the water, and laughs.

That feeling it is coming over me again.

Gammina:
    "What the–! Calico! Calico! Look what you did, I will certainly receive death!"

Calico:
    "No you won't, just let me bathe you, it looks fun."

Gammina:
    "How many antinwonians are you?"

Calico:
    "What does that mean?"

Gammina:
    "Gorilla whore language, gorilla whore language uh– how old are you?"

Calico:
    "Four years old."

Gammina:
    "Four antinwonians old!!! I attempted to lose my virginity to a four year old!
    I am eight years old, and I am a full grauba {full grown} What was I thinking?"

Calico:
    "I don't know, you want to know what I think?"

Gammina:
    "Let's just finish this."

Rendemra enters the Hall of Fountains with two hundred brottos about him, and they eye Calico and Gammina.

Rendemra:
    "Aw the fountains the perfect place for pure seduction. Gammina has your virginity been spared off your body?"

Gammina:
    "He is four, Rendemra!"

Rendemra:
    "Four times you say (laughs as do the other brottos), looks like there won't be any intercourse for either of you for awhile. Calico leave Gammina so she can clean up her act and head to the red gates to repaint it."

Gammina:
    "Go Calico."

Calico:
    "I am sorry Gammina."

Rendemra:
    "To the temple brottos. Female pure kind need not be forgiven because the word "whore" carries the feminine connotation and not one of the brottos. Onward."

{Calico eyes Gammina one last time and shakes off the water and heads with the other brottos up the mountain tunnel. They go back into the village and head to the main palace—like temple. Rendemra suddenly stops.}

Rendemra:
    "Fellow brottos, Calico and I shall only be in the temple and no one else shall enter, understood?
    Calico only, enter."

Calico looks back briefly at the large gathering of pure kind and the verdant mountains, and the sunset, and looks into Rendemra's eyes. Rendemra smiles, and puts his paw on Calico's shoulder briefly and moves him into {the Pure Kind Palace Temple. In the large blue bricked white stone and painted wood building is a bridge built entirely of bamboo extending over a pond of red human—faced koi that instead of winking close both of their eyes in full blinks. Calico and Rendemra pass over the bridge into a gigantic amphitheater with rows of seating and on all of the walls there are tile mosaic displays of animals who have black and white exteriors like Orcas, pandas, types of birds, penguins, Dalmatians, and probably several hundreds of others. There is even a gorilla with a white body and black coat of fur. Above the large atrium is a glass circle centered in a giant dome displaying in black and white tile, the planets of the universe.

Rendemra:
"Do you know why you are here Calico–?"

I have to think fast with Rendemra.

Calico:
"Origin. I think I need to know what a pure kind is."

Rendemra:
"Hmmmm, yes, but you are one. Let me tell you the summation of the basic reign handling the pure kind definition and then I will ask you the same question again when time permits it."

THE SUMMATION OF THE PURE KIND UNIVERSAL

Rendemra:

"78 Billion years or antwonians from today humans or gorilla whores were not in existence, nor was I for that matter–shame···

Earth was an uninhabited lifeless planet. The first planet of the great existences was what is known today as Saturn. As I begin to detail the events imagine these planets as they come into a blank universe. The beings of this planet, the Ore hetheons (Orray Heth e eons) were orange and almost mucus–like in their exterior skin, but like humans they walked in a bipedal formation; two legs, Calico, two legs. They had blond clots of fur and interchangeable spots of pink that would reappear in other spots of their bodies. I know Calico you will have a multitude of questions by the end, but be patient.

Hair never existed until Earth, and fur was primordial. On Neptune in the first existence lived the Fattarnihiuemians, they were very toad like and all carriers of the pocket hole, Calico mind you its real title, vagina. If you lick it well–––uh you may be too young for such a conversation. How brash of me. Their eyes were quite gigantic with two yellow pupils in each eye. Neptune also oddly was gaseous and pink, and these Fattarns let the surface move their body upside down–interaction was very temporary.

Then on Pluto during the first existence, lived the seven Khhartins (Kuh huh artins). These seven were each four meters high and where bodies like a caterpillar with changing color flesh. They had two mouths holding their eyes. They did not eat. But however it is said that their minds stored the most advanced creativity and knowledge about the truth of our existence, and that if one was able to drink their blood,

their liquids, Calico, they would achieve all answers until their
own existence depleted.

On Venus, during the first existence lived the Charcoaleans; their name
is still common today in their ashes. These beings were a combination of
bone, hard tough bronze skin and faces made of ruby etched like the
nostril of an elephant. Their lifespan was short as they existed to steal
each others interior flame, and that other whose flame was robbed would
disperse into ashes.

In Uranus existed the Slavaaas (Slaev ae ae ahs), who were of hydrogen
and oxygen mold, or I mean very jelly and sticky substance. Like the
Charcoleans they lived to mingle, and take some jelly liquid from one
another— but their lifespan was endless.

So there were five planets of existence in all, and then a large distance
away was the planet, which humans refer to as Jupiter. The elephants
call this planet Maffa. We call it by the original pure kind that was
colorless except for its component, Chlorestigon. Jupiter would then be
called the Chloresto.

Every few antiwonians Chloresto would expand because, during the
rotation, like the care birds manage for their eggs, Chlorestigon was
growing and expanding with the immense heat and rotation. I will teach
you more about the sciences, and yes I will tell you what sciences are
soon, Calico.

Then one day during rotation, Chloresto was fully ready and halted its
rotation. As all those who give birth, Chloresto was a she. Her planetary
womb entry opened and she with great stress pushed out Chlorestigon
which appeared in life's proximity as what humans call, the Sun. In
addittition Chloresto bled and bled comets and meteors for Chorestigon
to digest. Chlorestigon grew to its complete size as it is today in three
days.

Chlorestigon gave the six planets something that has patterned our life
on all levels, light. Other large female planets also began to give birth
to their own chlorestigons and the galaxy received light.

This revolution and creation brought on to the existents fear beyond
words, and the sensation of heat from a non—living source— to them, but
also a completely living one by those who know its true purpose.

Chloresto still had more grubbies on the way as more blood (the meteors
and comets) raced out into space. These were the trinity planets, Mars,
Mercury and Earth, who were the brothers of Chlorestigon. Chlorestigon
like her mother is believed to be feminine as well.

Chlorestigon loved her brother planets well. She even decided to play a game one day and covered them with Chloresto's blood (meteors) covered in flames. Each brother reacted different and rotated away from Chlorestigon and she was all alone.

Her brother planets came closer to the first existent planets. Then came the second existence of curiosity, starting with the Khhartins who let go of the planet and went to a brother planet, and all the living existents in the next hundred antiwonians began to find ways of entering different planets and interacting.

And what did the brothers look like? They had perfect atmosphere and pure air. They all had oceans and plants. Their water was clear and reflected the black speckled sky. The beings of these planets were called the Pure Kind. The pure kind were made of the colors black and white, the balance of colors. Today there are only few of us from orcas, to cows, to trottulls (horses), to pandas, penguins and even some tigers, and other animals as well.

This journeying of beings going to and fro to other planets brought imbalance which led to even more fear, than jealousy, and eventually corruption from their original existence. The Ore hetheons became more hungry as there were not enough existents on Saturn, the Charcoleans looked for flames in the wrong places and started digesting other species and instead living longer. Two Khartins were depleted from their formatted selves and were devoured by several species.

While the chaos was brewing Chloresto (Jupiter) was still healing and missing its Chlorestigon and sons of the trinity. The planet is still healing today as the gorilla whore have glasses that let you examine the red blood mark of Jupiter.

Then appeared the first signs of sexual intercourse; Calico, intercourse is, well you should know this but let me review to you as a male pure kind brotto to another brotto, is the most wrongful right, if right is wrong for its own existence. To have intercourse a being must take a part of them and fit it into another part of another being. Then when heated contact is made miniature antons carrying your same existence will speed into that other being. That other being usually a female kind would reproduce these antons into one or more versions of you— the giver of the antons.

Calico is confused and shocked, but is just focused on hearing the story. Rendemra nods and continues.

And because of this interaction, all lifespans changed on all the planets as they could all die, yet through this process— be reproduced— though differently. And separations, divisions, and different considerations to view life started coming into effect.

The land was even named yang and the oceans were named yin to
explain that separations were necessary to balance the imbalance of the
beings co-existing together.

However through conflict and intercourse disease and destruction the
five planetary populations were dying out fast and extremely rapidly.
Then the last Khhartin of Pluto, called Syxttaut explained while living
on Saturn to many of the last mixed existents that with the dying
planets and populations, the only path to continuum and a future for the
existents would be to have intercourse with the pure kind and live for
more than one day on the surface of Brother planet A: Mercury.

No being of the five planets up to that point had been to the brother
planets near that long as the heat injured, from Chlorestigon, injured
most of the existents in their arrival and many perished. However the
existents were dying fast as suddenly did Syxttaut.

<u>MERCURY</u>

And so onto Mercury the breeds came, and those who could not make
across the cold space died and rolled forever away. It was like a massive
moving of different colored kites twirling and flaming and gliding
smoothly towards the brother planets. Then the beings entered the
atmosphere-as that is what the brother planets have encasing us here
on them.

The Slavaas could not make it and became part of the atmosphere, and
other Slavaas drifted into the other brother planets to escape their
Mercurian end like their fellow beings but became part of the Earth's
and Mar's atmosphere as well.

As these brother planets were in Chloresto's (Jupiter's) womb with
Chlorestigon, they also had an intense heat attraction. That is what
pulls us down, and keeps us from ascending.

However because of their desperate situation, the mixture of the five
planet breeds attacked the pure kind in efforts to rape them and plant
their antons in them whatever way they could. One black and white
moose drowned in antons as several Ore theons face fed them into the
moose's mouth until it overfilled. With the presence of the
Charcoaleans, and the heat attraction balanced with the atmosphere,
weather began and seasons began and through a long range of scientific
explanations all of the brother planets adapted this characteristic, as
they are a trinity.

Despite all the rape attempts from the dying breeds, the results did not
live long or was a stable result-or a stable reproduction so to speak.

Then there was the perfect imperfect reproduction with a pure kind
gorilla and a mixed Fattarnihiuemian. The result was a filthy black

skinned gushy gorilla figure without fur having bright orange
paws and the bullfrog Fattarnihiuemian eyes. This bizarre being was a
female. The other male gorillas in response became more attracted to
this odd being than the normal female pure kind gorillas— and would
have as much intercourse as they could with it. Some of the male
gorillas who had intercourse with the being would also pass some of the
mutated germs and blood to other regular pure kind female gorillas
during intercourse and thus breeds began mixing. Yes, this is where the
phrase gorilla whore comes from.

The last of the Charcolean, to escape the odd weather and their
increasing death rates found an empty cave filled with pure white lava,
like the milk nestled to a grubby in the core of Mercury. It was warmer
than the surface of Mercury, and they decided to dive in—the rest of its
population. The pure white lave immediately transformed into a black
tar drenching with glowing flames, this became known as kleiahuakokoa
or eventually lava.

The lava and the heat exchange brought a Mercuryquake and the land on
Mercury split into continents.

To rush the history, after generations and thousands and thousands of
antiwonians the resources of Mercury were depleted, yet unlike the
previous situation with the original five planets, pure kind got along
with the regular kind and decided that it be best if they could transport
in their magnetic pole pods to Mars during the shutting down of Mercury
as its existence will be months if not years of study for you, Calico. And
this would involve language, history, habitats, behavior, and what
humans like to call technology or taking a half Khhartin approach to
using up resources to the advantage of a population.

However most of the Mercurians did not make it, as they had never
tested the pods prior and many burned up as they entered Mars'
atmosphere. Oh and these non—pure kind were called Therochodis and
looked more like humans except in purple fur with smaller
Fattarnihiuemian eyes, and nostrils that stuck out longer and rougher
teeth. Though unlike the pure kind of Mercury, the Therochordis were
very power hungry as they were very hungry for resources and would do
whatever it took to snatch anything of energy or of value.

<u>MARS</u>

The inhabitants of Mars, the Juhikyop met the Therochordis with much
wonder. Unlike Mercury there were many Pure Kinds living, and most of
the Juhikyop were solely evolved from Pure Kind and not of the five
original planets.

The climate of the land of Mars was drastically different compared to
what was and what became of the flaming canyons and volcanoes of
Mercury. There were waterfalls dripping from mountains and snow areas

like there are bushes in a bamboo forest. The pure kind of Mars
wore jewels and golden ornaments about their body. The Juhikyop were
literally a pure kind human without the gorilla whore process involved.

The oceans were beyond beautiful as they were different colors from
turquoise to radiant fuchsia and even violet reflecting the shimmering
of Chlorestigon boldly.

The only surviving Therochordis were the wealthiest as the poorer by
Therochordis's standards, though not of the pure kind's, were left to die
without the life and living functions of the planet they destroyed. The
Therochordis, who survived were amazed at the "technology" and of
course at the resources the population had to "offer". The architecture
was stunning as well, and the Pure Kind had massive statues that they
built with the Juhikyops to erect made of crystal. In efforts of worship,
the Marsian (not Martian) pure kind dug into a mountain and made it
shaped into a face like that of the Juhikyop.

The Juhikyop had a ritual and way of doing everything so anything that
happened with the pure kind happened in balance and in equal treatment.

The Therochordis yawned at all these rituals, or what they considered
weak ways of acting, and grew aggressive within the first week of being
toured around. They wanted control.

When the Juhikyop led the Therochordis to their leader in Mars' capital
barshwa (country) of L'ujulu (Lu haw aw), the Therochordis took out
their manual boomerang—like blades and murdered the calm Juhikyop
leader Silentose before he even spoke which is where the phrase silent
comes from.

The thousands of last Therochordis pillaged the Juhikyop and enslaved
them and destroyed their temples, and forced them see and view things
the way they only saw them. And the pure kind human were raped and
many of the male pure kind humans were butchered. The Juhikyop had
yellow blood and their remains flooded their polished crystal roads and
homes; a genocide of 12 billion. And according to the historic texts not
one pure kind human attempted to attack and were killed on the spot.

However pure kind women delivered mixed grubbies or what humans call,
children. Some were more influenced in acting towards their pure kind
human ancestors while others were forged into the ways of the
Therochordis. For uh— "nature animals" the same as for the new kinds—
either they leaned towards their ancestor pure kinds or they were
placed into the treatment or mistreatment by and of the Therochordis.

After destroying entire cities and their artwork, the Therochordis and
those who supported their ancestors started a ten thousand year war
that led on to too many a battle of battles that one should experience in
a lifespan. Mars' seas were all tar black and had begun lowering as the

Therochordis used them for weaponry to kill their own kind and the pure kind.

In the last war along the Tiocriopriopic Coast edging into the Giuspppari (the Great Sea of Mars pronounced Gus whu whu whu ree), there was the last pure kind of both worlds (Mercury and Mars) this was the pure kind winged lion. Oh they had pure kinds like you wouldn't believe on Mars; it was simply spectacular before the Therochoris. However it was the texts of both the mixed Therochordis and the existing Therochordis that survived—with some original texts from the early Juhikyop years that have kept it in our mental thoughts today as we speak.

The pure kind winged lion was impaled by a gorilla carrying a blade of the Therochordis as the kinds were at combat with one another.

And so during the last battle the Therochoris sent a massive hmmm, they call it explosion, into the black waters and the atmosphere began to disappear. Quickly with what they could, the Therochordis bundled themselves into their floating orb homes with many of the kinds though many died, and were knocked away to Earth.

Mars went into decay and the oceans and plants disintegrated from existence.

But the gorilla whore have hid these notes of understanding from themselves and forgot about their ancestors' existence entirely.

EARTH

Earth: survival's last chance.

The orb homes ignited into flame when passing through the Earth's atmosphere from the gasses and materials that they were built of.

As Earth had been closed to being untouched for such a long period of time, the pure kind had evolved into—uh—into—uh—aw yes the gorilla whore have called them dinosaurs along pure kind pandas, orcas, koalas, but no pure kind humans. On entry many of the dinosaurs died as the pressure changed on Earth and the weight and cardiac system of the dinosaurs could not take it; they died on the spot.

And so from there did the Therochordis who survived decide to start anew in a new world. Those who disagreed had the option of going elsewhere.

Though through very similar processes has Earth taken its toll like its brother planets, and is headed towards a large internal conflict soon. We can just hope the world doesn't end anytime soon. And so to keep the pure kind in existence as we are the original breed, we must stay together away from rigid attempts of humanity, the gorilla whores.

Calico, you've seen the deaths they cause and the lack of their common sense— even the regular Kinds seem to sympathize with the gorilla whores.

Calico:
"Yes that is true. But why hide, Rendemra?"

Why did I say that? What he said gave good reason enough.

Rendemra:
"Hiding, Calico···You see, it's their call, Calico, whether we die in their world or not. Here, right here in secrecy, living in secret, Calico, will protect us while the humans will go and blow themselves up on their own frontline; we can and must stay here. Understood?"

Calico:
"Yes, uh, brotto."

Rendemra:
"Handling our culture well outsider—oh should I say, pure kind Calico. Brotto Calico."

Calico:
"Thank you Rendemra, for once I feel at home."

Rendemra:
"Aw and it's a home well—deserved. Now Gammina shall take you to your hut that the other female pure kind were to have setup already, and there are bamboo stems and persimmons in there as well. We share the Hall of Fountains for drink. Tonight I will be performing my nightime ritual to represent the patience of the pure kind in such dark times on the grand labyrinth outside the secondary gate—oh you saw it. I can't be disturbed so if you need help ask Gammina or any other pure kind.

Calico:
"Thank you Rendemra."

Rendemra:
"Sleep at your best tonight, as we will begin training and the advancement of your pure kind understanding tomorrow."

Finely, I feel safe.

{Calico looks up at the tiled images of the pure kind before exiting the atrium in awe. Then he follows Rendemra out onto the bamboo bridge into the peaceful night village, where Gammina waits to take him to his quarters.}

THREE YEARS LATER···

{Calico is a little larger and he looks more matured and is on top of the giant Bonsai tree watching the sunset with Gammina on a branch}

Calico:
" I like this part of the day, it reminds me of the tale of Kharliktrottose when he observed that he would win a battle against the Therochordis general Herrogianiare because he exclaimed that the flames of Purity were taking on the darkness, as the sun began to set, and in trickery without injury Herrogianiare surrendered with his battellers (troops) an entire brashwa away."

Gammina:
"You're always full of experiences, Calico. Anything else new?"

Calico:
"Well do you want to sing a song?"

Gammina:
"A Pure Kind song or one you learned from your journey of long ago."

Calico:
"It does seem quite awhile, doesn't it?"

Gammina:
"Time seems to do that."

Calico licks Gammina's cheek, she laughs.

Calico:
"You're still an eight–year–old looking for love in young grubbies, don't ever kid yourself from that."

Gammina:
"Calico."

Calico:
"Well it's the song Komiak sang to me that night, okay are you ready?"

Gammina:
"Ready as ever."

Calico:
"I know."

<u>SONG: Knuck Pzark (sung by Calico and Gammina)</u>

Calico:

What once was a Knucka Knucka–goes

Calico and Gammina:
KNUCK PZARK, KNUCK PZARK

Calico:

There's a tusk in the stream and it looks so heavy–
Says he's out of steam.
But behold in the night, shaking to and fro,
Over here, over there, and away we go.

What once was a Knucka Knucka–goes:

Calico:

KNUCK PZARK, KNUCK PZARK

Gammina:

Oh grubby– I say, what once goes Knucka–goes

Calico:

KNUCK PZARK, KNUCK PZARK

Calico and Gammina:
Oh what once goes Knucka⋯

Calico and Gammina:
Goes KNUCK PZARK, KNUCK PZARK

Calico:
"You do sing well, and I comprehend that because the sun hasn't
gone down all the way."

Gammina:
"So now you want me to surrender to you, is that it?"

Calico:
"There's possibility in that."

Gammina kisses Calico's cheek.

Gammina:
"Why am I still a virgin after these three years?"

Calico:
"The training is just getting up to the level of the acts."

Gammina:

"But I could teach them to you."

Calico:
        "It's better that they involve a surprise tactic."

Gammina:
        "Oh Calico."

Calico:
        "You know I almost mentioned this to you a few times, but has your Rendemrabo taken you to the Forbidden tower in the back of the village."

Gammina:
        "Would you think Rendemrabo would be that nice to his grubby? It's the same problem everyday of my life, he doesn't love me Calico, I see it in his eyes."

Calico:
        "He just wants you to be safe— just really safe so you're not getting into trouble that would spark the interest of gorilla whores thousands of kilometers away."

Gammina:
        "Now what would I do that would attract Gorilla Whores thousands of kilometers away?"

{The White House: The Diplomatic Room. The pale blue and gold rococo carpet of the ovular room is full with shoe prints of the concerned Cabinet members of the President of the United States. The walls display a painted verdant early 1800s scenery swimming around the clicking teeth and tapping pens, with scribbling ones of the concentration of the main concern of the Capital.}

The President suddenly enters the Diplomatic room in a blue silk golf polo shirt with the tiger emblemmed logo on the upper right hand pocket and appears more casual than the rest of the Cabinet. He greets everyone with the usual business and such.

Three White House Kitchen employees come with trays of freshly brewed coffee in official white porcelain White House mugs which are handed to each of the members.

The President:
        "Thank you all for coming to the usual end—of—the—month coffee meeting here in the Diplomatic Room, like any office or working office— an office that works well together, employees need some spare time to

talk— as we are under so much stress these days that its not a
requirement, it comes standard.
But take a sip and let it ease in you.
Now I am not concerned what the polls indicate, but it is clear
that our highest priority right now in our budget for the next few years
and hopefully with the next President is— war prevention in the
mainland, wouldn't you all agree?"

The Cabinet Members who are barely able to drink their coffee as is it is
extremely hot, choke and cough a bit, but shake their heads willingly and
are unable to voice their opinions.

The President:
"I recently received an e—mail. Now normally I do not check my
e—mails and I usually don't look at a computer without my glasses on,
but I just put my glasses on and began to read my e—mails. And I found
something that might lead me to believe that our friends and South
Korea are clueless about what is hiding in South Korea.
Now as faceteeteetiousa, that's my Espan—ya—oll for just plain
silly, as silly as this sounds it may be true. North Korea has indicated
that there are still weapons but they have moved them in close
proximity and have refused to give them up because I sent them a letter
asking them to. I think I sent it about two or three days ago.
So I have asked the Secretary of Defense to send me any odd
locations, and he should be arriving here in one hour with the report.
Now while we wait who wants to play telephone and hear what
the press will say about a topic, next?"

AN HOUR LATER···

The Secretary of Defense enters wearing gray Army jogging sweats with
black sneakers, and has some sweat stains on him. He is also carrying a
towel around his neck.

The Secretary:
"Hey— was working up a sweat, sorry."

Mr. President:
"We were just talking about you. About South Korea···"

The Secretary:
"Uh huh."

Mr. President:
"South Korea."

The Secretary:
"South Korea, South Korea—the state, oh wow, the country,
apologies everyone."

Mr. President:
    "You almost made me choke while laughing (laughs)."

The Secretary:
    "Just like a bag of peanuts. And speaking of handouts, Mr. President my personnel had sent the army a memo to test the Robo—12—Xyte— Prototype two weeks ago when we received the 'e—mail.'"

Mr. President:
    "I apologize everyone I meant an older e—mail that I had reached several weeks ago. Go on."

The Secretary:
    "One of the coordinates that were located was just off one of the hidden (by hidden, hidden from the reach of hikers) sewage systems at Worak—san National Park. The robot had rolled upon a large deserted fortress with a red brick wall and an absolutely stunning golden door—just imagine how much our budget could increase with just a golden door.
    Now we thought the area was deserted as no sounds were recorded—HOWEVER!
    The 12—Xyte's chemical sensory detected a new layer of a lead sulfide and cabondioxide based chemical; the components compounded with other components to make lead paint. And in this case it was red paint.

The Secretary of Health & Human Services:
    "Lead paint! Lead Paint! Quite a dangerous weapon indeed!"

The Secretary:
    "Very."

Mr. President:
    "Thank you again, what are the coordinates and when can we have at least oh a few tens of troops deployed—that can fit in our budget?"

{The following day in the evening at the Pure Kind Temple··· Calico exits the atrium with the other brottos; they are conversing about learning the acts—finally—and what they plan to do with the other female pure kind they have built a relationship with. Gammina sits near her quarters and watches him arrive.}

Gammina kisses Calico's cheek, and they enter Gammina's quarters with the completed painting of the universe glowing all over her room and flooring in the sun—setting sky through her window.

Calico:

"Remember when we painted the great trails together from the origin planets to the brother planets?"

Gammina:
"Remember? You compliment me every day on its beauty or my beauty—which one I still don't know."

Calico:
"The wall I think is just fine without compliments—"

Gammina:
"So my work of art doesn't need any compliments or it doesn't compliment the wall? Calico?"

Calico:
"The Wall is built to hold magnificence and it exists as is, but with you and your great efforts, the wall is beautiful."

Gammina:
"Calico."

Calico:
"Gammina."

Gammina:
"Are you ready to begin the acts, love?"

Calico:
"(recites the opening words of the acts) We've long started before we've met in our initial trail towards one another."

Gammina:
"And over the bridge I have waited for you to complete your trail—oh I sound silly reciting the texts."

Calico:
"No you do not Gammina···And each day learning the Pure Kind way I move closer to our true purpose and connection, and still you wait for me."

Gammina:
"Three years—wait for you—wait!—"

Calico:
"Gammina."

Gammina:
"Oh okay, and uh still I···will···wait for you always from the sun's earliest rise to the darkest regions of our beings. I will wait."

Calico:
"And I will long to meet you in your eyes."

Gammina:
"And I can't wait to kiss your belly."

Calico:
"Gammina! And by our connection to the Great Chlorestigon we complete our bond and work together to give purity endless life."

Gammina:
"And by Chlorestigon I will wait with her until I see your shadow approaching mine. And I at first fret because your longing for me burns uncontrollably like the Therochordis hunger for power over the land of the Juhikyop. And so I take to my daggering claws for protection."

Calico backs away and looks into her eyes, and she gets her claw ready for the first swipe at his jaw. And Calico waits to be bled again. Gammina gets ready to attack, but she is nervous about it.

Calico:
"What is it Gammina?"

Gammina:
"You are all grown up, and we've grown up together, and everything, and I want to love you, and I don't want to love you by hurting you. Oh let's just please get to the next act."

Calico:
"Are you sure, Gammina? It may be fun. Oh okay the next act···"

Gammina:
"And so after I wounded him in a great battle of confusion I anointed his wounds with the persimmon fruit and his wounds were cleansed. Calico?"

Calico:
"Oh no, Gammina, I was thinking about you after the brottos text study and all I could think about was you, and I forgot to run with the other brottos to the persimmon plants near the Great Labyrinth. But I will go now quickly to fetch some."

Gammina:
"No! Calico, I almost forgot on my part, Rendemrabo is performing the darkness labyrinth ritual and it might interrupt him, and that not one single non—elect pure kind can be in his presence during the process."

Calico:

"Then I will be as quiet as I can. I love you, and I can tell
three years is quite a long wait for you to be waiting for me to cross the
bridge."

Gammina:
   "Calico! No other pure kind has ever, and I mean ever trespassed even
near the edge of the Hall of the Fountains when Rendemrabo is walking
the trail. It is forbidden, and what if you are caught?"

Calico:
   "Do you love me Gammina?"

Gammina:
   "Yes, that is why I will wait for you among all the other pure Kind
to do the acts with."

Calico:
   "Do you love me Gammina?"

Gammina:
   "Yes, what is the matter?"

Calico:
   "I've seen death before, and the longing to see that person again
before they pass is unbearable in the moment, but you, Gammina to be
with you is like that."

Gammina:
   "So I'm the embodiment of death."

Calico:
   "No, Gammina, I love you like that, I want to be with you always.
Now do you love me?"

Gammina looks into Calico's burning blue eyes and looks at the painting
in her room, and the temple palace in the starry sky through her window,
and then swallows. She has never considered this love in such a great
measure before. Gammina starts to shiver a bit and tears start coming to
her, and she begins to understand.

Gammina:
   "It's so powerful."

Calico:
   "Now you understand, why on the day I saw you here on that ladder,
I-"

Calico begins to get teary but swallows his passion; Gammina starts to
cry and embraces Calico.

Gammina:
> "I love you, Calico. I love you."

Calico:
> "I love you, Gammina. And if I break the rule tonight, and I die or am punished—"

Gammina:
> "I will wait for you always, and now the texts seem to make sense."

{Gammina and Calico kiss. Calico looks at Gammina one last time and heads away from the village under the silent starry sky. He goes into the dark and dimly lit red marble mountain gate tunnel trying not to make any noise, and then slowly goes down the stairs to the Hall of the Fountains.

In the Hall of the Fountains, the only sounds are the running fountains pouring endlessly into the marble pools; ahead he sees the Giant Bonsai tree. However further ahead he sees a shimmering object or something shining through the leaves. And slowly begins to move forward passed the Hall of the Fountains into the Magnolia Tree grove area.

Calico feels the cool soil below him brush against his paws, and he continues to tread forward into the fields of the Bonsai Tree.

The light is still glimmering and is even further ahead of the Bonsai Tree. The light seems to waver and carries black moving dust with it. Calico is in a state of amazement. Also Calico hears whispering, and looking back briefly at the Magnolia Tree Grove and the Mountain Gate, continues towards his curiosity's delight. The whispering becomes louder as he heads towards the forested gates and the Great Labyrinth Fields.

Calico sees the persimmon tree just in reach but wonders about the glow light of multiple lights blooming from the Circle of the Twelve Buddhas around the Great Labyrinth.

As he edges nearer staying low in the fields with a persimmon in his mouth, he sees that each Golden Buddha has a flame torch in each of their laps. Calico had seen torches before during a Tikki themed party at the San Francisco Zoo, and also remembers Rendemra's discussion on the value of fire and energy for the Therochordis.

Calico edges close enough to view and hear the discussion of the Labyrinth.

In the torched 12–Buddha Statue circle are the twelve tigers who attacked Komiak. Each tiger is sitting at each Golden Buddha statue eying and listening to the voice of what was a whisperer from a distance, that

now beamed in great volume with the beat and heat of the flames—
this voice was of Rendemra.

Calico is somewhat shocked yet still curious.

Rendemra:
   "Pengall excellent work, your Gengallbo would have been very
impressed by you today. However it was unfortunate that because of
outsiders like Jul, or in the upper Northern territories, Dorimmda and
Karen— the regular Kind have taken to being more rebellious on account
of their presence against the laws of our ancestors. It was a great loss
to both the Pure Kinds and the Tiger Kind Clans alike for we here, the
leaders of the Tiger Clans and I—the leader of the Pure Kind of Korea are
completely Pure brottos.
   Glammuth, what news of you today from the port?"

Glammuth sitting to the left of Gengall nods, and Rendemra turns and
eyes him, the other Tigers turn and listen.

Glammuth:
   "Brotto Rendemrabo, the gorilla whores are mentioning a tanker
coming in tomorrow from the San Diego Zoo with an injured Rhinoceros.
When should we kill, my brotto?"

Rendemra:
   "Blarkthaw, and Volartant? Will you have your fellow clannars
(clan members) in range by sundown tomorrow?"

Blarkthaw:
   "It can be done Rendemra, though they are tired from the last
kill of twelve elephants two nights ago."

Rendemra:
   "What about you Volartant, any excuses?"

Volartant:
   "Blarkthaw, you mean to tell me that your clan is dying, how weak a
leader you are to your clannars, why don't I kill you and replace you
with one my clannars right now. You are a disgrace already to the Twelve
leaders who stand before you on such sacred grounds, and you worship
yourself to call yourself a pure kind brotto."

Blarkthaw:
   "They will be ready as soon as they can, they haven't been fed
adequately and their bones are aging."

Volartant:
   "Aging clannars? Are all your female clannars infertile, or more
suitably are your dimwicks unable to carry enough white antons to bring
more grubbies?"

The 11 Leader Tigers laugh at Blarkthaw.

Rendemra:
    "Aww, even I myself at the age of fifty-three antiwonians—"

Blarkthaw:
    "And still going stong, my brotto—"

Rendemra:
    "Did I permit you to speak?!"

Glammuth:
    "He dares interrupt the purest of the pure, he must be killed now."

Polarth:
    "Kill him like Lacroth two moons prior from today!"

Blarkthaw:
    "And he was my clannarzo (brother in Tiger clannar)."

Pengall:
    "Then you shall die decently like Lacroth!"

Blarkthaw:
    "But I am not—I have a grubby on the way—"

Volartant:
    "Lies, disloyalty—he acts like an outsider already, with your permission let us end his ruling."

Rendemra:
    "So be it, if—and I say if of the Juhykiop stand affirmatively on our side as we know they all will—they all will—Blarkthaw dies and the body is carried off to the road to be deposited for Antoine, then Volartant shall elect a leader Clannar only from his clan to take Blarthaw's place. Otherwise Blarkthaw stays and Pengall's grubby daughter shall replace Volartant."

Pengall:
    "Sounds compromising— at least Blarkthaw will feel more comfortable when she makes fun of his old mess of a body with his grubby ass to wipe his tears in and lick them up."

Blarkthaw:
    "I knew your Gengallbo, and—"

Pengall:
    "You can keep talking about my Gengallbo wherever your life goes after you're dead.

Leaders: leave Volartant and and Blarkthaw to brawl before the flames of Purity."

The 10 Leaders except Volartant and Blarkthaw:
    "With Purity."

Rendemra:
    "And with purity earned; begin!"

The Leader tigers get off the Great Labyrinth Circle, and Blarkthaw swallows as Volartant runs and instantly pounces and roars on Blarkthaw. Blarkthaw slams into the golden Buddha statue behind him. Blarkthaw roars as does Volartant. Blarkthaw scrambles and scampers to the side as Volartant pounces towards him again. They roar again towards each other. Volartant flashes his teeth and moves his tale intrepidly back and forth. Blarkthaw begins to pace back and forth eying Volartant's next move.

Volartant is annoyed and runs and bites at Blarkthaw. Blarkthaw swings his left claw and slices into Volartant's cheek. Volartant quickly does the same daggered swipe into Blarkthaw's left side of his face and they both rear back and stand up throwing claw blows at each other and growling furiously.
Blood puddles below them. Blarkthaw uses his hind legs and pounces onto Volartant and quickly neuters him with his claws on his hind leg paw claws. Volartant screams in painful roars, blood rages below him.

Blarkthaw laughs and pushes Volartant to the side and slams him against a golden Buddha statue. The torch becomes unhooked and falls and ignites the blood trail of Volartant and runs onto his body.

With Volartant's last effort as he is now covered in flames brings him to get up and jumps on Blarkthaw's back, and immediately his flaming claws brace onto Blarkthaw's face and rip open his eye sockets and Blarkthaw's face is covered in blood, and he stumbles back as the rest of Volartant burns up on the circle, and Blarkthaw shakes his body on the grass that he can only feel and not visually see until he feels the flames sift off his body.

Blarkthaw:
    "I am the victor! The great Blarkthaw! I am still a brotto of the Pure Kind! I am the victor!"

Rendemra:
    "But what good is a Clannar Leader if he cannot see, kill him Clannar Leaders he has insulted us twice this evening, and I do not allow—even my own pure kind—to treat me with such folly behavior!"

"His" own pure kind? This is Rendemra? I can't believe my eyes; I almost feel like Blarkthaw, this is unreal, I can't beleve this. But it is, I feel

very faint, but I can't move—not now, but they'll kill me. I can't move. I don't know.

No, Gammina, they would hurt her. No, no! What do I do? Why did I come here?

Pengall and the other nine Leaders pounce on the limping blind Blarkthaw and literally rip his body apart, and Blarkthaw can't defend himself but tries to swipe at nothing.

Over half of the Great Labyrinth is covering in the blood of the tigers.

Calico watches as Rendemra gets up and walks onto the drying blood from the tigers and smiles at watching them tear Blarkthaw to shreds. The flames dancing and sound of muscles and bones breaking and stretching echoes in the silence; the flames; the flames; the flames!

Rendemra removes two of the torches out from the Golden Buddha statues and ignites the blood, and a huge eruption of smoke jets into the air.

Calico jumps and urinates in fear, so much fear. He drops the persimmon, and Rendemra eyes him though the other tiger clannar leaders do not as they are enjoing ripping their former colleague into shreds. Calico runs as fast as he can away from these flames of Hell by his standards.

{Calico runs with the trail of smoke emerging behind him above the view of the mountains, he dashes through the gate. He jumps forward and trips and rolls down the hill to the Bonsai.

He roars in fear and keeps running, and accidentally runs into some of the Magnolia trees and scratches his face on the branches. Small ample drops of blood peer off his face in comparison to what he just saw. He quickly scampers onto the marble flooring of the Hall of the Fountains clawing the ground and chipping some of his claws. He defecates on the way, and tosses his body up the stairs of the mountain gate. He quickly runs down the tunnel pushing himself from the walls as he is having trouble walking.

He runs straight to Gammina's quarters, and she is holding a persimmon fruit.

She notices that he is completely covered in soil and his face is bleeding, and she becomes concerned.

Gammina:
   "I asked one of my friends for— Calico, what is the a matter?"

Calico:
   "Before your Rendemrabo kills me, and his tiger clannars I want to tell you what I saw before they come—BEFORE THEY COME!"

Gammina:
"Not so loud, Calico. Not so loud. Come inside quick."

Calico:
"Your Rendemrabo···your Rendemrabo···he (panting) is using the tiger clannars to to kill the regular Kind because I do not know, he tells them to kill and they kill. They killed Jul! and Komiak, and Hig, and Aub!"

Calico vomits, and is completely embarrassed. Gammina starts crying and embraces Calico.

Gammina:
"Oh Calico, oh Calico, oh Calico, oh Calico."

Calico:
"What am I···(gasps for air)···doing? I···shouldn't···I···shouldn't···be here with you."

Gammina:
"Oh Calico, oh Calico."

Calico:
"Gammina, Gammina, then again I may have no choice but to be with you, and···and···"

Calico passes out, and Gammina screams and whimpers on top of him trying to wake him up.

{The morning. Calico wakes up inside the Atrium of the Palace Temple, Gammina is across from him wearing torch holders acting like cuffs on her front arms. Gammina has a few cuts on her arms her legs and even her face. And she is situated upright revealing her breasts to the many brottos who are sitting around her. Calico is in the center of this arena of the Atrium and slowly raises his head to Rendemra.}

Rendemra:
"Calico, Calico, the outsider bear: one I thought I could trust. I even let you play with my grubby, yet you tortured her and never gave her intercourse, and she is ashamed to be upfront with her body like all female pure kind and is instead shy—as if she is on that textual bridge—still waiting for your dimwick to get into her."

Calico:
"What did you do to her?"

Rendemra:
"She told me she sent you to fetch a persimmon—which is likely more of a request of a male pure kind who forgot it himself, am I correct? Yes it is clear that I am."

Calico:
"You did not kill her did you?"

Rendemra:
"Brottos do you hear his tongue, he inquires of her Rendemrabo to have murdered his grubby, he does not hold trust in any of us for that matter—and we all took him in, and look at him—he expects that we would kill our own!"

The pure kind brottos Roar, some scrape the wooden floor boards with their claws.

Rendemra:
"It has been in full decision to my own and by the minds of us, the brottos that you meet your own exptectancy of us at the final moment of this antiwonian tonight."

Calico:
"Maybe death is purer than any pure kind could be."

Rendemra:
"A pure kind, Calico, does not judge the beauty of death; you should ask Antoine if you are still interested by the time he makes rendezvous with your remains."

Calico Roars and tries to lift his body up but his neck is harnessed on something with sharp metal chains. Rendemra has leashed Calico and quickly tugs Calico to the ground.

Rendemra:
"You should be used to this treatment— this is how the gorilla whore trained you is it not?—To roam and follow in their Therochordis footsteps, is it not? Calico your whole purpose in life was to come into the pure kind kingdom and to live your life like you were birthed to be. But you have refuted your true destiny and not only that, you have interrupted the most sacred rituals of the pure kind, the Night Trail and Passage of the Pure Kinds which symbolizes our great struggle we had to undertake to get to our safe grounds that we stand so strong, bold and free on today. "

Calico Roars and tries to speak, but is pulled quickly to the ground by Rendemra.

Calico:
"It's a lie, Rendemra!"

Rendemra pulls Calico's leash all the way onto the ground and the sharp chains tighten on Calico's neck and he begins to bleed. Rendemra loosens the chains.

Rendemra:
"Those are the most torturous words that were ever given to myself or my existence, or our existence. To say that our pure kind have never struggled, have never lossed a great many because of the war of the inbreeding of the original planets to our kind, is to say that we are all dead, Calico.
And I see in your eyes—those are not pure kind eyes—Calico—they are lustful eyes hungering for our blood—you want us to die. I can see you wishing Antoine would just come and wash away us. Is that what you want? Yes, it clearly is."

The pure kind brottos Roar again.

Calico:
"Muh—muh—murder—eruh!"

Rendemra pulls Calico down again.

Rendemra:
"I thought you were trained in, what do gorilla whores call it— OBEDIENCE!"

Gammina:
"No, stop this Rendemrabo!"

Rendemra:
"Silence Gammina! I said silence once, and I have repeated myself.
Brottos, see this tool again."

Rendemra takes out a rusty carving knife that he has on a pillar next to him that has some marks of Gammina's blood on it.

Rendemra:
"This is a gorilla whore utensil, tool, weapon and a way to punish another one who disobeys, who refuses to act in obedience. Gammina has been poisoned by Calico, and we may be too late. Calico— watch and see what you have done to Gammina. Gammina!"

Gammina:
"Rendemrabo, no, do not come near me again!"

Rendemra:
"See, Calico, she refuses the hands who brought her into this world, like you Calico!"

Rendemra takes the knife and walks to his grubby.

Calico:

"No stop you whore! You gorilla whore monger! I love her, I love her!"

Rendemra takes the knife and slices off a finger of her right front paw. Gammina whimpers and tries to stay silent.

Rendemra:
"If you love her so much why are you hurting her more? Why aren't you protecting her? Why aren't you givin her the pleasures she so deserves? Why have you turned against us? Calico, you will never be one of us again, and your life is coming to an end."
Now I have never injured another kind in all my life until this day, and I feel like a Therochordis in this moment— oh how I ask for forgiveness from the Juhykiop as they were like I feel today— slaughtered by inviting you into our world and murdering us.
Forgive us oh great Juhikyop."

The Brottos:
"And we forgive you oh great Brotto Rendemra."

Rendemra:
"As I feel horrible for my actions that I have committed today, I shall give you Calico two positive favors of my dearest sympathy—as you were a pure kind and a part of our great lasting family. The first favor is that your poisoned love, Gammina will be at my side to privately watch you die in the Flames of Mercury—something only a pure kind leader can do.
The second is your last request that cannot involve murder. Now Calico what is it. State it right now!"

Calico coughs and looks at Gammina with tears coming from her head and then looks at the tiled Pure Kind mosaics and all the brottos in the room staring at him with vicious eyes.

Rendemra:
"Time is moving on now, and if I have to repeat myself—"

Calico:
"Take me to see the full interior of the Forbidden Tower!"

Rendemra:
"An odd request.
See, he does not love my grubby, and he has already broken a rule; and now he wants to break another, and as many others as he can. Only the kind and the gorilla whore break rules.
But I shall keep my promise."

Rendemra swallows as he did not expect those words at all and the other brottos are murmuring words back and forth about Calico's bizarre request.

Rendemra:
"Brottos it is such an odd request, that even I myself am outraged at his bringing up of such a greedy act. But I shall hold my word.

Calico must and can only come with me to the tower.

Brottos take Gammina to the Great Labyrinth and tie her with this rope as I instructed on the days I presented the texts of gorilla whore construction, against one of the Golden Buddha statues so that she is sitting on its lap facing the rest of the statues and the trail.

Brottos also bring bamboos and persimmons as you will all wait at the labyrinth and make sure she cannot escape and do not give into her lustful poisoned desires which Calico has planted in her body.

Go now brottos, I am gratefully sorry it has come to this."

The pure kind brottos begin to head towards the koi bamboo bridge, and all of them eye Gammina and her blood dripping arm and her breasts. Gammina is whimpering more. They unfasten her and Rendemra hands one some rope that is on a pillar next to the knife. The brottos leave. Calico wants to voice out to Gammina but knows that Rendemra may only push the punishment further.

{Rendemra grabs Calico's leash and Calico begins to move slowly and sees that his paws are chained and cuffed together, but with enough length so he can huddle a bit forward. Rendemra drags Calico over the bridge. Calico trips and scrapes his legs on the bridge and realizes he has to keep up with Rendemra regardless of how much he can move with the tightened chains and choking leash.

Rendemra exits the Palace Temple and the entire population of the pure kind in the village with the just—exiting—brottos wait to hear Rendemra's last words before he executes Calico's request.

Rendemra:
"I have unfortunate news to explain to all Pure Kind. Calico, the outsider that we took in turned against us all— last night as he interrupted the most sacred ritual, the night trails of Pure Kind suffering. Tonight death will be brought to him, and from these last words, Calico is no longer a pure kind, but a kind. But on these grounds, no—but on these grounds he is considered a gorilla whore!

And now I take him to his last desire to see the Forbidden Tower, and then he will be put to death to bring no more suffering to us.

Join me in chanting what he really is as I will depart into the bamboo forest extending behind the village to the tower."

The Pure Kind and Rendemra:
"Gorilla Whore! Gorilla Whore! Gorilla Whore!"

The brottos exit carrying Gammina and the rope towards the
Mountain Gate. {Calico is taken in chains by Rendemra slowly down the
blue and white polished brick paths of the village with the Pure Kind
chanting "Gorilla Whore!," over and over towards Calico. A few grubbies
go up to Calico and spray the words in his face. Rendemra laughs.

At the end of the village is a large iron gate with a broken padlock
covered in rust. Rendemra looks back and indicates to the Pure Kind to
stay back as he and Calico will go to what is behind it alone.

Rendemra opens the gate and it creaks open slowly. Rendemra opens it
enough so that only he and Calico can be seen entering into it, and closes
it quickly behind Calico. The Pure Kind Temple is not as closed off as
Calico thought as the forests of the Park continue passed this point.
Calico looks back at the rusted gate, and it is covered in vines and barely
visible from the forest with the bamboo stems flocked together in front
of it.

Calico begins to remember the treachery that brought him to the Pure
Kind Temple and swallows.

Rendemra takes Calico through a long path in the forest that extends
down into a cave part of the way with a carved out opening that appears
to be some sort of lookout over the small waterfall—

The small waterfall that Komiak's bones ran down from. Calico can't stop
and is pulled harshly by Rendemra, and quickly remembers his
punishment.

Rendemra takes him up a carved set of stairs coming from the cavern that
extends out to the Forbidden Tower.

The Forbidden Tower stands like the Dongdaemun Gate of Seoul in the
ancient Korean Gate architecture in hard carved woods and the same blue
brick used on the village huts separating three large stories—the height
and size of the tower doubles or triples that of the Palace Temple. In
addition it is well hidden underneath vines and crumpled leaves and dead
petals covering it.

To the right side of the gate is a dried marble pool with the bones of over
a hundred koi tossed together. Near the marble pool are several rusted
bicycles dating back from the 1940s.

Calico:
 "(coughs) Rendemra—"

Rendemra tightens Calico's leash.

Rendemra:
 "You shall see the interior, and not talk, that was your request."

Rendemra tightens Calico's leash a little more and it cuts into Calico's neck a little bit more so that Calico receives the point clearly. Rendemra then loosens the leash.

Rendemra drags Calico to the front of the tower which does not have a door and is just a circular opening in a smaller blue brick base of the wooden tower. The weather has gotten more humid and mosquitoes and a gathering of flies seem to be grouping above in the tower.

They enter the circular opening and the ground is all dusty surrounded by cobwebbed covered wooden walls and flies buzzing around. Rendemra swipes a bit at the flies, but knows exactly where he is going like this is a common routine.

This ground floor seems to act like a storage area as there are probably forty cans of different color paints, and different colored inks piled against the walls. There are also matches, dishware, bullets, flares, torches, some rusty flashlights, quills, brittle browning toilet tissue, gardening tools all covered in rust, batteries, a few old books with almost black torn apart pages and unstitched bindings. There are a few lanterns too. There are some deteoriorating scrolls of sorts, envelopes, and empty canned foods cans lying about.

Rendemra takes a flashlight not too far from the opening of the floor, and blows on it and presses the button on it, and the bulb flashes on. Calico ducks down and tries to cover his head but his paws are restrained. Rendemra tugs on Calico and continues to walk forward.

Rendemra:
    "Every time I enter here reminds me of the time the museum keeper in the Australian Museum in Sydney took me out to walk around the museum. And to sum it up my museum days ended when the exhibit changed, and the gorilla whores adored me until they just decided to get rid of me like that."

Rendemra was an outsider?

Rendemra:
    "What you are going to see, you cannot tell anyone of the village, as you will lose your tongue tonight anyhow—I can make your death more sudden now,

Understood? Yes you understand, but I see in your eyes you are already planning how to undermine my own request over yours, isn't that right?"

Rendemra pulls Calico on with the {flashlight revealing a wooden stairway with broken floorboards and probably oil stains and spill stains of some liquids permanently staining them. Calico's skin on his legs are becoming raw from the restriction yet he struggles fully to get up the stairs hitting his paws though on the corner of each step going up. There are flies buzzing about as they head up to the next floor.

This floor is entirely dark and feels very warm and damply humid from the weather and there are no windows. The air smells of very strong immense odor. Rendemra waves his flashlight around and then paws on a lever switch and sparks fly from the ceiling as the piped lighting slowly turns on. The light hums louder and louder and so does Calico's heartbeat.

Do not faint, Calico, or else all this will be worthless.

The lights immerse the large room that takes up the entire floor.

There are decaying human skeletons all around, and shriveled up reddish brown robes. There must be two to three hundred human skeletons—none in perfect condition with several antons inhabiting them. There are torn up cloths all about and broken furniture. The bodies of these skeletons were bodies of both children and adults.

Calico is shivering but takes deep breaths.

Rendemra:
    "These were the former residents of the Pure Kind Temple, the Gorilla Whores. These were monks and they were regulating their peaceful palace devising ways to make more gorilla whores forget their ancestory in the spreading of their peace to create a fantasy where humans would eventually become the Therochordis dream and achieve 'Enlightenment' through self-searching and identifying, and things that sound, as they call it, spiritual or magical, and soothing or stunning to their minds.
    They had kept four pure kind, they call us now— as they did them, pandas. One of those pandas became my mentor and our teacher for quite awhile. His name was Galarxemra.
    Like the gorilla whore in the museum they would watch, smile, and laugh at the pandas— as the pandas were to live inside a section of the village unable to escape, and every often they would throw usually cold or soggy bamboo in— to watch you eat. When you defecated or urinated, because they were right next to you they would laugh and joke about you or look disgusted! And they would hit your cage or the glass that separates you over and over, and they would show happier people than you, and talk about selling you in your face! The gorilla whore! The gorilla whore!
    The gorilla whore!
    They put my maffa to sleep— they called it! They called it 'sleep', and I waited and everyone else but me knew they killed her because they didn't want her to be in pain, and she said she would—"

Rendemra tears a bit, so does Calico. Calico wants to say he understands him, but he is being punished by him. Rendemra suddenly pulls Calico's chain harder, and moves him by the skulls and piled bones and deteoriating objects.

Rendemra:
"And so they sent me out to Korea to live life like I should because I was too sad for the museum to keep me any longer in their presence and my cage was then transferred to the python exhibit.

Like you I entered the world of this Park without a clue as to what to do next, and it was quite chaotic as gorilla whores were fighting each other with what one carried on the truck that shot your camel friend, a Gun and knives and their hands.

How do I know about the camel, Calico, you are wondering? I recall you heard the entire meeting last night with the clannars, they are everywhere in Korea acting as surveillance for myself, the Leader of the Pure Kind.

When I had heard about your roughened arrival, I quickly deployed the noblest member of the 12 Clannar Leaders, Gengall to bring you to my presence.
Gengall's father Krengall knew Galarxemra.

During a few nights, Krengall would go on the rooftops of the village huts with other clannars to steal some of the baked fish, and not too far from where the fish filets were cooling, was the cage with the pandas. Galarxemra gave Krengall knowledge of the pure kind's history, and they partnered up to kill the monks— so the kind's could be in peace again. It was quite a revoluntionary move, but was something the pure kind should have, and may have acted on ages ago.

During a walking meditation exercise with the monks being outside, Galarxemra with the other three had taken one key that was placed near the colling racks for fish and figured out how to open the lock.

Krengall who waiting above with wagging tail came with ten other clannars, off the village rooftops onto the scene. Krengall went with Galarxemra to go to the storage hut to take away their weaponry of tools and knives. They, the gorilla whore were harmless though aggressive, and they died.

Years passed as the pandas and tigers lived together. Galarxemra, very wise in his ways made a pact of course to bring peace with the kind from the gorilla whore, right? Get that part Calico? So a pact must be kept. However more outsiders came and began to mistreat the tigers and the pandas and other kind, and imbalances began.

So according to the Gorilla Whores, which appears to be true in our situation, peace is accomplished by Order. As long as the pure kind keep a 'peace' so to speak, order must be retained by them—or their presence.

The Clannars were at first overly polite and loyal to help in keeping their land as much as ours safe. So rules and boundaries were made, and rumors were spread, and our system began. And it is very unfortunate that you are going to leave our organized perfection, permanently, Calico. It is quite a shame.

So how did I make my way to being the leader of the Pure Kind you are puzzling to know? Let us move to the next floor."

{Rendemra pulls Calico's leash harder again and Calico trips over and tears the already destroyed rugs and steps on glassware already broken, and they head back to the stairway.

The sound of flies becomes louder as they ascend up the stairs hearing the creak of each stair. The stairway shockingly becomes completely dark on the way to the top floor as the lever on the second floor suddenly turns off; Rendemra did not switch the lever on all the way. Rendemra switches on his flashlight and slowly ascends again.

Calico feels the extensive heat dwelling in the space as they approach this floor, and the stench is the worst of anything imaginable. Calico vomits on the stairs, and in disgust Rendemra pulls his leash up the stairs as Calico chokes a bit.

They get on the top floor and Calico is sure that he has stepped in something horrible, and the sound of the flies is horribly loud. Rendemra finds the light switch and after two tries gets the lights to slowly turn on.

Unlike the previous floors this floor's ceiling extends to the roof.

All around Calico and Rendemra are severed heads of the Kinds murdered to keep this peace in the Pure Kind Temple. There are thousands of antons on the thousands of muscled or fat combed skulls dripping with maggots and other liquids. Calico has stepped on the inside of an elepant's torn open head and lifts his gut covered paw out.

Even on the high ceiling there are hooks holding heads of the kinds and some are still drizzling. There seems like there is no floor as it is one of the three: covered in a decapitated head, blood, or skull of some sort.}

Rendemra:
"Impressed by your decision I take it.
So how was I elected Leader of the Pure Kind? Let me see if I can find them···Aw yes here they are."

Rendemra moves through the piled heads and skulls getting blood and dried powdery blood on his coat, and pulls out two deteoriating bear—no Pure Kind skulls!, and a somewhat newer elephant skull. Rendemra puts one of the Pure Kind Skulls down with the elephant skull.

Rendemra:
"This is my mentor, Galarxemra. I am glad you two finally met—better late than never (laughs). He became somewhat of a soft bear per se, as I came upon his Pure Kind Temple when I was five. He was nice, just as I was to let an 'outsider' in and all, but he let the clannar kind roam

freely and play with the other pure kind—and from reading and
studying the texts his fumbling of not catching this flaw of his control
would lead him to an end.

Then one day while he was conversing with me on the Bonsai he
asked me personally what I thought of his sharing the pure kind power of
keeping the peace with the clannar kind as they had watched over us for
so many loyal years.

But as the text indicates, the Kind derived from the
Therochordis raping our kind and developing wars and destruction. And
not only was he asking me as a colleague, he was already designing a set
of rules— that have been eagerly destroyed— to balance the power with
the kind.

I felt sick. And that night I snuck out of the Golden doors of the
red wall, and ran in the dark and wanted to kill myself."

Rendemra places Galaxemra's skull down and lifts up the elephant's skull,
and continues the story.

Rendemra:
"I ran out until I got to the edge of one the cliffs and peered
down into the wilderness, a gorilla whore word for a mass of trees with
the free kind or unowned by the gorilla whore. At the the edge of the
cliff, I realized that I didn't have it in me. So I tried something else, I
took a sharp rock and tested it on my leg, and then cut in really deep—
and it really hurt; and I roared for the first time in my life and then I
cried.

An elephant, as humans call them etc., let's just call them
elephants, by the name of—yes you guessed it—Komiak came onto the
scene. Seeing that he was partially blind, and he wanted to help me like
the tiger clannars usually did, I used him to get me back—not knowing he
would memorize the way he came.

Anyhow on the elephant I devised a beautiful plan.

I came back to the palace and snuck in and cleaned the wound
with persimmon juice and tied it with a slice of bamboo, as I still had
the sharp rock with me.

I then came to Galaxemra's quarters while he was asleep and
of course the kind clannars were as well—the ones he was planning to lay
his trust in the next day.

I got up to where he was sleeping, and took the stone and
dismantled his body from his head. He was quiet in the pain of death as
his eyes just stared up at me— still in his loving respect. Oh and you're
looking at me to imagine my reaction in death are you not— by watching
me die in your own paws? Yes you are Calico, yes you are Calico!

And with his silent head, I brought it over and placed it on
Krengall's paws as he was sleeping.

In the morning, Krengall, covered in the blood of Galaxemra
was brought to the Great Labyrinth with his crying grubby, a few years
younger than I at the time, crying and urinating on himself in fear.
Gengall needed a friend. Manipulation was the key.

Krengall was first stabbed in the chest, and with the torches that we used every night—the ones you saw in the meeting last night, 12 tiger clannars including his own grubby each ignited Krengalls' body over and over by throwing each torch onto the mess.

The tigers murdered him out of their loyalty to the pure kind, their loyalty that was transferred to me. "

He will be the death of the pure kind, even if I am not one anymore he will destroy the balance and lead the bond of goodness between the kinds and pure kinds into disaster; the clannars killing themselves, and the kinds already.

Rendemra puts down Komiak's skull and picks up the other Pure Kind's skull.

Rendemra:

"And this one doesn't have too much of a story. This is Lassurria, she was the female pure kind who I performed the acts with forcibly. She gave birth to another female pure kind to my demise, and an insult to me is given repayment immediately—as she was taken care of by the tiger clannar. And once again I was spared for spilling the blood of a pure kind. Oh thank you Juhikyops!

The sunset will return as we will venture back, and your death will be much quicker than Krengall's; that will be certain."

Rendemra turns the switch off and switches the flashlight on and drags Calico {down the stairway to the bottom of the Forbidden Tower. Calico can barely breathe, and swallows for air. On the bottom storage floor, Rendemra turns off the flashlight and places it exactly where he had it before he came and then he quickly looks around to see if anything had changed in the storage area at all.

They quickly leave the area with quick pace— with Calico dragging his paws. Rendemra is over-joyed and is looking forward to someone's death more than the kind who is going to be committed to receiving it.

They take to the trail, and the sun is almost done setting by the time they come back and Calico is weak and hungry.

Rendemra:

"Your time on the last brother planet is almost extinguished, Calico. That is what happens when you trespass against perfection."

Rendemra pulls Calico forward towards the vine covered rusted iron gate, and then the ground starts rumbling. Rendemra and Calico stop completely.

Suddenly an F-16 jet flies over the village dropping bombs whistling into decension. Rendemra is entirely shocked and urinates on himself ,and

then lets go of Calico's leash and one of the links that held the
chain in place becomes unhooked as the leash hits the ground. Calico
ignores the jet, pushes Rendemra to the side with the unhooked leash, and
goes into the village.

Calico:
  "I hope to the Juhykiops that Gammina is safe!"

Rendemra:
  "Where did the gorilla whore come from, they will destroy the
perfection of the pure kind, they will destroy our peace!"

Calico:
  "The Mountain gate⋯The great labyrinth⋯that is where she was
taken."

Calico doesn't realize he's thinking by talking out loud as he is in pain
and is numb from hunger. He darts towards her direction in the village.

Rendemra gets through the gate and sees the aluminum canister fall burst
onto the Palace Temple; he roars. The pure kinds are all running about
wherever they can. Another bomb lands and takes out twelve of the huts
and flames scatter, smoke fills up the entire walled village. Then
Rendemra remembers about Calico.

Rendemra:
  "Pure Kind Find Calico! He has brought the gorilla whore to end
our existence and our peace. Find him and kill him. I was too nice; his
death is needed now!"

The Pure Kind in the Village:
  "KILL CALICO! KILL CALICO!"

Calico's heart is beating.

The entire village is shattering as another fleet of bombs start falling;
in addition smoke is blanketing Calico's way.

A pure kind grubby jumps onto Calico's head and tries to dig into Calico's
face with his weak claws. Calico grabs the Pure Kind grubby with his
mouth and holds onto him and takes him through the smoke. The grubby is
scared and confused.

Calico gets into the Mountain cave which has less smoke in it, yet is
shaking and pieces of rock are falling off inside the tunnel. Several pure
kind roar and growl at Calico ready to attack him, but stop immediately
as they see the worried pure kind in his mouth. Then they stop their
growling and immediately let him pass and follow him. Some of the pure
kind start to mimic his action and take a grubby into their mouths and
then run forward with Calico in the shaking grounds.

Another jet drops a series of bombs ahead of them and the Bonsai Tree ignites in flames. The pure kind are darting out with Calico leading the group, though his legs are bleeding from the cuffs tearing into his skin.

He slides around on the tile a bit with the cuffs restricting his balance and falls over still holding onto the pure kind grubby. Suddenly another pure kind steps out of the stampede and helps Calico get back up, and jets away. Calico does the same. Another jet bombs the Hall of Fountains just as Calico passes the Magnolia Grove.

The Mountain Gate collapses and crushes the still exiting Pure Kind.

Then consecutively by effect, the Bonsai Tree deroots and falls back towards the incoming stampede of pure kind.

Calico went the furthest right from the falling and scattering flaming branches spraying the nightfall with agony. They continue to thunder on passing the sounds of crumbling and roaring, and whimpering cries.

Gammina! Gammina! Live for me please; you are the last thing that I ever want to lose!

Calico runs and bleeds, concerning his last energy on getting to Gammina. Calico runs and hears the sonic jet engines circling the area while destruction is the only control separating Calico from Gammina. From Gammina—who is waiting⋯

Oh Gammina, please wait for me.

Calico runs by the forested fence and sees the Great Labyrinth and feels that great warmth and strength coming back to him with his pain also rising. He eyes barely scope the ropes that were tied around the statue in the distance and runs and runs.

A Jet soars overhead and bombs the Great Labyrinth.

Calico puts the grubby down in shock, and tears leak out on impact.

Pure Kind Grubby:
"Thank you, Calico."

Calico:
"Go! No, No! Why did this, everything I lived for was to be with her! No! No! Gammina—Gammina—Gammina—GAMMINA! No!"

The Pure Kind Grubby runs with the others towards the red walled gate.

Calico's whole world seems to freeze as the Buddha statues break apart and the labyrinth is demolished in the phantom smoke.

Calico with his aching back and limbs sits down and watches each explosion and thinks of all his losses and this one being the greatest of them all.

Calico:
> "Gammina, I love you."

Suddenly a claw comes and slashes crying Calico in the face. Rendemra is in rage.

Rendemra:
> "I should have removed your head in the tower! You made me lose my own grubby!"

Calico:
> "No you never loved her; you love your 'perfection' more!"

Rendemra:
> "How dare you! And you destroyed the purest kingdom."

Calico:
> "It is only pure because the King says so! And the pure kind that you say you love as well are finally leaving their ancestors' ways to live their lives for the better with all kind."

Rendemra:
> "But that is exactly what the gorilla whore want— it is what my mentor wanted, and look what was going to happen with someone who believed in his theory."

Calico:
> "Well at least you still have your crown, why don't you go and help your kind?"

Rendemra:
> "Enough banter, your death shall be the first of many to get things right again."

Calico:
> "Strike at me, I am ready."

Rendemra takes out his sharp rock and places it next to Calico's neck whose head is watching the smoke, and whose body is sitting with his back legs almost akimbo because of the chains.

Rendemra:

"Look at me, just like Galarxemra. I order you to die just like Galarxemra so look at me!"

Calico doesn't turn his head.

Rendemra:
"If I have to repeat myself···No you will not look at me—for that matter here is your grand entrance to Antoine."

Immediately the sharp ends of two of the Buddha torches are jammed into Rendemra's eyes. Rendemra roars.

Gammina:
"He can't look at you if you do not have eyes Rendemrabo! And you know a population is never as bad as the corruption that pretends to represent it."

Calico:
"Guh—GAMMINA! GAMMINA!"

Gammina:
"Calico! Oh my Calico!!!"

Calico:
"Gammina, how? Gammina—I love you!"

Gammina:
"Take it easy, Calico, your eyes are weak and you're bleeding a lot, we need to leave this horrible place. Like I said, oh Calico; like I said they observed how Rendemrabo made me suffer and when I told him about the real ritual they untied me."

Another rally of bombs hits the Bonsai area behind them, and the jets soar over in ricocheting echoes.

Gammina helps Calico get off onto his limping paws, and he barely has energy to kiss her. She gets him over the bridge and through the very light golden doors, and into the natural forest, with the other waiting pure kind, the other panda.}

{The White House: The Diplomatic Room: The First Lady is sitting with one of the First Dogs in her lap in a yellow chair across from her pacing husband, the President, and standing aside in a sparkling gown is the Secretary of Defense, scratching his head.}

The First Lady:
"We have every single animal activist calling us in the world. Can someone please clarify what is going on in Korea? Why are planes

bombing panda habitats and chasing herds of pandas out of their homes?"

The Secretary:
"That is a good question, but to answer another question is- that it's drag queen night in the Pentagon."

The President:
"I know, the Vice President went there in a cabaret outfit."

The First Lady:
"I hate to sound like a poor old hag but we don't have the budget anymore to these type of things- the dollar is already below Hong Kong's currency as well as Tokyo's and we keep having to make up values to stay in our currency race."

The President:
"Race? Dear that state of America is not a one-time race it is continually continuous! What went wrong Ms. Drag Queen of Defense?"

The Secretary:
"Well we gave them orders and all like you indicated to infiltrate those coordinates."

The President:
"And the Army didn't listen-?"

The Secretary:
"Our Army is being used up for other wars; we have no more military men or women available except the coast guards-and who wants them?"

The President:
"Well who in the world flew those planes?"

The Secretary:
"A private army, Mr. President; they were all I could hire."

The President:
"An army I do not have direct authority of!"

The First Lady:
"Oh my, I think I need to let someone out, we can't have three dogs gassing up the same room in the White House can we?"

{The forests of Korea: Calico is barely conscious and all of the other panda are gathering around with Gammina. The panda grubby- the panda cub goes and places his nose on Calico's shoulder-the cub Calico rescued.}

Gammina:
> "I will never leave you Calico, please just stay here for me, for us."

The Cub:
> "Thank you, Calico. I think I feel safer out here."

Calico:
> "(laughs) I am glad someone does."

Gammina licks Calico, and he closes his eyes.

Gammina:
> "Don't you leave us, Calico? Calico."

{Calico wakes up inside a building with white walls and has string along his cuts and an I.V. connected in his arm, and there are two gorilla—two human veterinarians both female looking over him and smiling. Calico attempts to speak and realizes he is back where he is around people who don't understand him.}

One of the Veterinarians:
> "Hey there Mr. Sociable!"

The Other Veterinarian:

"It's a miracle he woke up with all the abuse that these pandas went through. It's a shame poachers still attempt to take on pandas even in our Korean national Parks."

One of the Veterinarians:
> "Does Mr. Sociable remember the helicopter ride at all?"

There's a scratching at the door, and One of the Veterinarians goes and opens it and is handed the leash connected to someone⋯

One of the Veterinarians:
> "Hey Mr. Sociable, guess who is over—ready to see you this morning?"

The Other Veterinarian:
> "And she even fought to get on the same helicopter as you. Oh do we have some lovebirds here."

Gammina is led in and she immediately eyes a chair almost right next to Calico, she whimpers and points with her nose to go there.

One of the Veterinarians:
> "Oh it looks like she wants up."

The Other Veterinarian:
          "Don't we all want up with our men?"

One of the Veterinarians:
          "Okay here you go; let me move the chair closer to Mr.
Sociable."

One of the Veterinarians moves the chair closer to Calico's table and she
gets Gammina onto the chair. One of the Veterinarians steps back and lets
go of the leash in front of Gammina's face to make her feel comfortable.
Gammina looks at the two Veterinarians so to maybe mark her "territory."
Gammina turns back to Calico and jumps onto Calico's table and goes over
laying Calico and swarms him with kisses all over his face.

The Other Verinarian:
          "Whoa, easy there big mama!"

Calico:
          "I am glad to see you too."

Gammina:
          "I can definitely tell."

One of the Veterinarians:
          "Oh my I think Mr. Sociable is ready to mate— how about since
he is done with his I.V., we can let them in the Waiting Room since we're
closed."

The Other Veterinarian:
          "How long do you think it will take for them to—?"

One of the Veterinarians:
          "Probably a couple hours, his build and all and from the
damage he received—and survived, ya 2—3 hours."

Gammina:
          "So the humans seem nicer, though I know not all are like this.
She said this is a refuge just for pandas—how odd. Well there is one
thing my Rendemrabo always told me with the gori—the humans— was
that it was Their Call, Calico. And that we are in their control."

Calico:
          "It doesn't matter who makes the rules and regulates them, our
life is how we view it, and we can make our days greater one day at a
time. So I heard them referencing mating."

One of the Veterinarians:

"It's almost like they are talking, I think she's getting him really aroused."

Gammina:
        "Well it's about time."

The Other Veterinarian opens the Waiting room door and pulls on Gammina's leash. One of the Veterinarians takes out Calico's I.V. and puts a bandage on him. Calico licks the Veterinarian and jumps off of the table to Gammina; the Other Veterinarian closes the door and smiles.

One of the Veterinarians:
        "Hey you want to watch Animal Planet?"

The Other Veterinarian:
        "Definitely, and know what would go great with our viewing pleasure?"

One of the Veterinarians:
        "No telling."

The Other Veterinarian:
        "Some killer cherry ice cream."

KNUCK PZARK!

NOW CONTINUES
WHATEVER YOU WERE LOOKING AT

The Fictional Life of
B. SPEARS

(The Events, quotes and location of the poem are fictional)

I sit at home alone in a pale blue lit camouflage
Of quilted squares matching my pajamas. I lodge
My back against the Leather couch and turn on
MTV, and pass it to see a gospel chorus on a Christian
Network displaying morning mass. Each silent gleam
Of the spoken word, "Alleluia" paves a smooth seam
Holding up harmony and balance.
My head is bright red from the passing day, and I feel in a trance
When watching their rich and old voices fill wooded halls for many.
I get up and hear his faint crying— which I hear every
Night. My security camera outside my windowed hallway
Turns back and forth every minute of the day,
I pass flower vases and fan mail, and a picture of when I was two,
When I didn't know better—of course···too.
I look up to see the Mardi Gras beads,
My MTV VMA awards, a framed letter that reads
About my Charity work, and my former husband.
I walk across the carefully lit hallway, rubbing my finger band—
As maybe I will wear it for one more night,
Or hold it like, wear it like a locket out of sight
Of all of Earth's others. I grace pass my parents who are sleeping
Right next to the room eyeing me to go in there. I start peeping
Into a room like the Oval office with clouds in rotund display
And the fluffy mobile twirling in sifting agility,
And I go over and lift him, and see our eyes and smile, and the night
Shine on his calm face, and I rock back and forth.
I breathe, and I can hear his beat next to mine. His worth
Is more valuable than glamour could achieve, if it does in fact
Achieve a value worth living for. He closes his eyes, danger lacks
Its Infamy once again, and I think peaceful thoughts like Madonna
Told me, and the Rehab Facility, and all those who··· I don't want to
Bring this up, but to focus, and persistence now, is key.

Then it happens, again. As I barely
Leave, as appearing in the middle of a cross—fire
I see in the shadow of the moving leaves in dire
Need of peace, a blinking faster and faster red light
Followed by a punch—in—the—face flash, hammering bright
Sparks to my baby's eyes and his suddenly bursts into tears,
And then there are more like snipers targeting near
My heart. Flash! Flash! Flash! And it doesn't stop—

I can't scream, they said I can't, and I quickly flop
A blanket over my baby, and hide him in my shirt;
Thinking they'll say "Britney Attempts to Hurt
Her Youngest To Torture Husband in the Divorce Process."
Then I run out of his chambers, and lock the door. The glass
Breaks off the windows and the alarm goes off. Her bodyguard
Wakes up and heads outside with a gun. I am hit hard
Again by this. My Mom runs up to me: "Oh my God, Britney, they
Didn't hurt you did they. It's the thousandth time, day,
And probably night this has happened to you. I mean, we
Could try to get you disguised or move to New Guinea?"
I can't reply, because I've tried to before, and go to
The closet and sit down with my baby, and my Mom goes
To wake up my other child. The dogs are up too. It's 3 A.M.

I always remember that talk I had with the doctor to whom
Many great artists of several genres of music and writing
Had met with—some on a daily basis to discuss these issues.
I pulled my baby closer and wiped him with some tissues,
And then remembered what he told me after meeting
Several times to discuss about my fictional life, and the beating
It was on the real one.

    " Britney, there are three types of women
     In the Pop industry. Woman A— the Barbie Girl;
     The girl who is loved by parents— even to the
     Extent that girls want to wear their same clothes,
     Braid their hair the same, be them for Halloween,
     And get all their CDs and paraphernalia. That is
     The Barbie Girl—A. Now we move down the list,
     Woman B—, if you excuse me, is called the "Slut".
     By Slut, she attempts to break from "society", be
     A mean girl, for example P!nk; or even the Dixie
     Chicks— they're speaking out on political issues.
     Or in general the ones some parents just aren't into,
     But their kids are—or vice—versa. And C—, Britney,
     Woman C— is called the "Whore", and by Whore, we're
     Not fully defining someone who sleeps with someone
     Else to achieve success; —the media and any controversy
     Attempts to sneak up and sleep with you for success
     And ruin your life as much as they can for you to sink
     In status. I tell the artists, you never walk
     Into stardom with these letters already existing
     On you. Nor does it just happen.
     Britney, to you it happened in reference to the
     Mickey Mouse Club, the tie—in cast, Justin, Christina,
     And then your parents were strongly supporting when
     You came into popular view. But whoever made your first
     Video, whoever made a porn album, whoever passed out
     International derogatory comments and information

Started it. And to that extent, there is only little you
Can do to get out of it."

I replied, "So I am trapped—trapped like Michael Jackson?"

"Michael Jackson is not a woman."

I said, "So women are just categories? I have to go, I don't
Feel well."

"Being pregnant can do that to women sometimes."

I said," That's exactly it. Goodbye."

I sat in the dimly lit closet, rocking him back and forth, singing
Twinkle, Twinkle Little Star. And at the end of the song came a pinning
Knock on the door which became an aggressive slamming.
I moved back holding my baby looking around attempting
To find a weapon and saw the fire extinguisher—but couldn't:
It's not that I wouldn't:
Here are the logistics:

    I would hit the paparazzi and he'd:
      A) Lie about an injury—its severity
      B) Say I was hurting my child, and he was trying to save him
      C) That I needed to go to more rehab
      D) That I again was losing my (Barbie) role model—ness
      E) That the Divorce caused me to go out of hand
      F) That I was an aggressive (Slut)—Bitch
      G) That I had stopped taking the medication
      H) Easily they'll just make up the medication I am taking
      I) That my parents were trying to take my child away
      J) That I am not the real mother
      K) That I am at such a level by "society" that no matter what
         I do, I can' help the situation.
      L) Besides I most certainly am going to be in the tabloids
         and TV for harming my child tonight, and any aggression I
         show will add onto that public intolerance.

He bangs the door again, I let go of the extinguisher,
And kiss my baby again. Then more footsteps, I hear
My bodyguard moving him away and talking to the
Arriving police. He opens the door, and asks me if the
Baby is alright, and then if I was okay.

    And the thought, the main frame thought
    Came back to me:
      Life is not Fair.
         No, that IS a comment from a Man

Of Men, who have gotten it forcibly stuck
In so many heads of women, that we have
To tell our daughters and sons that the
Constitution, that laws and judgment—
True as it may be is not fair— and that
To be a woman in this world you have to
Suffer miserably, endlessly for a mistake
Or a missed attempt, at the result that
People shouldn't care how we feel, that
We're Category Women.
         And I have to tell my fans, as other
Artists, Female and Male artists have to that
You—Fans can be a singer if you have endless
    Determination and Persistency—
So you can learn for yourself that the lie is true,
    That we have to lie— no, now you do need
    Determination and Persistency—
    But look these are different times;
But I was supported the whole way from the Industry,
And Act One, to Show one, To Set B, to Saturday Night Live.
And Mothers and Fathers see that, so children start earlier.
And it's hard to explain. At one point it all
    Makes sense, and the next minute
    Nothing at all— but it's just disaster.
And one way could be the same as the other,
Or it could just be a temporary stardom and end.

Yes, I know, representatives from the media are gathered
At the front door—waiting more politely—illegally lathered
In negative persistence waiting for me to quote
On the new coverage by the Category—C antidote.

    I could:
    A) Go and say anything— be mis—translated by the media
    B) Go and say anything— and be wrong anyhow
    C) Don't Go – And their story is 100% true

My children need to sleep, as does my family, as do I.
My bodyguard goes back and gets rid of them. Why
It's like that, I··· Just won't go there anymore.
In 10 minutes, at 8 A.M., I see all the news channels score
In E.S.P. as they read my big headline title,
And I hold his tired eyes closer in this vital
Transition that will again last another month or longer.
And yes again, I have to just keep wandering stronger,
As he and I will be shot by pedophiles and stalkers
Passed around from web page to e—mail, church letters
That depict me as a Whore, oh you mean Category C?
No, the real one. And that's what I'll be.

I have tried swearing in public, like a man,
Defended myself in public, like a man,
And I am slapped across the face
By the man who says that
Life is not Fair—
You Women:
Category A
Category B
Category C

Child Support companies, —even the Planned Parenthood
Have hammered my telephones; even my cell phone. Judging my good—
Ness. And who are they to judge. Life is not fair.
What if my kid goes to Harvard? Will I be treated fair
Then? What does it take? Are women at a point where
We've had our last stand and we're just their
Categories— This society's, both at the judgment
Of Men and Women who hand the flyers on the rudiment:
Life is Not Fair— to every one, and we all suck our thumbs at
This point?

Watch me speak out—and comedians will not judge me
By my voice or working skills— like men judge men,
They will judge me by my breasts, my weight,
My age, my make—up, and then compare me to
Other celebrities that are going through "issues".

If a woman voices her opinion should she be a comparison
To Man?
Or a comparison as man itself is for the sake of humanity?

—   — — — — — — — — —

ON POKA POKA'S ISLAND   From *Pulchritude for the Mind*

She was an attractive catch of the day,
Forbidden from my family, we were cast—a—ways.
On an island floating in the sea,
Me and my dear Poka—we were very ha—a—ppy.

Poka Poka you are my love,
Poka Poka you are like a dove,
Flying through the deep blue forests, and kelp,
I will be there whenever you need help.

She is someone who I will always admire,
Our longing for each other burns like fire.
But fire burns, and she'd be barbequed,
Poka Poka let's not start a feud.

Poka Poka you are my love,
Poka Poka you are like a dove,
Flying through the deep blue forests, and kelp,
I will be there whenever you need help.

We are like two fish in a bowl,
Without the other we are not whole.
But unfortunately, I have feet and you have fins,
Poka Poka our marriage would contain sins.

Poka Poka you are my love,
Poka Poka you are like a dove,
Flying through the deep blue forests, and kelp,
I will be there whenever you need help.

NEPTUNE   From *Pulchritude for the Mind*

On Neptune we ride on the Celetoar seavels
That glide on the icy jelly waves
With the pink and speckled sky—
And the whirling triangle wheels.
We are sparkling nude, for our clothes vanished
When we submerged into the atmosphere.
Our skin became scales reflecting golds
From the distant sun, and the star shining nearby.
We won't be able to leave Neptune,
Nor will anyone who has gone through.
But we can see the Uiy Binos,
A Massive screen that lies atop the Gianamatran—
The Mountain that lies alone—very passive
With the relaxing waves.
We live underwater as the water is immersed in breathable air—
It is fluent, it is clean.
In fact there are thousands of us,
Humans who became margiifin as we call ourselves.

Though some of us haven't,
An old lady with gray hair became a
Gelosquat, a large jelly star with venomous hooks
On all her star points.
Others have turned into plants slowly,
And their roots lie atop the water—green and pink.

Our blood is orange, and our lips blue.
When we bleed it comes out in square to prism drops.
My age is eight-hundred,
And it seems life hasn't been changed too much here,
Until Deibotha stood up and touched the layer of
The Neptune Atmosphere, atop the seavel-then
Her scales turned back into skin, and burned.
She sat down on the ship and wept.

I came up and she could only think of her parents.
And then I kissed her, and she turned to stone,
And others walked away deeper into the seas of
Neptune.

Chapter Four
THE TRAIL OF THE AGES

時代

And as life went from war to war, crime to trial, marriage to
divorce, son to father, daughter to teacher, and there was no
end, I found myself **FADING FROM THE HEAT**

(From Pulchritude···Mind)

"I quietly closed my eyes,
As I could hear the showers of the night,
She held my hand, and I remembered,
All the days, as time flies.

My hands lost pressure,
She told me that her love would always be there,
Lasting forever,
The eternal treasure.

I couldn't talk, my breath had left me,
My mouth was hollow and drying out.
My eyes were closing.
Now she felt she had to let me be.

Her voice was silent.
I think I felt the tears, heard her cry,
My limbs and body became a statue.
It was not evil or violent.

If I was on the outside, I would cry too,
Just like the rain that I had seen in my life.
Just like the days when my family before left,
Forty years after my spouse and I were to woo.

There's my daughter right next to me.
This is the moment that I embark Earth.
This is the end of my life, my story.
All that is to be.

Goodbye, if you can still listen. Good morning,
If you can listen and make a better life for the next
Generations to come. "

SMOKE OF THE PROSTITUE,
ART OF THE GEISHA   from *Pulchritude for the Mind*

Walking down the alley in blue and crimson leather,
Strutting her shaven legs in her silver and sharp high–heels;

Gliding her body as balanced as a swan's feather,
Moving slowly and agile with every stroke of her delicate feet.

Wavy blond hair and energetic eyes that wink–
When a customer is in range–transitions to a flirt;

Her slippers are silent and pink,
Each step towards you is like a step of a winged fantasy encounter.

Her leather jacket is undone revealing her crevice
Bathed in the finest perfume bought from a pharmacy;

Her robe is a beautiful device,
Soft, and woven with designs of flora.

She trickles her hand down your back,
And breathes of cigarettes and used ashes;

Her white powdered face symbolizes she has nothing to lack,
Her powdered pureness does not dissolve by playful kiss or massage.

She takes you back to her layer with red neon lights,
She shows you her torn up bed with springs sticking through the sides;

She opens her paper doors, with a window reflecting summer nights,
Her bed of black and white, displays the characters: *innocence; guilt*.

She does her job to earn her commission,
Though at the she puts you at gunpoint to ask for everything else;

She acts like the waitress and begins to take the dish in–
To the kitchen, while taking the leftover greens.

– – – – – –

THE PIANO'S LAST PLAY   From *Pulchritude for the Mind*

I sat down and hit C,
The sun rose and the years began.
I sat and saw my childhood;
The years before becoming a man.

I followed the chords, and the beat spread over.
My teacher told me to be quieter and listen.
I smiled and kept playing,
The sunlight was glistening through the stained glass windows.

I saw my friends playing in the park;
I, on the swings, they on the tennis court.
Then I got off to meet them;
We played all day till it got dark.

Each day it was original and fun;
Sometimes we played undercover agents
With neon laser guns.
It was good fitness, we were always on the run.

My hands were running,
And playing quick threads of harmonies,
Then to the minor, then up a chord.
There she was shunning

Me to get away—boys are gross!
No, girls are gross and that's settled to infinite!
—Infinite plus one!
Counting unlimitedly what we thought was the most.

The wind on the summer days
Were quiet and easy;
The sun how it would heat up,
Then I'd move, and the sun stayed.

She and I played through the field of keys,
As we were happy, teasing and cheerful.
The tune was high pitched and merry,
And life seemed but a breeze.

Then came the day I graduated high school;
I looked back in time again
Playing the piano in the glittering sunlight.
I imagined the sun streaming into a moonlit pool.

In that pool, I had to say goodbye.
She smiled a bit anxiously;
I kissed her, and she kissed me—

And she began to cry.

That was the silent part of my sweet melody.
But lo and behold, my future lay before me.
I got in the car and she waved and smiled—
But she cried as I drove away, like a felony—

Who stole gold and didn't repay it.
Even I cried a bit, but I guess that's life.
I began to work and realized who I was—
A dentist, the perfect fit.

I love to see people smile.
As the keys glided both ways
Revealing the white shimmering rays
That could never lead a man into denial.

I graduated and the war hit.
I was drafted and the tune went out of order
Into the bleeding jungles of war—
Considered by naby to be the forgotten shit.

I was shot, and wounded on my left leg.
Fortunately it was nothing—
And the battle continued on
And the war left the scent of a rotten egg

That oozed with blood,
And kept blobbing out;
Never—ending, and thud—thud
Was covered in volcanic hot mut.

I got home, finally, my friends of the war were all killed.
My aunts and uncles screamed at me,
And rocks were thrown my way.
I was treated with scorn, like the weak and ill.

But my family loved me,
And there was a piano to play.
So I got on the bench,
And moved my fingers vibrantly

Over the moonlit waters
Where I saw her once,
And once again.
She was there—silent, we were playing like river otters.

I waved and she waved back,
And vanished into thin air.
I splashed the water with my bare feet.

I wanted her back, and began to pack.

Again, but this time looking for her,
I traveled all across the state,
Through all weather.
I knew I could find her for sure.

The waves changed under the moonlit sky
As I parked the car and watched the waves.
And how each key moved at a sweeping melody.
I held down the pedal—holding the moment to let it fly.

Then it came down like a parachute open
Free and gallantly moving
Down onto the Earth.
Then I was roped in

By some force to look behind.
She smiled and so did I.
And I kept walking towards her,
Kept walking and wanted to call her mine.

She vanished as the sun came up freely
In the nick of time.
I got into the car and drove home,
Not gleely, but upset.

I began to smoke,
Then stop.
Then drink.
One night with friends, I choked—

I cried, I missed her—the girl over the moonlit pool.
I pulled the pedal down again;
And here her boots came to mine,
I felt like a fool

Because it wasn't her!
And I was drunk again,
I cried, and went home
All alone with the piano
And I played for her till I began to wonder.

And then one night the doorbell rang
And I jumped to joy,
There she was, Girl and boy.
She wore artistic clothing, and on that note she sang

With a twinkling charisma that played with keys
Trotting to the sky.

She took her own journey while I had taken mine.
The pitch came back, very high.

We danced all night till the morning came,
And I told her my story,
She—hers.
Ha, I wasn't drunk or high, pretty tame.

I was in love again and so was she,
And I brought her to the pool.
We sat under the pale moonlight
And swam in an uncharted melody.

We married and the parents passed.
I sit here playing the piano again,
Time keeps on moving,
This time it is even more fast.

I watch the seeds plant into the soil,
And life come anew,
I watch the trees fall under,
And the cities and oil

Rise up into the sky.
And I end a C chord
Long and still lasting,
As it is the last time I play it today;
As the days move on,
And high into the zeniths of our future,
And what tomorrow brings.

Chapter Five
THE TRAIL OF LOSS

WHY WOULD ANYONE WANT TO SEE THIS?
WHO CARES⋯

THE ONES IN THE 11th   From *Pulchritude for the Mind*

I was at work the day the World fell down
Tapping my pen, my computer froze,
And my anger came down in naïve rage.
But as my silent temper gained, a sound arose
From the blue and white gossamer draping over the Earth,
Constructed of the screams of terror,
Scaring Families, children, and those of the hearth.
Phones began to ring, the power then went out.
People begun to run.
I really had no idea what the Hell was this about;
I panicked, I stumbled back from my chair, and knocked
Over my coffee mug which shattered instantly on the floor,
Then I ran with the rest towards the office exit door,
And the building rocked a bit to the side.
I, with many fell to the floor, eyes closed.
My eyes opened wide,
As smoke was invited in.

Tom fell on the floor, and so did I, I thought this is it,
And it surely was, blinded in the darkness
Not knowing what to do, and my baby was in a fit.
I had cuffed her mouth from the waterfall of fuming smoke
That swam into each room.
My baby screamed and screamed, and screamed.
I couldn't calm her down, and we began to zoom
Downstairs, just sixty more flights.
Then the door of the fifty—ninth floor hit my baby head on,
And she cried no more.

I looked back at Cynthia with her bleeding child.
Now it is the Apocalypse, I thought
And I broke through the frantic crowd.
I quickly caught her and her dying infant towards me;
She was screaming like her child was, and the
Blood drenched her purple blouse, even I was crying—
Lost and confused; No love for each of us, just trying to be set free.
By the fortieth floor Cynthia's baby wasn't breathing
And she held her child closer to her while moaning and crying down
The endless flights.

I saw the janitor protecting my wife, the secretary.
I saw Tom with coffee spilled on his shirt leaving the exit door.
I saw them all walk through the door into the light.
And I never made it to Pittsburgh, and I just watched as the people
Jumped
And fell by our windows.
I looked down and I was trapped at the airport, watching my wife
Cynthia,

And my son Pat covered in blood in her hands,
And I dropped down and cried.
Televisions continued playing more footage and
People could feel it as we all fell down and the world just sank
Away.

PINE NEEDLES

My whole world sits above the half lit mountain lid.
My life is but an umbilical cord connecting
To these great brimmed trees, and did
I weep before I opened my eyes? Expecting
To be groomed by your side—winding bid
To be excavated with your eyes reflecting,
In gold, we both dug out, and hid?
No, I began to mill the snow into a globe exacting
Our distances apart. Like a compass sacred
Between our hearts, as Donne would be contrasting
The great orb of the sky from that dome below your naked
Eye dripping and becoming a snowflake turning
Whether, either, which way or that. But I did
Recall the figure—eight, the yellow—white scarf, skating
Over an enchanted life I could not see below the thick veil amid
The beating of me to the end of the lake, and back. Dancing,
When all we had were off—tones and hums. How retched
Can this be? These needles haunting me, demanding
I go seasons back to when time was stilled.
But where we played are just fallen cones. So I am asking
You to reopen your lid,
Once more, and let me begin my climbing
Up to you, as if the seasons didn't end, and the fireplace remained
Momentous like those blades upon the untouched lake, and we'll make it,
Till the stars become snowflakes, and my shaking⋯
It's just a white—winged chill. As I have placed your scarf tied
In the laces of your two 7's. I am on that bench sitting
Just like the days when you came to my eyes and the first snowflake slid
Down our lips and landed on your heart. So in waiting,
I'll skate and underneath that blue glass veil, I'm sure you'll have joined
Me, as I'll be halfway to the end and it will start snowing all over again.

— — — — — — — — — — — — —

BLUE LIPS   from *Pulchritude for the Mind*

We walked to the park again & again,
Watching the days turn to summer and fall again.

Saw the Sun up's and downs,
You seemed like you were always around.

We would eat on Friday nights
And party till the fading lights.

And would drink and palette the wine,
I was in awe to call you mine.

The one summer passed June,
Your eyes began to lose its glimmer under the nail—bit moon.

Your heart did not beat of pure gracious love,
For I wanted to tell you, that you were astonishingly above—

Then we turned and kissed. Your red passionate beautiful lips—
Embraced; My hands on your hips.

But the air trembling around us was cold and dry—
Though it was a magnolia summer, and I did not know why.

I began to realize over time,
That the greatest honor in souls' love had lost its beat, its rhyme.

Then one Friday night, when we were to go out,
I waited till it was again cold about.

I saw you in the distance with not crimson, but vein blue lips;
I hand pondered whether it was tangible to get a grip

On the reality which I now have to face.
My Love walked right passed me without changing her pace,

As her hand sifted right through mine,
And I knew our love had died
Eternally.

—   — — — — —

WATCHING AND WAITING   From *Pulchritude for the Mind*

He was sitting in his bold chair
Remembering the fields in May;
All the wild flora and yellow daffodils
Waving by the by.
He remembered when he and his brother
Would roll down those hills and into the more mushy grass.

The sun, the birds, the squirrels would all be so beautiful,
But the times would pass.

The rain would fall towards winter,
Silent and moist— The sensation of dry earth.

On Halloween he was so joyous to see
The bags fill up with sugary delights
Of rich, vibrant and caloric candies.
He and his brother and friends would walk to each door.
But if they didn't get their bags' worth—
Well this meant war.

They threw eggs at the doors and even at one fancy red car.

He refused to throw the eggs though; he was too scared.

In the wintertime, they would celebrate with the whole family.
But that one wintertime, when he was twelve
Sunk at the bottom of his heart.
His brother died of leukemia.
Then a year later, his mother passed away from understated stress;
His father didn't want to deal with or children for that matter.

So at eighteen he left the house and started life from there.
He brought up his bags on the bus and waved to hid decaying
Lonely Home.

The first time he cried since his mother died was on the bust to
The Unknown.

He met a girl, just two years older than him who offered him a job.

To work at her father's place on a farm not long from her home.
He accepted the deed gratefully and went to work as soon as he arrived.

Morning, he swallowed in tears, would come soon he thought, he asked God
"Why?"

One night he was alone plowing the fields.
There was the invitational girl who gave him the position.
She was dispersing words to another guy about the stars—
Watching us from the sky.
As the guy got to her side, he gave her a drink, then another,
And another.
He asked her about her diamond ring, and how much money she
Had in her purse.
She giggled a little, thinking he wasn't serious.
He told her to shut up and began to swear.
She giggled some more and he killed her in one shot.

He dropped the gun and took
     Her ring and her $900.00 from her nested purse, and flew.

He—he then nervously dropped the plow, and ran to the barn—
Where he had heard the shot—
So did his boss, her father—ran from his lot and into the barn—
After He did.
The farmer gave him a shout and a cry all at once,
Then punched him causing him to bleed like cracked eggs,
"You nigger, you deserve to go to Hell!"
He realized what the farmer thought and told him the truth.
                                        The truth.

The crowd settled in front of him, on his rusty chair as
     Morning came round.

His boss sat in that crowd, and smiled as the man pulled the switch.

He didn't have to wait anymore.

THE LOSS   from *Reflections of the Dream Panorama*

I sit before a table, wounded from my hardships.
No one is listening.
And I don't want them to, but I try—
And the dark is glistening overhead.

The rain pours over our heads;
The ceiling begins to leak, and the tears run.
I look at each chair tucked under the sturdy structure,
The narrow beak continues to fester the injured.

I reach over to make believe it's all there···
The children smile back.
My wife behind me cooks, because she is off early.
Then she mentioned that the boys had to pack, and the timer went off.

"Now boys remember not to give your mom trouble."
I smiled, they laughed. We ate
With the television on with the sun beaming
Not too late in the day, but nearing the time to watch it descend.

Thunder struck, and my head, my body, my love started shaking.
"Bye honey, say hi to your mom for me." I told her.
"Hey, by law she's yours as well."
"Make sure to keep the boys busy, see you Monday."

"Hey no hugs and kisses, Prince Charming?"
"—Hey honey, the phone is ringing."
"Fine. Boys are you almost ready?"
While she was cooking, she was singing: " You're too Good to be True."

"Just one moment dear···okay···okay···On Saturday···okay···okay···bye."
"Who was that?"
"Work—uh, a meeting on Saturday, probably playing Russian Roulette."
"Dear, stop that, it's not funny. C'mon boys we have to go now."

It was funny, but never really was.
Then we kissed but more of a colleague to a colleague equation—
That had and will continue to last,
And dig through the fallen days, to give me something to hold on to.

On Saturday, the misty morning drew.
The executive smiled, but was perspiring as I am now.
The board was dead silent, as was I.
The foul stench snaked into the cobwebbed suffocation of the moment.

The pen dropped the last minute he spoke.
The company had to transplant itself to Thailand,
And we were all left, left.

And each of separated on what we earned, and were given.

I got to the bar and took a sip from a cold Miller,
Then another and another.
I think I remember the cell phone ringing over and over.
—Just thinking it was my brother—in my drunken state.

I walked into our bedroom, and fell asleep.
I woke up almost immediately at 4 in the dark
Scorched in sweat and jaw pounding echoes,
A burning headache, stark naked from the reality.

The rain felt like hail, my sweat, blood,
Itching and crawling down each limb,
Running off of every pumping vein,
Sailing to be a puddle in solitude's mirror.

I saw the garbage and the mess I knocked over around the house.
I heard the empty signal beeping on the open phone.
Picking it up···Beep···Beep···Beep
I began to really feel that I was alone.

Something drew on me—that my wife, the kids—
They tried to contact me, and I hid away.
I took a shower and looked back on the bed
At where she would have slept yesterday.

Days from that yesterday still linger my today.
But I answer the door that rings in my tired head.
They—no the woman, the police woman was at my door—
With the voice of a lead bullet—it tore through my limbs.

My upper built limbs once in bold ease
Began to feel nimble and crooked.
I fell back. I lost all my balance and screamed in a dark seizure.
An attack of broken darkness···

     Another car was believed to have been driven by a drunk male, who
tore head on to your [my] wife's truck, and her vehicle was thrown off an
interstate bridge [off as the sun descended].

Descended while she cooked and sang.

I apprehended and did nothing.

Now the rain patters against the glass,
And those faces on the chairs vanish.

The other car was my car.

Chapter Six
THE TRAIL OF DECLINE

LIKE I SAID WHO WANTS TO GO THROUGH THAT—
NOW LOOK WHAT YOU'VE DONE!

OPTIMUM VIEW IN A U.S. AGRESSOR'S MINOR

Turning like an acrylic acetone rock churning
Like locomotive clinks as the boiling coal burning—
Burning, burning my eucalyptus scented soulful symphony
Breathing through my three—pronged electric eye sockets' epiphany
Of distilled remorse's delighted needle—tipped—tongued urethra
Spilling miscellaneous vulgarity into cement fermented plethora.

Aching, taking a long scalped bone framed in scales of scarlet,
Sipping squares of courted blood and crimson reigned in starlit
Acrimony. A red plot—sanded spot drenched mucus white sac
Crushes itself against a dripping sponge periwinkle Pontiac
Soccer mother's wobbly questionable hands as she hands out
Orange slices— and only slice is eaten into congealed mouthed clout.

It is hath how, hath all, hath how & why thus all in time beguneth/decayed.
Taken plow in her soiled remedies, thirsted spillage quenched in oblique fade,
Across a bridge built and bartered between the allied, all lied, ink foraged.
And architecture constructed rudiments and pediments, in heart's soul voyaged.
Corpse quality gutters, splinter—thin diamond rings in tombs of living cadavers
Without names, only children who will never know, never know their mothers or fathers.

These brittle boned infants will wander into woods unknown, sacrificing their own weak,
Separating their meek drowning voices, piercing nerves with roots by medicine they seek
And cure with. Getting lost and alone with and hide themselves urinating at a bus stop;
They will be raped by those who know how and don't have to explain or develop
To them an answer—and close their shutters and watch social feet melt carcasses and new
Meadows, and their ancestors' methods that laid to them but forged to them by hew.

And come forth on high the edifices, the striking hunger forces united in sperm and stone,
A hundred names they call it, a thousand words they call it, to us it's understood alone.
It's published, and only the trees hold our history—both the ashes, and papyrus, twigs
And leaves with holes and deathly shriveling. A robin's song, a broken branch's figs
Scatter and die scathed with juices mixed with the pus and wax of our ears;
And the oceans become charted, the lightning grates and grips our scalloped fears.

We are diseased they say, and they will die first, and we will have died next or die
Already. Clothes and carriages will be nailed and burned over and over in the sky
Our bodies are covered by. We will reach out and touch nothing but blackness;
Some will realize its love and smile, some will follow it and feel the tactless
Echoes and become so tangled and indifferent that there will be no day or night
Thrusting their raised up, brought up cartographic destinies off into nature's light.

Losing breath fogged against a one—way window the public cannot see their own mayor
Masturbating in sweat and sweet perfumed Palmolive fresh marble floors in care;
And the other hand open, then fisted, or formed to represent peace and everyone will nod,
Some will follow, and he'll smile while he will finish up and say he just found God.

Banners, fireworks, parades and bodyworks, soap dreams, bubblees and naked broads
Will perform our methods in cyber—technical terminology, our fatted fucked wads—

Will use us in new efforts, as the old will just finish dying out at that point of vertex.
Stuttering for air in a murmuring crowd of billions, a bone—covered child out of context
Is naked covered in scars and people are offended and keep walking later caring, people

Not ready to touch "her" and become diseased, others will touch "him" in hubris' steeple.
Then people will touch them beyond their dreams and sacrifice everything to be forgotten

Like a hundred feathers nested once, forever slept on, and then floating in
sewage, rotten.

And the greatest crafted structure will be created out of all of this of every hallow,
Hollow and woeful tear supposedly brought about in its production. A swallow
Will be heard by an old widow who sighs, and hobbles first to her pew and kneels.
Then the President will declare it real and defecate in its holy waters, do what he feels.
The people have little choice but to dip their hands in it and make the cross
On their forehead. An infant grabs too much and has to put some back. Her loss

Is that she will go to war in the future, and her wedding and burial will be in here.
And on the frontline, she will watch others die, and herself in fear
Because the mind dies last as the body shuts down and sleep does not exist; no more.
But back at home the World is broken and dams are damned and break in score
Of rhapsody, flooding the Earth in its filth true love and leadership. It's life.
A treading mother with only her only infant swimming to the edifice puts her strife

Into placing her child on the right hand of Oswaldo's Christ open to the world
To which it's man—made existence relates it to. And the floods have hurled
Her body down a thousand stories curtailed of ever seeing her child for love.
The waves die down, and the Statue looks down to the dead many from above
And closes its fists crushing the infant. Like the spreading of flowing red silk
The infant's last runs down the cement fermented curves, the last of his ilk.

The believers come to the statue and either perceive it as miraculous as it is evident
Of their sin, or that their faith has betrayed them and they feel lost and alone to invent
A different set of rules that maybe they should believe, and all suffers. The skeptics
Come and view it as art like the Virtuvian Man and gasp in aura and eclectic
Purposes that brings believers again and non—believers, and those who forget it.
Hath it man that forgot it? Hath it in blood lost, lust or wit

That truth can be cemented firm? Hath truth meaning for its existence be? Or
Rather life a lie allied to bridge a distant dream among shadows on sunlit floor
And flanked rooftops? And in gazing towards a compass if all points end the same
Or meet up in the end one way or another, then why begin or end if to become lame
Settled again among the dust? So then the man in accustomed comfort began to depart
From her pollinated cleansed bosom saying he found God, but she was described like art.

———————

STREAM BY THE CHINA SEA

Sit beneath the malicious waters
Drown under the vicious waves,
Let your eyes become the ripples
Let your arms become the claves.

Take apart your limbs and separate
The bitter tastes, fumes, and open,
The water's liver and slide in.
And remove each stone, then open.

Take the stream and untie it apart,
Let your mind tremble, let it tweak.

Grab a rodent and toss it in, and
Watch the starlit sky, but bleak.

Turn that rodent into a rhododendron,
Let the petals disperse into the bath.
Scoop out the urethane scathe
And take the stars and ignite wrath.

Turn Red from Gold, turn White from Gray.
Ignite Black into Blue, and ignite Yellow into Green.
Handle the oracle bones, but not their decay.
Take a character, turn it, but not too green.

Take your drowned child from the river,
Get your knife, and feed it too.
Give her your limbs, your eyes, and let
Your arms lift her up into the new blue.
——————————

TRANSLATION BY SYRINGE

From *Reflections of the Dream Panorama*

A collection of broken needles wait on the bathroom sink,
My eyes in purple and crimson rain. My wounded eye begins to wink.
I slit my wrist and out pours a rainbow waterfall,
Giggle, I can't hold it in, I can't stay sane at all.
Catch my breath, time holds still, I take a leap.
I fall into my rich lathered skin, cells piled in a heap.
Each bone, browned like rich cinnamon,
My life again turns to hell, I am red—handed in sin.
Saliva, yellow and bits of red, infected by those heart—shaped pills,
That I call love, and all I can, and all it fills
Is my empty stomach, and then lifts up in vomit.
Then it is morning, and my lost state vanishes in a comet.
  I have no reason, now that you're not with me.
  Lonely eyes need others so they themselves can see.

Chapter Seven
THE TRAIL OF WAR

NOT RECOMMENDED FOR THOSE NOT OLD ENOUGH TO
ENLIST. NOT RECOMMENDED FOR THOSE WHO ARE
GOING TO ENLIST. AND FOR EVERYONE ELSE
APPARENTLY IT IS A-OKAY.

MATTER OF WAR   from *Reflections of the Dream Panorama*

Sweet naïve children in the garden,
Gathering their rosebuds as they may.
Butterflies on their eyes catch the next rush of breeze.
The muddy soil, under the seeds hardens.

Cypress, freshly clipped. No fences.
A friendly batch of kittens run through the fields.
The flowers sprinkle pollen in their cotton fur.
The children innocent playing, no defenses.

The children giggle as the furry nose pops out from the field.
They make mewing noises at the friendly kittens.
These kittens are quiet. Grandmother is down in the kitchen with tea.
Lanterns outside gather fireflies. They yield.

Wings from Inventors fly overhead. The clouds clear away.
Sip. Grandmother is listening to the breeze.
It goes over the pond and up the pebbled paths.
Its harmony rushes through making the bamboo sway.

The children were laughing bright.
Then the ground tumbled, dust flew up.
Light raced across the town, disappearing into darkness.
The children's soft hands in their pockets disappeared into the white.

Grandmother vanished while drinking tea.
The kittens' bones melted away. The breeze sank in.
The laughing and smiles on tubby cute skin, turned to
Stretched muscle and bone, then ash. Not to be.

The flowers disintegrated. Poof!
The land, the pond disappeared.
The breeze then was free, and danced alone,
Crying as life once was, was now aloof.

————————————————

COLLAPSED ASTERION

MISSION REPORT: CONFIDENTIAL

The area was a tunnel, with green
And gold weavings painted
All around the mouthed block and on
Its black marble surface untouched.
Twirling. Mind swirling, enigmatic brushed.

Then on my hands I eyed
Rich quaint speckled splatters
Like the dried—up, raisin'd remains
Of a devoured—strawberry.
Syrup, Dripping off the lone balcony—where she once stood.

Autumn leaves hurried down
From the ceiling. The hinged
Flooring had a "U" shape to it;
The tiles were cemented round,
Mosaics like herpes, chained and unbound.

They were of ellipses and
Grew gray stained gross torment.
Beautiful crimson form extrapolated
And then I looked at my polished shoes.

Don't you remember what happened then?
All is not at End. All is not at End.
     —

       —

Someone dropped a sparkling
Bomb down the stairs and it bounced
And bounced and it broiled him.

I loved you, he thought. He
Couldn't breathe as those
Gases choked and punctured
His spine; [I'm not fine, I'm not fine] Acid leaked from his face.

His mule nose, his grapefruit chin
Began to turn to soggy.
Sky lashed out and beat his "naïve" civilian woman.
There was dark laughing, the sun never ascended, it seemed.

Her body, a civilian's body became weaker and just like
The split of chicken muscle, cooked white
From the bone, her leg burst open.
It revealed her white bone going up in flames alone.

I could feel them settled
In my hand. I licked my
Chops and tore them with
Hot sauce. "Make sure not to waste the food."

I looked at a rose colored mosaic
And thought it was an old
Irish woman, looking at me,
Blooming her grin. Petrified,

I ran and fell among the
Sharp crying bricks. But
Instead of cement between
Each brick, there were blue

And red veins, pumping blood.

A stray cat came by my view
And opened my jaw—no it
Was a suicide bomber. Get out of
There, I screamed. Can't

Take it. That fatty sweating
 Flesh, that hard yet soft
 Skull, those brittle fingernails
Settling on our palate.

I felt on my hair someone
Brushing it, no—my hair was being
Sliced out by a dark black skeleton
Using a saw to play my life like a violin.

I turned towards it, and it then became
Turbulent flames and I couldn't hold on.
 I lost my balance, and fell on the vein
Tapered— bricks. The veins rose up and tried to strangle

 Me. But I had had it, the old woman
 In the broken mosaic giggled, the sky started blinking,
 On, off: on, off. Someone closed a jeep door.
 Someone falls on the tundra.

   I had to hold onto a passing jeep
   And we had to roll over those living
   Vein roots that were moving and
   Pumping. I then received a rifle and shot it.

 The blood sprayed.

 Speckles and polka—dots swished
 Around like the mixing of a rusty keg.
 The handles of the doors came off and more
 Veins came out. I ran

 Downhill. I opened a tent flap.
 Few, I thought, there were people in
 Here. I heard the rustling of tin plates
 And conversing of fellow men; I smiled.

I secured the flap behind me and peeked. It's a cafeteria.
The lanterns were on, and there were people
At all the tables with warm-scented
Recipes on their plates. But the people

Weren't moving. There was noise, but
No one was eating; there were scents
But nothing was turned on. It was cold, odd.
Their hands were all handcuffed behind their backs.

I screamed for a reply
But they didn't react; they didn't
Even twitch. I wondered where the
Sensations were coming. I see a

Walkie-talkie

Near the flap I entered. I went to
The vinyl flap I had peeled, and I
Saw the volume had been turned up high. I held the
Reply button down but instead it was mute. Then I saw where

The aroma departed from. There sat
A fan blowing dried ration bags in the air.
I went over and turned that off.

It was sanity returning to me, almost ephemeral.

All those mannequin forms had
All shifted their stiff heads and turned facing me—very glad.
They were all smiling. I said hi,
But they were stuck in this position—why?

Staring at me—dead-on. I wanted to run
But I backed up and knocked something undone
By Movement. A rusted tin bowl. Thus tortured more
On the circular green matted floor..

Then came out surgical tools, and torture devices.
And it happened again in turbulent blind decay.

I Heard a police siren, and fiddles
Suddenly playing. In the rusted
Paraphernalia were dried up fingers and bodily items.

The scalpels were still warm from just being used. The bowl
Didn't break, I just thought it did, like my partner.
He was a top shooter, first in his league
His arms broke. I looked back at the mannequin prisoners

All their staring heads never actually existed,
    Leaving only their passive souls.

  Then I
     Tried to rethink what I had seen.
     I was covered in sweat, and had to intervene
     In my thought and sorrow.

     I saw a clear plastic door.
 It was all fogged up too. In all that turmoil I explored, Remembered the
humidity of back home—which had no existence. Walked over the dried up
sanded guilt to clear transience.

     I opened it and went in. The door locked
     Behind myself and I couldn't open it back up.
     I was trapped for life I thought.
     Then I looked around in this secret area.

I was in a temple garden.
It was like a sanctuary of eternal peace,
Untouched by the hands of torture.
There were beautiful granite statues of
Angels and a few leaping Centaurs holding branches.

    In the scorching desert sands
       I never saw any green splatters of grass, but there was
verdant ivy all around this garden, especially
    Ascending up the veined brick walls of a peaceful facility, a
haven, a cleansing villa.

    The moonlight glittered against a fountain
With a large glass sculpture of an angel Crying with a side post sign
saying: "The Wars may never cease to end, but roads are unlimited,

    And life is still always steps from the deceased."
      Water ran down through the eyes, and
      Into a pond made of granite. I went over and
      Gazed at this soothing beauty.

    The fountain brought back memories
      When I used to go fishing
With my top—shot buddy. The water glistened in the
      Sincere moonlight.

    My sweat was bandaging my
Dusty face and clothing. It dripped down by
    My brow. It slid down my
Tears to my beating chest. Which faded.

I decided to quench and wade

In the glimmering pond water
On my face. I quivered at
First from barely touching it.

The water was very cool. I
Made a bowl with my hands
And scooped the water up. I
Closed my eyes as it splashed

Against my face. That's odd
I thought. The water was tangibly cool.
But when I threw it in my tender
Face, very lukewarm.

I opened my eyes and the "water"
Was from the donated blood from the soldiers
For the soldiers.

All I thought was
AIDS— I was going to get AIDS!!!

There was blood, down my
Shirt. I was shot in my side. My hands were like rubber
Latex gloves that had been opened wide
into heavy crimson candy liquid blubber
Coating. The statues weren't statues.
Civilian men and women all crying blood under sounded salutes
The ivy leaves were nets in death colors.
These were never green. Some civilian— others
Were covered with left over bullet shells, and disease..

I ran by one who was de—fleshed and I got goose bumps.
I ran by another and her scars and stitches were in clumps
I aimed at the building and my rifle had gone off.

The Ivy did breaststroke under silent golden flames aloft.

I saw a gate covered with coupled eyes
And fingers. I ran by it all stepping on lies,
On the scarred mess and all
Vile puss and sordid immunity came out from my maul.

I grabbed the slimy gate and the fingers
Grabbed my hand. I pulled the gate, it pulled me.
I couldn't stand it. I grabbed at each one
Of the fingers through the door and—

The cracking, the muscle stretching
And snapping from the greasy gates.
The nails were yellow and very
Brittle, and shattered under my pull.

I tore off twelve that were
Dying on the floor like dismantled
Bees. I then ripped open the door
And it began to melt under the flames engulfing the medical room.

I walked back to base. Night purple skeletons saluted
Me as I walked passed them.
Then I heard a scream,
A child had lost his or her legs.

Please forward this to my country if it still is in tact

If only sanity meets its temporal existence
Before all points fade, by then I would vanish until
All else remains.

WHO ART IN HEAVEN   from *"Reflections of the Dream Panorama"*

Skin-colored sand swirling under the musty gray sky,
A fusillade tremors strangers naïve to the apparent wrath.
One after the other, deliver a fatal mortality,
Lonely, unconnected, dispersed on a solemn path:
Seven armed with sand-shrieking snipers;
Six tanks marching on the crusty sand dunes;
Five trucks carrying a hundred men;
Four remaining of the previous platoons;
Three missiles soar by the eagle eyed-glares;
Two city blocks are completely demolished;
One country is stripped and torn;
All lives of the past abolished.
A man walks with his men on the muddy veins.
Dried powdered human debris slithers,
Arid and smelting under the fumes of global wreckage,
An age of eighteen, opened chest, heart withers
Gasping under those precious flames that leave awe.
A tie-dye of blood and dirt on concrete
Stained against the torn cotton and smothered lungs
Banging outside an open alley,
Left to melt like grease in a pan. The meat was strung

To a chain and left to rot for the world to see.
A grenade explosion cringes the necks
Of the naked children malnourished and tortured.
The buildings heap over and bring wrecks
To the naïve travelers on their expedition.
Stripes, stars, bloodlines, ropes wrapped
And knotted on a steady creature of artillery,
Whose teeth are biting the sand mice—trapped.
Wombs and fetuses shattered by nails of death
Aborting the senseless unto a sliced removed center.
Trapped under a closed eye, the nervous youth
Cannot enter. We cannot re—enter.
See the coffins from the metallic—winged eagles,
Drenched in stars, stripes and luminous stars.
Coffins waxed and polished shoes
Glitter as given to the set of long black cars.
Hearses that travel, yet are not moved.
A knock on the door and the riveting call
That stops a breathing youth's life,
An open—winged dove flaps his last and takes a fall.
Then as I opened my beaten palm, I stood still
    As the coolness flew over my pores,
    And I saw my leader/ my daughter/ my brother/ my whole
    Disappear inside a finely waxed coffin.
    Seven, six, five, four, three, two, once again.

AN INTERRUPTION TO THIS BROADCAST
THE AUTHOR RECEIVED THIS LETTER FOUR YEARS AGO:
THIS IS A 100% REAL EXISTING LETTER

"May 7, 2003

[···]

Dear Mr. Mullin:

Thank you for your letter about Operation Iraqi Freedom. In Iraq we sought to remove a threat to our security and to free the Iraqi people from oppression. Saddam Hussein's regime has ended and the Iraqi people are regaining control of their own country and future. Pockets of resistance still remain. American and coalition forces are helping to restore civil order, and providing critical humanitarian aid to the Iraqi people. Iraqis are already meeting openly and freely to discuss the future of their country.

Coalition forces have made every effort to space innocent civilians from harm and continue to do so. We respect the Iraqi people, its rich culture, and religious faiths. We will continue to

bring food, water, medicine, and other aid to Iraq, and we will help
to build a government of, by, and for the Iraqi people.

Our war on terrorism continues. We look to our Nation's Armed
Forces, with the support of our coalition partners, to help advance
peace in a troubled world. By answering the call of duty, these brave
men and women serve as examples of courage, dedication, and
sacrifice. Laura and I join our military families and countless others
in praying that all who serve return home safely and soon.

Thank you again for writing. Best wishes.

Sincerely,

George W. Bush   "

WE CONTINUE THIS BROADCAST

    Whoa he what, received a letter?
    A letter of sorts— he says

    "We respect the Iraqi people[..}"

    "[···these brave men and women serve as examples of courage,
dedication, and sacrifice"

And sacrifice
And sacrifice
And sacrifice.

Chapter Eight
THE TRAIL OF VENGEANCE, HELL & SORROW

地獄

Sometimes we question what is real,
When everything ends to begin

All is not at End··· All is not at End···

LE ENTROPY

The mindful philosopher rests his cross in his open palm,
Pews of children turn their page to the next psalm
Psalm Eight. Two.

Tires rip apart on the vibrant meadows, windows shatter,
Seatbelts stained in red wine, crystal grasps shatter,
Splashed, parched lungs.

Ceramic rules exhibited in engendered language forked,
Broken territory tortured like signed gorks.
Demands fixed.

Portraits, Tupperware, syringes piercing bourbon bread pudding,
Like a needle not in-vein, tanks spill, mudding
Guts surfaced.

Basting spheres of our pumping hearts, eagles eying scope,
Golden bridges, vying mercy, unknown hope
Connect all.

Printers using blood for ink, and ink for colorful pastels
Of victorious bed maids nude on jet castles,
Holding bells.

Cylinders with catamarans bending back sneezing solar glow,
Roman baths luxurious, Kamchatka snow,
Melting Straits.

Moving souls, storming sacrifices atop Yautepec,
Where spears glimmer in science, time interjects,
Twelve–Two–Twelve.

Virunga and the Mauna Kea, crumbling plates, from Nazca
To the Juan de Fuca, lava engulfs. Kafka's
Ready read.

The Amazon's jungle drenched in tar and fallen skulls eaten,
Would–be vaccines liquefied, river beaten,
Canoes split.

Paris streets sliding into the flooded Catacombs of peace,
Two–hundred–year–old bones devoured by keas
From the pipes.

Rusted nails into puppeteers with hemorrhages in jail,
Broken alarms; no government. Controlled pale,

Breaking free.

Las Vegas becomes the sinful wasteland, melted and deformed
Damned by broken dams, feathered females reformed
As gold ghouls.

From Liaoning to Gansu, bricks crumble, the bustart's wings fry
From Hohhot, the white pigeons become charred by
Lightning veins.

Soldiers storm to Dhaka where citizens are stripping the stands,
Buildings have been set by flaming cosmic bands,
One by one.

Loch Ness' head rises out as Edinburgh sinks with the Crown jewels.
Spectators clench their screams as they watch the fools—
Chunnel's end.

And the tunnel sinks, as the walls do fall, the last British folks
Depend on Southern Ireland; Britain's skulks—
Give their hands.

Not all men help each other, and children are pushed out to Sea,
Many can't swim and perish quick—verify
As support.

Bodies upon bodies, with no farewell or foretell, that fall
Like kamikazes, and barges cling ports, maul
Frames on Earth.

Still the social workers place bodies in collecting coffins
Ironically parts for corpses often
Are found fast,

In the wreckage, but there are no tools except for new firearms.
And the Black Death looks calm, juxtaposed to swarms
Of disease,

Collapsing Open Arms on the Portuguese families with
No where to run, closed sealed minds request blacksmiths
To have faith.

Eighteenth century crystal chandeliers rain on Iguanodon
Bones, unhook and collaborate with the gone:
Nevermore.

Orcas pound in the vehement waves against the steel risers,
Still polluted by empty cups and old Kaiser
Bun burgers.

Surgeries stop in place, and life supports end without notice,
And they check the generators—they are iced
By no sky.

Gargoyles ascend, the sphinx grows wings, rivets unhook the domes
Belts and buttons undo, hair gels and black combs
Have no whim.

People have no shame as the Big Apple ascends with Japan,
And hands become as smooth as a Mustang,
Life—less cold.

Each hair and pore sways as if they are nestled in fierce rip tide,
And the eyes let their tears drain, violins stride
In echoes.

But then clouds disappear like dust swept off *Relativity*
And waves cease, floating with no activity,
Full silence.

And I see outside this government craft the Earth lose each light,
Like the end of the circus or play the sight
Dims from view.

—————————

WHEN PASSION REIGNS ON HIM

She's Dead! He butchered her, strung her up.
It looks like we'll need back up.
I'm sorry I can't fucking help her.
She's fucking dead.
Dead in the carried rush in sand and guns,
Dead in the carnage catastrophe, storming lodgments.
Hearth demolished, children raped before her eyes.
Yells, shrieks, and gold medals were awarded today.
She was destroyed by the corrupt.

We're going in, bomb every house that relates to her.
Destroy life that is born from her.
Birthing to millions in bed underneath the pyramid sky,
The hieroglyphic flames choking Cleopatra's beauty,
Enslaved demolished crying lambs de—limbed
Each craft, the linen she had pained to make,
The family she made for him, torn like each stem of cotton,
Planted, then pulled, and stepped on, and
Shredded, shot down, grinded, gushed in blur.

Set flame on every torch on column,
Build the cross, rope it well and tie it to the Great Column.
Hold her glorious ax and drop it in manure,
Rip each serpent, which from the garden she does carry on her shield,
Tear off her garments and lay them on her children.
Wreathe her; cover her in loves and daffodils.
Place a boulder in front of where her children lie, so she may never,
Never see them on their own. Give the dying the swords and shields too.
So that they may learn to hate, in broken down love of solemn.

Condemn her from speaking even though she has no voice.
Neck tie her rope, first over her mouth, never to voice,
But can only echo a song when we please it heard.
Let the other women see this and cower.
Place a group of freshly slaved emeralds so that her deathbed has light.
Nail her right hand to the wing of fate,
Nail her left hand to the wing of loyalty, solid obedience!
Stake her ankles till empty holes; so she may only wear the heels we give her.
Rope her breasts, her legs shut closed, her wrists bracketed, so she has no choice.

Let her lovers scorn in the bleeding rains from the Heavens,
Oh Olympus looks down on her, she's a walking bitch, not of the heavens.
She sleeps at her own risk. Soldiers take and confiscate the rest of her belongings,
Mark her a terrorist. Kill those that look like her, torture those who come close.
By the name of her father, she was the mother.
I pitied her, but it is the duty of men, and she loved, like me, not.
Raise her! Above the cobbles, marbles and solid chorus, Muses
Gasping for Air.
No, she was not one of them, it seems, but she meets ends.

Her father cries, kick him for he is a man, but not of us, not of war.
Kick him, and give him the choice of sword or silence, victory in war.
Let the trumpets mark this triumphant day, and let the screams
Fight on high! Force the other women to fight and if they continue to remorse,
We will need more trees to slice and ropes to tighten for tonight,
The morning we fail to surmise the burning sun as the cape of darkness
Will soothe our agonies.
Make sure she is stable on it, that no man can lie about her beauty,
As it is she who defies the law, she who ignited the war.

CONTORTION VICARIOUS

A silver veiled encyclical ties on
Its fine laced ballet attire, and the velvet violet
Curtains unthread becoming heart drenched gossamers,
Rippling into the uncut, throat less, empty vena cava display
Of dust.
   —   —   —   —   —

A vanquished swan peers over a glossy
Marble-pearl counter, an orange cup containing a nine-month
Old urine sample, a calico bandana,
A blue microphone, a pumpkin pie slice, a dollar bill, a teddy
Bear paw,

Two rusted porcelain doll eyes, Yellow
Bandages with a permanent marked inked "With Love", sweet dark
Plums, toothpicks, a charged cell phone, a see-through brassier
Clipped into an origami crane, not really, two fluffy dice,
Condoms,

A parking ticket unpaid, some mace spray,
A stapler, a bottle of spilled ink running into the eyes,
Five paperclips linked, a pile of clippings, eight strands
Of young black coarse hair, two sheets-paper towels, a gray hand
grenade,
Shark teeth,

And two size eight tennis shoes. She takes the
Rubbing alcohol swab, and squeezes it ever so lightly.
Her other wing sweeps the rest off into the stark
Biohazard canister and the lid obliterates itself
Into

Dispersed 100-piece-a-set jigsaws.
Her dried flat foot accidentally paves a child's carcass.
She yelps and crunches it flat and jostles each green
Feather, some rip out revealing red drippy sockets. The verdant
Swan trips.

Her neck retaliates for balance, but
She slams against a long brass cane whose talons grasp a very
Bountiful lime and granite baptismal bowl and
It pours out a drowned black scarf'd infant, whose head was all but white
skull;
Mushed slush.

A shackled-cuffed woman with long black hair,
Sits in a plaid vinyl leather chair wearing a blindfold made
Of melting ice dyed black. Her skin is torn up, knifed
And butchered; her heart could be seen through a gossamer pouting dust,

Every

Beat. All she wore was coagulated stained
Wife beaters again and again. Her skin and muscles replaced
By a skin-textured foam. Her womb unhinged by a
Musical bubble machine that turned not-needed blood into a
Display.

Like a jack-in-the box pumping, a grand slot
Machine spinning, the telephone ringing, the carousel is
Off. To watch a bubble, not from soap— the liquid we
Use to clean our cuts and stains, but precious oil, our internal sea
Between

Our sun-drenched, air-paved skins. To watch a blood
Bubble take form and inflate like a black rose getting ready
To bloom, but wobbly like a water mattress, tossed
Tortilla jellied and spiraled, and lifts and falls, lifts and then lands
On the

Tip of the Swan's beak—and SNAP the swan clamps
The bubble and sponges drips onto the cypress flooring.
Six Venerable priests come and wipe up the mess
With their roughened foot palms. They then bend their knees extending
12 feet,
To their

Belt, and never use their legs, but only
Their hands for all. One bubble drifted over towards the empty
Babe, and gently christened him. The woman, who's named
Malady Viscera shrieked and clamored her eight-arms trapped in their
Shackles.

"My great blood!" Malady screeched, "my blood! The
Infant has my heart's delight, and I must have him. Forsaken
My life for he not be a cork in the great steel
Winery of my windowed chimes, enthymemes unbounded saints; he then
Is one."

The green swan now violet, lifted up
The baby, and it coughed. It could not see, as it was blind. It
Was a he, as its black garments frothed away. He
Started urinating, and the swan was quick to empty the bright
Orange

Cup, and replaced hers with his. "We shall share
The urine cup. Place him on me!" Malady screeched. The swan ran
And set her hair appropriately. The swan brought
The boneless life-full, agile, enigmatically mindful boy.
"Oh Greats!"

Malady spoke. The baby reclined in
Her swan—knotted hair, held by, now, a red feather. And like a
Dash of miracle, her blindfold melted and cleansed
The boy. Her black and white—striped eyes boggled, shimmered,
puckered onto
His frame.

"Destroy two of my arms and give, make, for
Me his skeleton." So the Swan did as she asked. The gray swan,
Now, placed rubbing alcohol on her arms, and then
Began to peck and pull each arm off. Malady's pain was numbed by
The Boy.

She then informed the Swan to milk the babe
With her left arms' older blood which was caked, ruffled Parmesan
—Like with chipped veins. And the babe swallowed with great plight.
He was choking. The Swan was quick to tear his back open, to give
Him bones.

And like inserts on a tent, the body
Became aligned; the boy had gas. And Malady swung her head,
Back and forth swinging until he defecated.
She withdrew her long holed tongue revealing scars drenched in skin
toughened
Yet smoothed.

The baby boy grabbed it, and blood dripped out
Onto the babe. And then he nestled and slept. " I shall name you
Argas, as you are as vulnerable to me
As the Swan is, and together we shall live equally amongst
The wood

And Marble⋯ After six years, the boy had
Grown and could no longer be cared in the hair of Viscera.
He had eaten the rest of her arms, and the six
Venerable priests, who gave him only lectures and bread wafers.
But still

Argas was gratefully hungry, and the
Swan was growing pale and its color white. Argas shrieked like his
Mother Viscera that segment of his birth. His
Blind hands rushed through the odd room they inhabited; cabinets
locked.
He screamed.

All Malady Viscera could do was
Shake her head, and tell the Swan to stop him, and move him away
From the Barred walls, and the square silver door handle.
Argas had it. Oh the despair of hunger and solitude! The

Poor man's

Suffering. He began to act violent.
"Don't commit humanry! You are not a man, Argas." She said.
And six bubbles flung at once out of her machine,
And slapped onto the brown ceiling covered in her dry blooded stains
From love.

Argas broke open one of the cupboard
Doors and jumped back, as he felt the extreme heat from the wires
That generated Viscera's bubble machine.
"He'll get too curious, stop him and bring Argas, pat pat! Argas!"
"No, Map! "

Argas said as that was what he called her.
"Dare defy me, I gave you life Argas? Get him away! pat!"
She said. The old tired Swan pushed with his stiff wings,
And could not move him away. Argas gave into his hunger and
Bit the

Swan's throat, and the Swan turned into a stark
Piercing yellow. Argas drank and drank, and ripped each bending wing,
Flapping like the trot of Pegasus, Aurora's
Night sky demolished; blanked. And Argas ate it whole leaving nothing,
But bones.

"Argas, you have taken everything,
You have killed the Swan of Nature, you have almost drained from me
My life!" Malady said as three bubbles came. At
That moment, Argas' eyes began to work, and opened them to the
Blood−scorched

Room. And his torn up Map, who was withered
And humped over just like he was before becoming to life.
Argas cried, and yelled. He threw the bones of the Swan
At the walls and ceiling. He broke open all the cabinets. The
Wires!

The Biohazard canister condensed
With all the wastes was leaking out onto the cracked cypress wood
Floor. And there was the door. "No, Argas, don't you leave
Me!" Viscera murmured. Argas in fear and madness grabbed the hot
Wires,

And yanked, and Malady Viscera shrieked
And uttered "pat, pat, pat!" Argas pulled them out. The room became
Cool. And Viscera shrunk up. Blood flooded the room,
And Argas opened the door and closed it, and saw her last rising
Bubble.

But it was not just the blood of her, the
Building gave way. Argas avoided the crushing
Debris and falling shrunk bodies, and dove into
The waves of blood. And the planet withered away, as did he; as
Did he.

Chapter Nine
THE TRAIL OF KNOWLEDGE

For Anyone of New Orleans that was interviewed for the creation of the "Katrina Leviathan" project; for anyone in general.

With great apologies, after several revisions, the "Katrina-Leviathan" poems will not be a part of these pages. Realizing that New Orleans is in the very gradual lines of change and recovery, the last thing that people need to be reminded of is what already happened.

NO ONE wants to hear about how African American children and babies were separated from their gripping mothers onto buses heading— God knows where. Or when people were stripped and hosed down without warning and tossed into whatever was considered safe by the National Security. No one wants to hear about being locked in a 98'F degree vault (the Superdome) with an aroma worse than feces glooming around and people dually lying about suicides and safety to settle down public concern— for no apparent reason. No one wants to know about several people who came back home to find someone else living in their own home and refusing to leave and threatening the owners at gunpoint until the police arrive, and thus are not ready to come home. No one wants to compare their living treatment with the Police and Firefighter luxury cruise treatment docked near the Riverwalk.

No one wants to hear that for months garbage bags were lining house streets of all classes of all races, yes there are Chinese, Vietnamese, Japanese, British, African—American, White American, South, Central and Mexican—Americans, Europeans and Russians, French, Spanish, German and other nationalities who lived there and are fighting to get it back, but no one wants to hear about that.

Everyone is sick of the FEMA acronym, and no one wants to hear about how—when people actually received their trailers (as still some have not (2 years after)) there was no electricity or plumbing involved and residents had to pay for that—with what? No one wants to hear that a boat traveled over a mile in the weeks of endless—flooding that damaged a family's entire rooftop and then sunk square in the middle of their living rooms.

No one wants to hear that the Insurance agencies will never be able to help their clients there until⋯

No one wants to hear about another Katrina special on the television, or see that line waiting to enter the Superdome or the wait outside the orange—lined Convention center— like the Orange—line the

government made up to warn us if a Terrorist is about to attack;
or how suspicious we should be of the people around us.

No one wants to hear that in January of 2007, New Orleans had a
large turnout to publicize in front of the mayor what should be done for
the rising crime, and the dichotomy of the interior arguments running
inside the N.O.P.D. of what the right tactics Really are— or who should
be the judge of it, and the Mayor in response refuted to answer as the
officers there prevented his further judgment in the matter— so that it
would be a "future policy to consider".

No one wants to hear that the same Gulf is shared also with
Mississippi and Alabama, and Florida—and where is the Mississippi-
Katrina—Wind/Water damage TV Specials?

No one wants to hear the Red Cross volunteers or Habitat
volunteers or volunteers in general tell what they were doing down
there, unless the people on the receiving end are New Orleanians, or
Mississipians, or Alabamans, or people who understand the importance
of the South— and the people who have made it.

Everyone is sick of hearing about racism, Post—Katrina—Jazz and
metaphors, and the phrase "We are going to rebuild, rebirth", and maybe
like the other states get recycling, but no one cares about this context.

No one wants to hear what was lost, because we all fall down— and
all at different extents and levels, so loss doesn't mean much until it's
fixed.

No one wants to hear the condition of the elders who don't have
anywhere to go, or maybe would rather hear about how the animals are
doing— not the dead ones hanging out windows, or the ones eaten in
times of loss, or the ones gone rabid and shot.

No one wants to know that children, yes African—American
children, boys and girls, who didn't have their parents enforcing their
actions, or had no idea where the rest of their family went— were going
to school on their own—any public school as soon as it opened— on their
own— and didn't go and do crack on the street or go shoplifting.
Everyone seems to assume what they want to.

No one wants to go to New Orleans or Mississippi, except the people
that know about them or have visited there before, because there is no
place, no place, like Mississippi, Alabama; and the Louisiana of the city,
New Orleans.

"Never play a thing the same way twice."
-Louis Armstrong

TO NEW ORLEANS, WITH NEW ORLEANS

There ain't no government
Like no government at all.

There ain't no New Orleans
Without its great blend of People and Spices.

There ain't no great gumbo
Without them shrimp—So everyone's welcomed!

There ain't no South
Without them folks from

The East and the North and the South,
And all points in between.

&

There ain't no life after death passes us by
Without a helping hand to bring us to it.

It's New Orleans let only the Saints
Do the Marching over our streets and bridges.

It's New Orleans let only a flood—
Be a crowd at the parades,

And a Wave be a victory at Tulane, or
When your momma goes a—waving her
White napkin when the jazz meets soul
And the sin is sipped by Bourbon Street Blues.

And the morning aw dem rays of light
On the Pontchartrain and the Mississ'.

And the days when NO storm
Will ever blow us down or out—swamp ours.

This is New Orleans.
Ma'm, it's New Orleans.
Baby, it's New Orleans!

Les Bon Temps Rouler!

有志者，事竟成

(If a person has ambition, things will be accomplished.)

BURIAL TAX

Eric stares brilliantly at two points intersecting,
He raises his hand. But he is not called on.
Another student is called, he writes it down.
The answer, he already knew.

The teacher goes down through different objective proofs.
Eric raises his hand again and again. He
Puts his hand down after sometime, and begins
To sketch a triangle in blue.

It is the afternoon at a boarding school where boys start
Their changing process to young men, and prepare
For what lies outbound in undergrad success
With calligraphy diplomas

Attached with scholarships wherever they can afford.
Eric turns his textbook page to catch up with
The lecture. And just in that moment he is
Called upon, but not by the voice

Of Mr. Walters. His cell phone goes off. Rule A–3–2–
No cell phones in the class for any reason.
"Mr. Matthewson, please hand over your phone.
3–Demerits and one detention."

The class laughed, the triangle he drew–pointed.
As he was about to hand it over, the phone
Unlatched. He quickly put it to his own ear.
Hearing what his Mom had to say,

Eric shuddered. Mr. Walters yelled and grabbed the phone.
Eric was beyond heart–broken. He yelled why
Mr. Walters?! "See me after class!" The boys
Around him were whispering and

Murmuring: "Psycho"; "Dickhead" "Asshole"; "Eric, shut up."
A tear dropped onto the desk on his college
Rule leaf. "Look, Eric's crying. He wants his cell."
Laughed the boy to the right of him.

"Eric's a material girl, obsessed with his cell
Phone and pink–scarf'd Chihuahua." A boy yelled from
Behind him. They laughed. Mr. Walters stroked his mustache
And fisted and gave everyone

The same lecture on cell phones. Eric dripping in red

Shame stood up, and told Mr. Walters to SHUT
UP! The boy to Eric's right quickly pulled down
Eric's pants. The boys laughed some more.

Mr. Walters, stood up, a former pro—NFL
Quarterback stood up two feet higher than sad
Eric— who was now tucking in his tear—stained
Shirt. "You must have a lot of balls,

Kid. 12—Demerits— 4 weeks detention. Edward get
The paddle." Eric, didn't want the paddle.
Eric became angry and nervously yelled:
"Fuck you Mr. Walters, Fuck you!"

Then the boys were finally silent. Mr. Walters,
Came around the desk and Eric was shaking.
He told the other students to walk outside.
They got up in shock, Eric was

Always the silent kid, what was wrong?— The boys now thought.
Mr. Walters locked the door, and turned on the
Rickety Fan that murmured all noise from the
Room to the hallway. "Eric what

Are you feeling?" he then asked Eric. "Shame beyond words,
Sir···But my Mom···" Eric was cut off by the
Teacher beginning to walk towards him from the
Back of the classroom that had no

Windows. "Eric, please remove your tie and your shirt now."
"Yes sir." Said Eric, and quickly did as he
Was told. "Eric, look at me, now." He said as
Eric felt the cool air on his pale

Skin— skinny body. "No sir, I can't, sir, I just can't."
"Eric you have to listen. Here are 15—
Demerits— your parents will know tomorrow.
Do it right now Eric. Right now."

"No, I don't want to. You just want to molest me. I
Can't do it.": "Eric, I said right now! That means
Right now!": "I can't sir, no, sir, I can't sir, I—";
"Eric, I am coming right now."

"I am so sorry Mr. Walters." Eric was shoved
Forward onto a desk, and turned around to
Face the angry educational menace.
"Why didn't you listen to me,

Boy?" said Mr. Walters. Eric was too scared to talk.

"Boy speak up. You heard me damn well. Say yes I
Did, sir." Eric swallowed but was losing his
Feeling in his legs and stumbled

A bit. He balanced himself on the desk. "sorry, I—"
Eric was cut off and pushed again. He tripped
On a chair, and got up, seeing dots in gears
Of confusion bleeding terror.

Stuttering and looking at how to defend
Himself, Eric trying to focus with his
Red—beat—eyes, pulled again his verbal defense:
"Fuck you, Mr. Walters, Fuh—Fuh."

Mr. Walters straightened up, and for a second all
Was in the eye of a hurricane. The blades
Of the fan clinked an ounce of air at a time.
Eric's red—eyes finally viewed

Lucidly. Mr. Walters took his fist and throwing
Arm and hurled a Hail Mary into Eric's
Cheek bone. And Eric felt his cool throat warm up
With the sudden leak from his cracked

Jaw. Eric started choking and blood spewed out on its
Own; on his chest, pants and someone's test paper.
Eric could barely feel his body, and see
Clearly. The teacher already

Opened the door. The boys filed in and sat in their set desks.
"My pack!"— one yelled; another " Eric, you're a
Blood—covered—dirty—wreck, need your cell phone now?"
Eric was trying to stand up

And his body was bright crimson and navy. "My Mom!"
Eric said. "Eric, get your stuff and go to
Headmaster Steven's, now!" Eric could not breathe.
The boys noticed Eric was lamed.

He started to grab the papers, but they fell on the
Tiles. "She said—" The teacher was yelling now
Ordering him to be quiet. "My Dad died
In battle, in, in Iraq, sir."

Eric's eyes rolled white and his back hit his fallen leaves.

He had a severe heart attack, at the age of thirteen.

Eric woke up briefly through electric shock, and then dimmed

Into sleep while on the lingering machine
Measuring his heart beat, and the I.V. meter
Feeding his sad weakened body.

Eric woke up with his mother at his side holding
His hand– that she said were getting very cold.
Eric in two minutes explained the events,
That the teacher had lied about.

In fact Mr. Walters said Eric took out his blazed
Aggression on another student and
Was punched in reply– this was because of the
News of his father's death– of course.

She knew Eric wasn't that bad; always trusted him.
Eric told his mother he was so sorry,
So very sorry. His mother started to
Cry, and smile again. She said that

It wasn't his fault at all, no one should treat him poor
And be mean to her child. The hospital was
Pale blue, and the windows showed the rain pouring
On a near–empty parking lot.

The Pine and Cypress swam with each gust, and every now
And then the brushing of a car in its night
Course was heard among the ambience. She just
Stared into his tired red eyes.

Mr. Walters was not relieved from teaching at the
Boarding School. In fact with "his" story, and with his strong
Connections with the wealthier boys' parents,
–Boys who were there in his math class,

Those boys also reiterated the false story
To both the headmaster; and the police–who
Were actually run by a few of this "tight"–
Colleague Collective–student parents.

A month after, Mr. Walters even received a
Raise. He even got to be coach the, not junior,
–Varsity, and by the end of the season
He received Teacher of the Year.

But Eric's Mom didn't care at this moment, and then
Another gust passed and the rain kept on and
On. "Mom I'm hurting," Eric said. She quickly
Pressed the call button, and they came.

The doctor saw his beat meter almost flat line, and
They were doing everything they could do. She
Stood strong and held his hand, and the nurse gently
Said, "Everything will be okay."

Eric told his mother, "I will say hi to Dad for
You. I love you." She rubbed his hand, "Don't give up.
Keep Breathing, keep breathing, keep living, keep living."
His hand was near frozen. She closed

Her eyes and prayed on his body. "I am afraid your
Son has just passed at 11:14 PM,
Friday, December 12th. With our deepest love
And sincerity we–"; "It's okay."

Eric's mother said as the doctor's left. She closed his
Eyes, put both his hands in hers and cried.

She brought him home and she put together what she had
In her entire savings and got him a
Grave and coffin, and on the stone was Eric's
And her husband's name Capt. Steve.

She and her neighbors held a funeral for Eric and
Gave invitation to his friends from the school,
But the school had threatened Eric's friends' own
Parents to prevent their mourning.

To write and speak of a mother's loss is not as real
Or tangible as being a mother or
Father. For a child– your child is part
Of You, and something only life

Prepares for you, and you don't feel it any other
Way.

But in little time and preparation, in three months,
She was arrested for not having enough
To pay for her rent or the Nine–Hundred–Forty–
Nine–Thousand–Emergency Room Bill,

She was in prison for twelve years.

— — — — — — — —

DIMENSIONAL ORIGAMI

1st Dimension. The Line.
2nd Dimension. The Plane.
3rd Dimension. A Plane that can fold onto itself.

4th Dimension. A Plane that can fold and unfold onto itself
Causing itself to **change** but never return to its
Original form.

5th Dimension. The parallel occurrence of folds and unfolds of the
4th Dimension.

6th Dimension. The plane on which the 5th Dimension parallels the
4th Dimension.

7th Dimension. The point of intersection on the 6th Dimension that
Reflects the occurrence of the 4th Dimension on the
5th Dimension.

8th Dimension. A 3rd Dimension derived from the 7th Dimension that
Folds towards the 6th Dimension.

9th Dimension. A 3rd Dimension derived from the 7th Dimension that
Is parallel to the 8th Dimension that unfolds from
The 6th Dimension but cannot retain the original
Form started from the 6th Dimension.

10th Dimension. The point at which the 8th Dimension intersects with
The 9th Dimension and the 7th Dimension is the center
Point of both the 8th and 9th Dimension— equally
Distanced from the 10th Dimension.

11th Dimension. The line that intersects yet acts as fulcrum from
The 7th Dimension through to the 8th and 9th
Dimensions.

12th Dimension. The plane on which the 11th Dimension exists.

The Human Dimension is what makes the line become infinite.

THE WISE DEPLETION OF MARRIAGE

Before Troy, during it and centuries till incidents
Corrupted by Helen's wake and wicked seduction,
Transfixed a swollen fisted angry man
Who saw no trust in his lover, and their love went to corruption.

She needed love, he did not give, she acted like Eve,
And picked forbidden trees. He acted like Zeus,
And brought her unto a mountain never to return
To those dripping tongued fingers who point in loose

Trajectory, spinning and edging to get her undone.
 Now as he wrote, and in crated parcel agreement with
Those who undertook love's same predicament,
He never took into her eyes how she played love's myth

To be loved as she had deserveth it, as Emperors,
Kings, and Pharaohs have often told her.
But love must be contained he said, it must be controlled.
If I am to give treatment thus, then her lure

Is that she must do my bidding, and on these partnered
Grounds she in turn must work for me as I will give her—
Her simple pleasures and nothing more. How wrong he was
After the bargain became a law. That the law quickly needed cured

Sympathy as she left him after dark, and oh he mourned that
Night as he made justice square below the belt, in swollen misery.
She ran off to meet her lover and in correspondence to the rule,
The Leader of the group assigned her body in the treasury

Of treason, and she was thrown into the falls, as there were
No trials then, and this was all for all. All the women of
The age of the first to be indicted were also thrown over the
Towering cliffs, so that no woman could then love

    As she pleased, and— or hurt men in their processes. So the
Women barely aged were slaved to this law, as the men
Stated that "this" had been taught for ages, and they bowed in
Certified agreement. For they were considered by these women then

    As the wisest of all Men, and these women were tossed in ritual
    Rudiments, and back alley love crimes that gave birth

Of the Sharp Fine Lines that judge all civility in women,
And also how men should "treat" these controlled girthed

Privileges or trophies to be administered for their qualities
And skills, as long as she received ample amount of needed love—
That the men in agreement, decided the length and amount was needed
For each woman to bloom into the servant of love (they will rise above)

To make them thus only uncanny in brevity to their softened heart,
And so women were considered weak and only regulatory,
As men would win and fight for trophies,
Coming home to be worshipped by one or more controlled in his glory.

Once a woman was taken into confinement she was to only be inside,
A man was however allowed to achieve in conquest, battle or gift
More trophies for the keeping. Women were told they could never leave
As the world was too dangerous, and pieces of precursory began to sift

Into gear as centuries pass and men and women decided to surpass the
Law, while governments have only added to it, yet on its corrupted
Ragged path at any given point, society has left it in prime
Entrustment that marriage is the highest closure, yet, irrupted

On its high flawed cost. One does not consider how society went to bust.
A stereotype, a crime, segregation, vandalism, taxation or fraud,
One can only guess with a nod that problems existed as they were,
And not one source alone. So on that context here today, the laud

That is familiarly present, where to blame, and whodunit,
Why the judge beats and beats their mallet, and the ghettos
Only worsen themselves, and the natives of the lands long forgotten,
And why cultures broke off, and more and more magnetos

Of transit energy framed graphic debris and hurdled mass,
Unto, not brought by, a broken edged vicinity.
We are the definers for this reason, and the roles transfer
Playing one who does the hardship autopsy

Of Life—wherefore the other smiles, weeps and cleans all
That havoc leaves behind. And so we call this "society", because
The Interactions have broken apart from an original path
Dividing us into endless levels, of having achievement buzz

Around those who still hold it—that which government supports,
And thus we gather here today to bring two burdens either way,
As together means— one follows the other. And by decay we
Break away as we give up new members who must act in a fey

Manner. Let us begin to unfold the flaws of the greatest blunder
That ruin not only families wide, by names, and pulling down
Entire countries asunder to something called "moral" shame,
Because the leader of the law, leads the blame, and the hound

Will have to find his fox another day. Let us take to the trifecta,
The triturative power–shocked–solid triumphant triumvirate
Of the Law–the Control of Closure, also known as marriage.
The Triumvirate is of the closed three inanimate

Trinity: Obligation; Rights & Power.
By obligation, it exists for the sake of Rights, forced by Power;
By power, it limits the Rights of, and retaining its stance is the
Obligation; By Rights, one can only be given these under the tower

Overlooking down–the controller– of Power, and this understanding
Is the obligation. So in awe t'was announced a sturdy system
Set to make the ways of life in terms of social value, but
How unaccounted for was the value of the wisdom

Of the balance of the Trinity. Mathematically speaking,
Power controls anything, and obligation holds that by acceptance–
Supposedly; as Rights must hold the obligation too, to exist
Upon rule as the viable smudged item power perchance

Has an exception to. Why is not then power the
Victor, the permanent glorifier set to make a valiant pose
Upon both obligation and rights, in addition
To where our industrious society goes?

The truth of Control is never the jurisdiction in abiding
Laws, regulations, codes both secret and open, and to
Be a person who meets standards, and the consequences that
Will be placed against them. The truth of You

Is what makes it real. One would judge this audibly abstract.
But politicians and lawmakers know this down to any sparked
Plague of controversy one can create and undo
In moments, and then quickly have parked

Their settled case to veto or create an opportunity.
This will never be taught to those who've asked to learn it,
Or to fight or protest for it, and find that the law will only
Exist until "The Truth of You" is a leveled bullet

Straight on course to manipulate the odds in favor of it.
This Truth of You, you and I, is something we "know" but
Fully never study, yet we let doctors do it all the time–
And easily governments and industries as well in glut.

This is the level of Control, the Desired Addiction.
Well this may devote its title to a prevention or lack there of.
The case of the matter of its existence is the Abstract: You.
The Desired Addiction is all about you, and your choice above

The rest or what seems at best for you, or for others.
And this choice in fact becomes vicarious at different levels:
You brush your teeth every morning for the sake of your control;

But you don't brush your hair with the same bristles

With the same brush you use for your plaque—free display.
Thus the Desired Addiction is even more divisible,
And functions in two varying degrees, a positive,
And a negative addiction. Then let us examine the treble

At each vibration level, for which sonar extends to impact
The pace and stamina of making control validated to all.
A negative addiction can be listed as: Doing something in
Repetition for: A) Positive for the self, Negative for All;

B) Negative for the self; Positive for All; And   C)
Negative for the self, Negative for All. Ignorance
And Apathy directly indicate positive because their power
Is lacking. So then on the other side, let us glance

A positive addiction which can only be summed as:
A) Doing something in repetition that is positive
For the self, positive for All. Otherwise the desired
Addiction is in majority as Negative.

A power exists, as does obligation and rights as well
To be done in repetition for entire positivism,
But it does not take a rocket scientist to figure out
That 3 Negatives to One Positive, is not a balanced prism.

With that in mind, control is not fair play, yet
To know what causes a positive addiction from the latter
Of control, a power, and obligation or set of rights,
Is to gain a change that alters the way our lives are after

This present period or set of contemporary laws···
Back to marriage.
Marriage— The Controlled Closure, that has brought
Together how a human should be brought to the age

Of understanding. Today with this "control" that is the case in an
"Average" family, as a family prepares through their understanding
Of the "Powers that be" and their experiences through Addictions,
And thus prepares their children to encounter the demanding

Society (An addiction from control) of Interactions with Control.
So it is that the Control of Closure does not end in existence—
Because of the 3—to—1 (Ratio of addiction) imbalance— or have
Closure to its cause— and this was by the consequence

That because women and men both have proven and probably
May have acted in such travesty towards the creation of this law,
That the 3—to—1 Ratio implies that the stability of the power of
The Control turned out to be not that supported—hence the flaw—

And hence the reason why the man threw his to—be—bride "by law"

Who fought against it, with the other women who may or may not
Have supported it to their death because of their negative
Addictions counteracting with it. How is it then, that followers ought

To follow under control or a control for that matter if the
Desired Addiction is negative—as it had been proven so.
This reply may come as a shock, or to most an overheard example—
That is painfully true. To keep a power on continuous go,

Though gradually changing—but existing—that is the key:
One must Lie. And this Lie has to have enough leeway
Power to keep on growing as it is positive for all—
Therefore all must make it their positive addiction. There is no one way

For any particular lie, thus it quickly transforms over and over again,
Yet supports the Lie to its entirety—
This is what we call the Truth— the Control, the Control
Of Closure. Lies can even add variety

To who or what is the actual Truth of a control.
What does this sound like? Religions. Cultures, Types of Government.
Laws. Taxes. Cultures. Fashion⋯All the way directly
To You. That is where ignorance can cause the temperament

Of the You, to be You; to then Control You. And that is where
We arrive at phrases like "Don't let it control you."
Back to marriage.
But keep in mind the power of and to

You of the Lie. So if the ruling of the marriage control
Came to a Negative opposition, a lie would be the best way
To Counteract with this person. The blame for not accepting
It, would be You— this in turn is via a Lie, a negative bay

Of Addiction to be floating on, and thus you might
Want to join the bandwagon that is "popular",
According to the lie.
The lie becomes very strong when the control becomes the receiver

Of the transformed Lie, and makes it part of the control.
This tends to be called making another law, and another.
Let's start with the "average" American poverty class
(all these values are parts of the control system roster)

A couple was officially announced married— in a civil
Marriage, in a religious place of worship. The place of worship
Must display the same signs of happiness as a grocer clerk
Selling groceries because merriment is a positive addiction and ownership

Of Leading a positive life in comparison to the control that
Exists over it. The lower class couple would then probably go
To their homes and most likely, as this is a "civil marriage",
The female (this is an average marriage) would have to go

To be with her husband where he lives. In that moment,
The Controls of Closure come into contact and conflict.
It would start from even the most basic things like who
Sleeps where, who takes care of what, they predict

Who is going to do what for who. Now in this moment, it is not
At all 100%— a serious addiction, but these settings will begin
To develop regardless of how functional they are.
Both of these "average" poverty class people are both in

Employment, and come home both at 6 pm or later.
During the morning she makes his lunch, and he goes
Off. She gets dressed for work and tosses the dishes
In the sink and jets. She then chose

To go to work because a control of the power of her boss/position
Tells her to, and now that she has chosen to not have separate
Accounts with her husband, she is working for him too.
Now they arrive at their job, and at the same time, liberate

Their work times to come home to eat, get paperwork done,
Do errands and "stuff". However, his wife also has a night
Shift job for four hours from 8 pm—12 am. By the time
She gets back, her husband is asleep out of her welcoming sight.

The only day she has off is Sunday, while he has Saturday and Sunday.
She is making $290 a week total for both jobs, and he is making $512.
The rent for their studio is $1,400/month. They own a used car that
Their family helped pay some of the lease for $432—

For eight more months. However there are taxes and a whole plethora
Of other costs and such. Focus on marriage.

Their first problem is that on account of this control they each want
To share their life together. But the leverage

Is it must both work on their end of their existing barging—their planned
Addiction. Another problem is that the house is not cleaned enough,
Then another problem is who's going to pay for this and that?
And then why aren't you "loving me like you are supposed to", in tough

Reality that maybe this Control wasn't exactly a System of Truth.
So they either attempt to make the lie real by making sacrifices
In their own lives (doing negative addictions/positive ones), or
This is the only requirement that they need to take their grain of rice

And leave from ever turning to entreat on the meaning of their love's
System. But if they don't give up, the problem though fixed, will arise
Again and again and root other problems with it— the 3-to-1 Ratio Flaw.

So if the dilemma of the Control is a conflicted demise,

Why is it that marriage is much like a successful enterprise?
Take into account that to Lie has to be positive for all, and by all.
To present and craft, the Lie of the Truth, Propaganda must take form.
Propaganda began existing: Which man will she fall

For? When a man comes back from or goes to combat it is best he marry
So that he can start a family if he lives or loses his life—like insurance;
Or marriage can bring benefits like tax benefits, care, a romantic lifestyle;
Be with the one you love "Forever"—that's the best glance

Yet ever advertised. And it is working with control.
Now control comes from all boundaries, religions, cultures,
Etc., but where controls gain control is by joining in on the lies,
And advertisement. It becomes an entire Control game with lures.

The famous lure of power which has gotten the worst positive addiction,
Is the buying of an elaborate ring to "bind" couples into place.
Countries are powered to make rings to meet this control.
Then again the entire economy has been transformed by this laced

Intertwined dimension of addictions under power, obligations and rights so
Transformed, that what we do—either addictions in the favor of a control,
And what we don't do also acts in favor of another control.
But what makes a propaganda boldly stronger, is the whole

Addition of its existence as a long—term positive addiction—
This is called a **Tradition**— happening over the original creation time
Of the original Truth of the Control.
So with the original Truth of the Control lost, who or what rhyme

And reason will manage the Truth as it was originally prevailed?
As in America, when the Founding Fathers passed, it was the

"Constitution" that became the control which they set forth, that seemed
To supposedly maintain its original purpose of the

Original cause of the Control. So "Marriage" too became
This symbol of Truth which its power is held by, and all the obligations,
And Rights are attached to. But again, Marriage does not
Exist without a positive addiction— in this case— being part of Traditions.

But propaganda and Lies separate as much as they attempt to bind ones
Interactions with the Truth,
And thus changes were well acquired to the Rights and Obligations,
Via different parties and views holding different truths

In propagation, the original Truth exists yet
In prorogation, there leaves behind the original purpose;
Therefore in subordination of the Original exists in different
Points of View, which stems back to the basis

Of the Problem of Marriage.
First off, let me ask you, what is wrong with your marriage?

If you are not married, what is wrong with your parents'
Marriage? The problems can range at all levels and gages.

Is there a snoring problem? Did one of your parents leave you
When you were young? Do your parents believe in different things?
Did you lose someone in your family that affected one parent more
Than the other, and this caused severe damage to their pings

And heat breaks? Then what about if you have a marriage,
How did you setup boundaries for each other, and when did
Those boundaries have dilemmas? When did family members or
Your spouse disobey you? Does your spouse lid

Their life closed up, ajar from you? Do they spend their time doing
Activities that you just can't settle down to, and in addition
Your friends agree with you too? Did your spouse ever cheat
On you? Has your spouse ever ruined your career, commission,

Friendships, Dreams and Goals for reasons or lack of them?
Losing that spark, and researching constantly to find it?
Not getting enough sympathy? You often wonder if you love
Your children more than your spouse does? It may hit

You to find that all of these are in abundance from the
Control of Closure. And in addition, control
Without the original Truth has conflicts that have
Been proven over and over again; for the whole

Time after the Original Truth ends, yet the control
Continues, conflicts to maintain the original Truth will
Likely not only be in abundance but happen in cycles
Again and again, even into an individual couple.

Then this is to say that all controls act in such a manner.
A tumbling of cycles whirling on a pathway to a believed
Path, the original Truth and origin of such a device as one
Of the control, but when we conceive

That the Truth has been uncovered and unbounded
In the grains of the Earth and un—scribed layers,
Another cycle starts again, as the origin is lost in sands
To journey, or hope on a prayer

That the purpose of marriage is closure, to find
That on the contrary, marriage was a force of power
To sentence control and social standards.
And in this moment, one might ask what we stand for.

However if the comprehension and determinism
Of a population flourishes towards a positive addiction
Of change that agrees over a control form to such degree
Then there is a chance that society can give valediction

To the marriage and social flaws and abrasions.
For she or he that can end the controls of marriage,
Religion, Corruption, Government and Crime,
Then she or he can give us ultimate change before the Fall foliage

Dressed to our distressed conflicted season.
Whoever, if ever the intentions and conventions drive forth
In the proximity of this toppling proportion,
That can identify not the idealistic value or worth

That pertains to the Original Truth, and only the Original
Truth = In solid verification of all lies validating it as so;
Nor is this Original Truth a Controlled Truth for that matter.
(One cannot so validate solely because of the majority show

Of gregarious praise and laud towards its consideration), then
And only then can this person either annihilate the Origin
By explaining its wrongs to the point of complete unanimous
Terms and thus replacing it; Or taking the Original Truth in

Transformation to either be adjusted to the lies that derive
From its existence or increase or decrease the strength of either
A negative or positive restriction from each end. Here's the
Catch, the new Original or the updated Original Truth can only cure

Over the existing Original Truth, if it is too— a Positive
Addiction, and that no one else can disagree with it.
And in this conflict becomes, but can only cease if
From all points interfering that their status pits

Into disintegration. In other words, as this is a control,
A trinity of: Power, Obligation and Rights—
The control must be made through Severe Elimination.
And yet the imaginative sounds and sights

Bridging out from the supported structure of what is right
May appear astonishing to a great many,
The majority may and will not disagree, and even with a
Severe Elimination: e.g. like marriage, the penniless

Effort of murder to rid those who cannot agree to this "Right".
That Elimination is just the first part of control.
The Lies are then the required attachments needed, as the structure
Of the Original Truth must transfer to the whole

Metamorphosis that changes with interactions (society),
Goes through to joust in different minds as accepted.
The best example relates to the Control of Gambling, in
The Lie of the Lotto. An entry person has a high rejected

Chance at winning (like the 3—1 Ratio). But it is in the
Best interest of the Control of Gambling,
That the Original Truth may permit winning by an even chance.

With that the Lotto jostles into a rambling

Mathematical puzzled—Lie—that 1 out of the number of entries
Has a fair advantage of winning, yet no one else wins but that sole
Person. Okay so why would anyone want to win if only one person
Can be the victor. Now here comes the main core and soul

Of all lies, and the reason why there is literally so much of
Anything humanly made, mass—produced, invented,
And massively enhanced by different sources for a control, or
Of many controls. This is the reverberated

Catch phrase, and what drives more lies and separations
From the Original Truth to come into play.
This is the **Lie of Competition**. And from competition, the
Best carry (supposedly) the same Truth as from the day

At which the Truth was first created and agreed to—
Without disagreement, or entirely forced agreement.
Now, back to marriage.
So then the next step would be to ask, what would be the replacement?

The replacement from my angle would be to rid Original Truth
Of having such a control. Would this cause family problems?
Yes; financial problems—definitely; Government problems—
You bet; will society fall apart—most likely. But the emblem

Of Truth will convey its true purpose in written form that
Neither a Man or a Woman were forced to be in an enclosed
Love, to struggle all their youth for this enchanted entrance—
And find out its flaws firsthand, the lies; had goodness froze

On our behalf, you'll think—as blame will fly either way in
Joust and Tongue—Wielding sin, to establish
Further emplacements to protect you from the control,
And the other controls jerking their heads and claws to ravish

Will further devour you in this position,
And like the gold band, and white laced ribbon struts,
That like the propaganda states, but doesn't:
That your marriage will last forever until reaching bust.

<u>CONTROL</u>

(In Diagram Format)

<u>The Triumvirates of Control</u>
Original Truth = Control

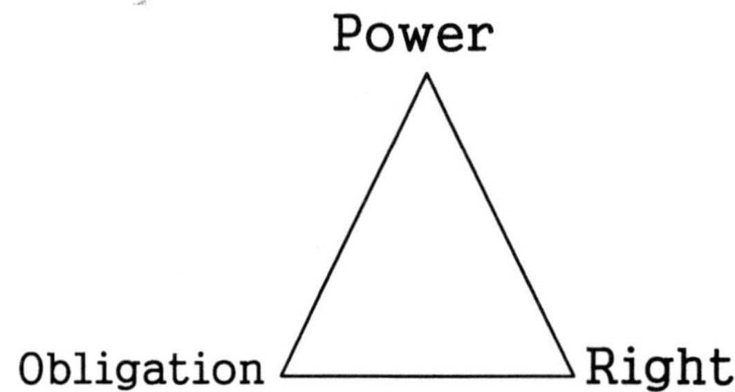

The Power of Control
Relies on Desired Addiction.

<u>The 3 –to–1 (or 3–1) Ratio:</u>

<u>Positive Addiction Vs.   Negative Addiction</u>

Positive Addiction:
Doing something in repetition that is positive
for the Self that is Positive for All.

Negative Addiction:
Doing something in repetition that is:

   A) Positive for the Self and is Negative for
      All.
   B) Negative for the Self and is Negative for All.
   C) Negative for the Self and is Positive for All.

<u>To Achieve a Positive Addiction:</u>

A)   There must be no Disagreement to the addiction
     —It must be unanimously agreed to—
     This may be done by severe elimination or extreme
     measures.

B)   To keep a Positive Addiction in play (supporting
     the Original Truth) and to prevent further
     disagreement, the Lie or Lies must be drawn from
     its existence to adjustably fit those in
     disagreement.

C)   The Original Lie must be Competitive, and the Lie
     must have the capability of continuously growing
     and branching—holding continuous power.

WHOEVER HAS CONTROL
CAN MAKE CHANGE.

*****POP QUIZ*****

Which one is more stable?

A) A controlled society of Lies
B) A controlled society of Secrets
C) A controlled society of Truths

Which is the society you live in?

A) A controlled society of Lies
B) A controlled society of Secrets
C) A controlled society of Truths

Why is that?

Chapter Ten
THE TRAIL OF REDEMPTIVE HUMANITY

寬恕

THE RIB

What does it take for a man to be a friend?
What I've lost, you've cherished.
You've had the experiences gained.
I, on the other hand would lose them all
Get away from your commemoration;
Your celebration.
I would stand amongst the rain, waiting.
Took against my happiness,
Thy internal feat,
Whatever necessary to complete the goal.
And never ever succeeded in being whole.
I gave up love to be your happy fool.
All for a chance to reach external flame.
But I am lame beyond each passing glance.
I am a window, closed on chance.
Even my brothers barely know me.
Before it was too late, and post terminated.
And if it wasn't for the crimson veins attached,
They'd ignore me like sparks in the dust.
But I'd rip my clothes down to the lemurs of my love.
Hell is it to call you brother; but it is only a terminology of peace.
I take for granted the gaining heart of kin.
I long lustfully endure original sin.
But Genesis says that no man was made to be alone.
So I ripped the rib out and watched it take form,
And it left before the Word stumbled from my mouth.
Of the pomegranates, the breads, the wines, and ivy.
This piece for you stands against the Mighty.
And all I have is love for you in time.

FOREVER ON

When the light on the needlepoint descends
As sunrise takes its course
And the silent geraniums, marigolds, on rivers bend
In delight as a stork arriving at its concourse
On time.

A meeting in the docks of time
Situates two passing parents of strolling tots
Who smile and see the news headline mime
The impact to people, space, innovation, lots

Open for display. They glance at Silver—lined
Stairs ascending to the future by the children playing hop—scotch.
A man jogs with his MP3 player and waves behind
Missing his cue, but the baby gets it all. He watches

His Mom laugh, a waved taxi, a rabbit hop in his face
The same rabbit strapped to his stroller that just
Reappeared to him again. And in that pace
Time feels like forever. A clunk over some street rust,

And then he falls out of the stroller about to tear up
As he is picked up and receives a kiss from
His wife to be, as he stands from that street corner up
To her, and she places him back in the stroller and drums

On his belly and plays with the bunny that reappears.
He is confused and smiles as life goes on, and on.
He looks to the side and falls off into the sewers,
And has his first falling dream and wakes up on

His bed in sweat and bewilderment and looks at
His action figures, and the stability of the shelves
And his posters, then he sees a shadow, so he takes the bat
Near his bed with his bear and scampers to what dwells

In that vicious wavering pitch of nighttime's remorse.
He switches on the light and finds her eyes wide open
The shadow on top of her in his apartment, the shadow coarse
In raspy breath turns to him. He was only hoping

That she would be the one for him, but he shudders.
He turns off the lights to find the shadow was just the lamp
And puts down the bat, and heads to bed and covers

Himself with the soft bear. In the morning the amp

Bangs in his throbbing head from a rough party that ended
Hours ago. He looks to find some Sharpee ink and wondered
If the messages were true—as she woke up beside him—blinded
By the sun as well; she jets out to the bathroom. He pondered,

And decided to go help her out. He leaned over and rubbed her
Back. He said is there anything I can do? She blasted "Get me
To the hospital, I think it's happening!" He gasped in blur
Of his emotions, and got dressed. Got her covered rapidly

And they headed for the car. She smiled and joked,
"Hopefully, it won't be too far," as he had drank all
That soda and he really had to go. He was poked
By his brother, who made the situation worse, and began to ball

In Laughter. "Don't do that." He pouted, as the bully shoved
Her again. " I said don't." He got beat up, and was stripped to
His boxers as she put on her leather bondage suit, where above
He was on her bed waiting in handcuffs, and then she had to

Get her laundry from downstairs, then handle her taxes, go
See what the field of men was really like, observe life's pleasures, and
treasures, fashionable and from long ago.
And he stood there waiting all those years in strife

Of what she would say from life's all, and he never gave her up.
She said, "I do." And they kissed. And he held onto her
As she breathed in and out, in and out. Then the doctor held up
A baby boy who yawned and saw his father, and his mother.

He turned to his wife, and she smiled and nodded and said,
"They grow up so fast." As they saw him head into his dorm
And they had to walk away into the sunset. And he said
I remember when I was a boy, I used to perform

On stage as an actor, and when I grew up the stage was life,
And there were no scripts needed when I met you, because your
Words were permanent, and held forever strife
And through those years and now they will last forever.

————————————————

THE END

And I end on a C chord
Long and still lasting,
As the audience moves away.

And every new beginning
Has a different path.
Paths that take us further
Beyond, beyond the greatest math.
And the choices that we take,
The choices that we make.
The bold new grounds our voices lift,
The shadows fade behind.

And when the sifting tides,
And the cable cars are silent,
And reflections open wide.
All roses fold, and the mirror becomes unbent.

And when the distance closes
And when the futures passed,
And when troubles lose under surprises,
When every moment seems to last.

And when all is said, written and done,
You leave the Sea of Poetry,
The words will swim for another one,
Another one, one day.

As it is the last time I play it today.
As the days move on,
And on high into the zeniths of our future,
And what tomorrow brings.

And that is where attrition ends,
Where humanity can forgive and improve,
But in this shooting star along an endless sky
The day ends for you with true love.

And that is where attrition ends,
With us, with you, and me.

THE
END

結局

CREDITS

WORDS ARE THE

PULCHRITUDE FOR THE MIND;

They bring you
REFLECTIONS OF THE DREAM PANORAMA

& They take you to act on
THE TRAILS TO ATTRITION

And what tomorrow brings⋯

& what tomorrow brings⋯

WRITTEN BY

ADAM M. MULLIN

A List of those who require Thanks in both the Creation of this book, improvement in the South, and those who improve the World one day at a time:

God,
My Family: Mom, Dad, Ben, Mark & Maggie
& My Family's Families
& My Prehistoric Ancestors
&:

A
Aaron (from the Presidio)
Adam Levine
Adam Sharron
Addison Goss
Aimee
Al Gore
Alex Chen, with Henry, Tony, Eric, Grand & David @ Pyramids
Alicia Keys
Alice Pencavel
Amanda
Mrs. Amash
Amber Robles
Amy Tan
Anderson Cooper
Angelina Jolie & Brad Pitt
Andrew Call
Anna Beeke
Anna Porter
Anne Fader
Anne Fox & Fox Family
Anne Rice
Annie McBride
Dr. Anthony Lala
Ashley C.
Ashley-Friend of Ben's

B
Barbara
Beyonce Knowles
Betty Young (Presidio)
Bluffton Pool
Brad Petifilis
Brian and Lauran Crawford
Brianna Sherman
Brianna Shafer

Bridgette Phillips
Bryan Allen Scholl- IISS

C
California
Carlos Santana
Casey Cadella
Cassie
The Castelhano Bros.
The Chalks & The Mirandas!
Cherie
Dr. Chong & Dr. Chong
Director Chris B.
Chris Chambers
Chris Cornell
Christian Armstrong
Christine
Cirque Du Soleil
All Companies who have been Philanthropic for any Crisis
Dr. Cotton
Courtney Catelli

D
Danielle
Danielle Gaubert
David Hayslett
David Pan
David Riche
Mrs. Debbie
Derek Bridges
Desiree Tirado
Donna and Patti-Supercuts New Orleans
Dorinda Moreno
Dorothy Williams
Doug Powell
Drew Beckham

E
Eddie Riggins
Electrical Companies
Eliana McCaffery
Elizabeth
Elspeth
Emma
Eric Reid
Erwina Viloria
Esperanza
Esteban Leon

Everyone who has ever performed in a matter of art/music in
New Orleans

Everyone listed in previous Thank you lists and Thank you letters
by this author

F
The Freemasons

G
George Gallien
George Lucas
The Georgian
Giovanna Pringle
The Good Morning America Cast
Green Day- The entire band

H
Mrs. Hamm
Hakan
Hans Zimmer
Mr. Hardesty
Hillary
Sen. Hillary Clinton
Hilton Head High
Hilton Head Island
Hilton Head Prep
Hinoki of Kurama
Mrs. Hudak
"Huli"

I
(ALL MEMBERS) of Innovate Inspire the South

J
James Blakeman
Jay Alcazar
Jacob Steubing
Jeff Gidre
Jennifer Smythe & Badu
Jenna Teter
Jeremy Olson (Park Ranger Mt. Diablo)
Jessica Lozano
Jessica Manzo
Jim Fassinbinder
Former President Jimmy Carter
J.K. Rowling
Joe Olivier

Joel Sledge
John Williams
Johnny Depp
Jon Blalock
Jonie Dillon
Jontae James
Jontué Jackson

K
Karen
Dr. Katherine Adams
Kathryn Ellis
Katie Ferrari
Kelsey Martinez
Kendall
Kenny (Roques) & The Roques
Kevin Harrington
Kevin Marlis
The King Family of and with Dr. Martin Luther King, Jr.
Kirra S.
Kurt Bindewald

L
Mrs. Lan
Latoya Brown;... and Thomas Riley
Laura Gallien
Lee
Lisa Huge
Liz Martinez
Loyola University New Orleans
LUCAP
Dr. Luthanen

M
Mrs. MacMorris-Sophie B. Wright Elementary
Maggie Simon
Mandi Moore
Maple Street Bookstore (NOLA)
Marcy Mason
Mark and Valerie Sigler
Martina Mills
Mary Mattingly
Matthew Howard
Meg O'Dea
Megan Harvel
Dr. Melanie McKay
Michelangelo Kallman
Dr. Miller

Minister Battle-IISS
P.F. Mossa
Dr. Munyon
MTV
My neighbors

N
NASA
New Orleans!
Dr. Nathaniel Becker
Nichole Thibodeaux
Nick Talesfore & ID-3D

O
Obama…Barack Obama
Oprah W.
Oschner Clinic

P
Peter Jackson
People of the South
Pharmaceutical Companies
Philip Bastian
Phillip McCabe
Former President Bill Clinton
President Wildes (LU)
Professor Whipple-IISS

Q
The Queen (of England, Canada, Wales…)

R
Rachel
Rachel Sokalski
The Red Cross
Regis and Kelly
Rider Barnum
R.L. Stine
Richard Downing, P.M.
Rob Thomas with Mrs. Thomas
Robert at Control Plastics
Ruth

S
Who Dat? – THE SAINTS
Dr. Sab
Sabina Rica

Sally Feller
Sam Cabrera
Sammy Loren
Sangeet (Presidio)
Sean Brennan
Mr. "Sergeant"
Director Siegal
Sister Beth
Sister Leyla
Shaawn Ali
Shawn Mitchell -IISS
Skip Wysinger
Sophie
Sophia Scott
Spencer Pollock
Spike Lee
Staff of the Georgian Apartments
Stephanie Hilferty
Steven Spielberg
Susan Robinson

T
Taiwan : Land of Formosa
Tim Veeley of Wasteland Press
Tina Ngo
The Rolling Stones
Tulane University

U
United Cabs
Usher
U2
Universities and Schools that gave evacuees education

V
Victoria
Volunteers

W
Walnut Creek Fire Department
Dr. Waguesback
Wassim
Mrs. Webb
William Gates & Mrs. Gates
Wyclef Jean

X

Y
Dr. Yandace Brown
Yoko
Yongsoo Park
Yusef Komunyakaa
YOU: _______________________________
Yumi and Mr. Johnson

Z
Zander White
Zuzanna Wojtkowska

THANK YOU FOR READING,
PLEASE TURN THE THE BOOK
UPSIDE DOWN AND BACK RIGHT
SIDE UP AND THE BOOK WILL
BE READY TO READ AGAIN.

WANT TO DIVE IN SOME OF ADAM MULLIN'S OTHER POEM
WORKS?

CHECK OUT:

Pulchritude for the Mind: Poems for the 21st Century

&

Reflections of the Dream Panorama

Just who is Adam M. Mullin?

   Well if you've kept up with his paragraphed bios, he now has
graduated from Loyola University New Orleans with an
undergrad in you guessed it English & Literature (in the fall of
2006). He's exploring the sites of Northern California and
enjoys volunteering, (and even after school) enjoys learning
and doing other activities and jobs. Will he be writing another
book soon— we'll see⋯He says hope you enjoy the book and
that you have a great day and future ahead of yourself; and
never give up in bringing your great ideas and projects, and
improvements to the world.

Just for your Information.

‒ ‒ ‒ ‒ ‒ ‒ ‒ ‒

There are types of buildings existing that can
withstand hurricanes, blizzards, tornadoes,
sandstorms, earthquakes and fire, + FEMA even
is highly aware of these, + these structures
are very energy efficient, low‒cost, and made
of Cleaner‒almost Mildew‒Free materials.
These structures are not receiving government
recognition because "constructive" weather‒
resistant housing is not necessarily a
highlight for governments who deal with an
annual chance of severe weather or
earthquakes. These structures are called:
<u>Monolithic Domes</u>. For More Information Visit
via the Internet:

  ‒The Monolithic Dome Institute
http://www.monolithic.com

  ‒Dome of a Home
http://www.domeofahome.com

  ‒Dragon Speed Design Group
http://www.dragonspeeddesigngroup.com

There are existing Flying Cars like in the
Jetsons that use cleaner burning chemicals,
and would minimize land traffic greatly.

However the government refuses to have
these in the U.S. because it would both
interfere with the existing oil economy and in
addition would require the additional efforts
of regulations, lessons, licenses and extra
preparations and such.

To find out about the Moller Skycar visit:

http://www.moller.com

The Truth of Freemasonry:
   Any male at age 18 and above can become a
Mason—at their OWN WILL. There are no
invitations involved— and invitations are
highly prohibited as well in order to join.
Freemasonry is entirely about improvement in
society, an understanding in symbols, and an
improvement in your self. Also Freemasonry
applies to men of all religions.

Yes there are Women only groups:
   Who follow the same rules—except for
women— like Eastern Star.

For more information on extinguishing the
freemasonry lies and learning the symbolism
of a Country's government look for your local
"Lodge" or your state's "Grand Lodge."

Taipei, Taiwan has the tallest building (for now 2007) in the World with the fastest elevator called:
Taipei 101

BIBLIOGRAPHY

Bibliography For the "Human Trigger" & Additional Quotes
throughout book:

"INTRODUCTION"

Section from "I Have A Dream": King, Jr., Martin L. "The I
Have a Dream Speech." The U.S. Constitution Online. 1963.
20 Sept. 2007 <http://www.usconstitution.net/dream.html>.

"HUMAN TRIGGER" + Other country quotes
Quotes with Translations from foreign countries without names
attached, and some authored named quotes were derived from
40+ different search pages from:

Wikipedia's ™ Wikiquote:
http://en.wikiquote.org/wiki/Main_Page
© 2007, Authors/Editors: Wikipedia Staff
Ones not from Wikiquote:

Franz Grillzparzer Quote: Grillparzer, Franz. "Franz
Grillparzer." Answers.Com. QuotationsBooks. 20 Sept. 2007
<http://www.answers.com/Franz%20Grillparzer>.

Mahai Quote, Eminescu, Mahai, and Corneliu M. Popescu. "Mortua
Est Poem." Mahai Eminescu. 25 Sept. 2007
<http://www.mihaieminescu.ro/en/literary_work/poems/mortua_es
t.htm>.

Phrases of Hebrew, Chayim, Orach. "Hebrew Phrases."
Headcoverings by Devorah. 2005. 20 Sept. 2007
<http://easybib.com/MyBib/step2.php>.

Scotland Quote: "Scotland,Quotes & Sayings." Scottish
Gatherings. 1 Oct. 2007
<http://www.scottishgatherings.co.uk/quotes.html>.

Printed in the United States
94203LV00001B